ALSO BY HENRY LOUIS GATES, JR.

Thirteen Ways of Looking at a Black Man
The Future of the Race
Colored People
Loose Canons
Figures in Black
The Signifying Monkey

With Kwame Anthony Appiah
The Dictionary of Global Culture
Africana: The Encyclopedia of the African
and African American Experience
Encarta Africana

Opposite: Kibweni Palace ruins on Zanzibar, Tanzania
Overleaf: A mosque in Mali

WONDERS OF
THE AFRICAN WORLD

HENRY LOUIS GATES, JR.

WITH PHOTOGRAPHS BY LYNN DAVIS

ALFRED A. KNOPF   NEW YORK   1999

THIS IS A BORZOI BOOK
PUBLISHED BY ALFRED A. KNOPF

Copyright © 1999 by Henry Louis Gates, Jr.
Photographs copyright © 1999 by Lynn Davis
All rights reserved under International and Pan-American
Copyright Conventions. Published in the United States by
Alfred A. Knopf, a division of Random House, Inc., New
York, and simultaneously in Canada by Random House of
Canada Limited, Toronto. Distributed by Random House,
Inc., New York.

www.randomhouse.com

Knopf, Borzoi Books, and the colophon are registered
trademarks of Random House, Inc.

A portion of this work was originally published as
"Rope Burn" in *The New Yorker*.

Library of Congress Cataloging-in-Publication Data
Gates, Jr., Henry Louis.
    Wonders of the African world / Henry Louis Gates, Jr. —
1st American ed.
        p.   cm.
    Includes bibliographical references (p.   ) and index.
ISBN 0-375-40235-7.
1. Africa—Civilization.   I. Title.
DT14.G385   1999
960—dc21   99-18496
                                                            CIP

Manufactured in the United States of America
First Edition

This book is dedicated to

KWAME ANTHONY APPIAH

and

'WOLE SOYINKA,

who have, since 1973, patiently and lovingly ushered an exile into their African worlds.

CONTENTS

Pyramid at Meroë, Sudan

ACKNOWLEDGMENTS

While I have taught African literature, I am not a scholar of the history of Africa. Accordingly, to write this book, I have tried to distill into a general discourse the extensive scholarship of hundreds of excellent historians, archaeologists, and anthropologists, whose work I have tried to acknowledge in my notes. My research assistants Eva Stahl and Miranda Pyne facilitated this process enormously. Ms. Stahl traveled with me throughout Africa as we filmed, photographing historical sites as we went along. Ms. Pyne helped me to sift through and understand the complexities and nuances of even the most arcane scholarly debates about the origins and progress of various African civilizations. Ms. Pyne also identified and located the historical images that supplement Lynn Davis's magnificent works of art commissioned expressly for this book. Without their assistance, this book would not have been completed. Superb works such as the *UNESCO General History of Africa*, *The Cambridge History of Africa*, John Middleton's *Encyclopedia of Africa, South of the Sahara*, Ali Mazrui's *The Africans*, Valetin Mudimbe's *The Invention of Africa*, John Reader's *Africa: A Biography of the Continent*, *Africana: The Encyclopedia of the African and African American Experience*, and *Encarta Africana*, among others, are ideal sources of historical information

providing far more data than I could possibly have marshaled here, and I urge readers to consult them for further research. Wole Soyinka's *Myth, Literature and the African World*, delivered as a lecture series that Appiah and I attended as students at the University of Cambridge in 1974, and Appiah's *In My Father's House: Africa in the Philosophy of Culture* are two of the most subtle works of cultural criticism about Africa that I have encountered. Several scholars, including David Anderson, Kwame Anthony Appiah, Roderick Grierson, Tim Kendall, Harold Marcus, Ali Mazrui (whose superb documentary series, *The Africans*, helped to inspire my own series), Kevin MacDonald, Suzanne Blier, John Middleton, John Hunwick, Martin Hall, and Emmanuel Akyeampong, along with Michael Train, generously shared their reactions to early drafts of these chapters, helping me to understand complex historical matters with which they have grappled for most of their professional lives. I would like to thank them all. If I have failed to understand their advice and sage counsel, the mistakes are mine, not theirs.

Film is notoriously a collaborative art by definition. It is said that a film is made three times: in its outline and treat-

Collapsed pyramid, Dashur, Egypt

ment, in its shooting, and in its editing. I was fortunate to be able to work with filmmakers who were superb in every way, stellar and professional craftspersons deeply involved with bringing stories of ancient Africa to a contemporary audience. Jane Root, then at Wall-to-Wall Productions and now the Controller of BBC-2, flew from London to Cleveland just to discuss my idea for this series over breakfast, and decided that morning to produce it. Ben Goold, the series producer, took my admittedly vague desire to film "the Seven Wonders of the African World" and turned it into a series of journeys into the African past through which an African American could contemplate African history and its relation to his or her own past. Three directors—Helena Appio, Nick Godwin, and Nicola Colton—taught me, each in their own ways, how best to utilize the medium of film to tell a story. Appio—an African living in England—was especially sensitive to the myriad variety of black identities. The cameramen, Richard Rank, Gerry Pinches, Graham Smith, and Smith's assistant, Sue Cane, taught me how to treat the camera like an audience of one. Smith is a painter with a camera, and the series's quality and much of its visual unity stems from his way of seeing. Research notes from Antonia Hinds and film treatments provided by Ben Goold and the associate producer, Katrina Phillips, helped to shape the direction of this book, structured as it is around my actual journeys in each country from start to finish. Nicola Moody at the BBC and Jonathan Hewes at Wall-to-Wall expertly supervised the editing of each film. I am deeply indebted to both.

Joanne Kendall, my faithful and expert secretary, as always typed the several drafts of this manuscript, and she and Peter Glenshaw, the Assistant Director of the Du Bois Institute, managed to keep my world at Harvard from coming apart during a sabbatical that took me to Africa seven times in less than a year. My agents, Lynn Nesbit, Tina Bennett, and Carlton Sedgeley believed in this project from the beginning. My editor at Knopf, George Andreou, and his assistant, Benjamin Moser, patiently helped me to realize what it was I was trying to say through several drafts, a message buried deep within a first draft twice as long as this book. My wife, Sharon Adams, held my hand through all of the anxious moments filming the series and writing this book, and put up with the uneven quality and brevity of daily phone calls on a satellite phone from the most obscure regions of Africa. Our daughters, Maggie and Liza, welcomed me warmly upon all of my returns and generously applauded the art and music I had purchased, even when disagreeing with my taste. They suffered my absences with remarkable grace and forbearance, and I thank them for loving me, despite all of my faults.

Many other "wonders" of the African world remain to be filmed and analyzed for a general audience. I was sorry, for example, that I was not able to film in my beloved Nigeria, which I refused to do in protest against the brutal military dictatorship of the late Sani Abacha and its threats upon Wole Soyinka's life. I hope that this book and television series only serve to generate even more sustained treatments of Africa's history and culture, a story that has only begun to be told.

HENRY LOUIS GATES, JR.
Easter Sunday, 1999
Montego Bay, Jamaica

x

WONDERS OF
THE AFRICAN WORLD

1

AFRICA, TO ME

I go to set an example to the youth of my race. I go to encourage the young. They can never be elevated here. I have tried it sixty years—in vain. Could I by my example lead them to set sail, if I die the next day, I should be satisfied.

—NEWPORT GARDNER, on the eve of his emigration to Liberia in 1826

One three centuries removed
From the scenes his fathers loved,
Spicy grove, cinnamon tree,
What is Africa to me?

—COUNTEE CULLEN, "Heritage"

In view of the present world catastrophe, I want to recall the history of Africa. I want to retell its story so far as distorted science has not concealed and lost it. I want to appeal to the past in order to explain the present. I know how unpopular this method is. What have we moderns, we wisest of the wise, to do with the dead past: Yet, "All that tread the globe, are but a handful to the tribes that slumber in its bosom," and who are we, stupid blunderers at the tasks these brothers sought to do—who are we to forget them? So now I ask you to turn with me back five thousand years and more and ask, what is Africa and who are Negroes?   —W.E.B. DU BOIS, *The World and Africa*

By almost common consent, the modern world seems determined to pilfer Africa of glory. It was not enough that her children have been scattered over the globe, clothed in garments of shame—humiliated and oppressed—but her merciless foes weary themselves in plundering the tombs of our revered sires, and in obliterating their worthy deeds, which were inscribed by fame, upon the pages of ancient history.

—HENRY HIGHLAND GARNET

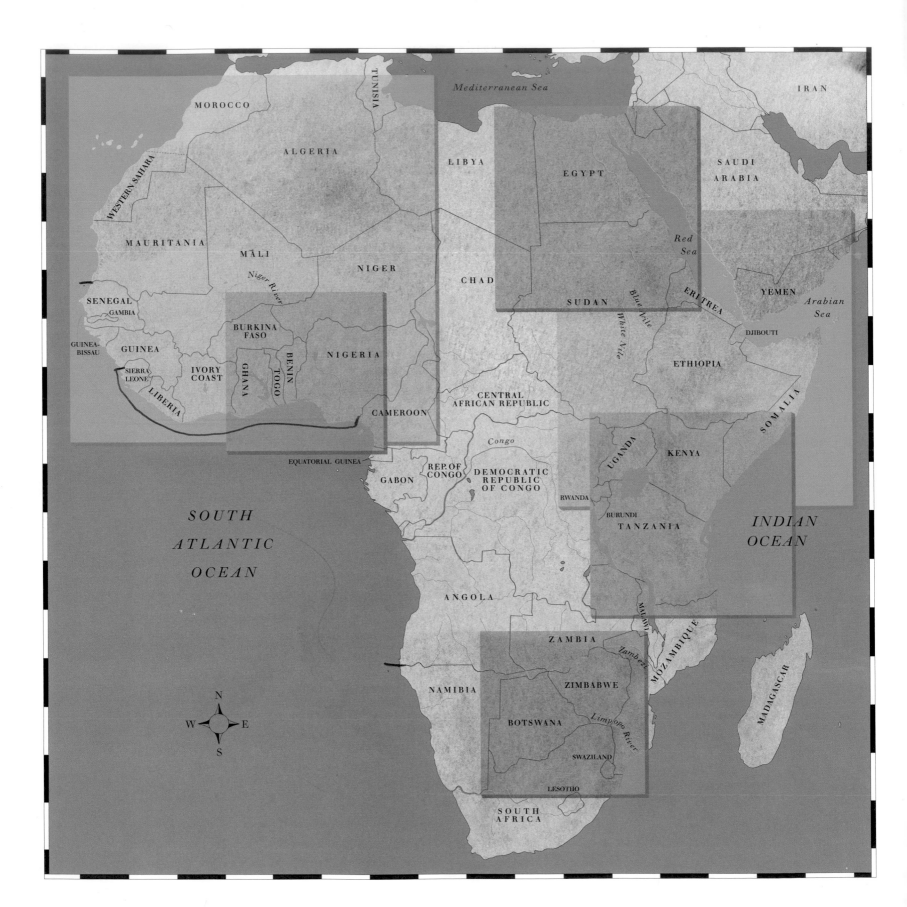

"So, Daddy, what in the world am I supposed to have in common with *them?*" my younger daughter, Liza, shouted at me within the confines of our suffocating train cabin, furnished by the BBC and Zambia National Railways. It was more a cry of frustration than anger. In 1994, we were on a 3,000-mile train trip, filming an episode of *Great Railway Journeys* for the BBC and PBS.

"Nothing!" her older sister, Maggie, responded on my behalf, hoping to preempt any possible response premised on our commonality of ancestors, of black skin, thick lips, or kinky hair. "They live in mud huts," she continued, "they are covered with dust, their clothes are ragged . . . they don't even wear shoes!"

What *do* we have in common? I allowed myself to wonder in silence, seeking to avoid the smug intensity of my daughters' gaze as they dared me to *try* to think of a convincing response, even while some part of them might have been desperately hoping that I could.

As I sat there, amused at my daughters' honesty, despairing to think of a clever one-liner that would deflect the enormous challenge of their question, these couplets from Countee Cullen's "Heritage," standard in black literary anthologies, kept dancing through my mind:

> What is Africa to me?
> Copper sun or scarlet sea, . . .

> Africa? A book one thumbs
> Listlessly, till slumber comes.

And then that curiously ridiculous refrain:

> Spicy grove, cinnamon tree,
> What is Africa to me?

I had never really appreciated Countee Cullen's poem before. I had never actually liked the sentiments it expresses about our African heritage—the emotions ranging from ambivalence, at best, to revulsion, at worst—shared all too frequently by my American Negro ancestors and my contemporaries, their African American descendants, in the privacy of their families and in ritual settings like the church, beauty parlors or barber shops, sororities or fraternal orders. The African American's relationship to Africa has long been ambivalent, at least since the early nineteenth century, when 3,000 black men crowded into Bishop Richard Allen's African Methodist Episcopal Church in Philadelphia to protest noisily a plan to recolonize free blacks in Africa. Inexplicably, I suddenly thought of my father, who proudly received the "I ain't left nuthin' in Africa" award every year at my mother's family reunion, and I burst into laughter.

"It's *not* funny," one of my unrepentantly American daughters, now exasperated, shouted at me as I reflected on our standing family joke about my father's aversion to Afros, dashikis, and most things "African."

"I know, I know," I halfheartedly pretended to apologize through tears of laughter and sadness. Truth be told, I wasn't sure that I could answer that question honestly without resorting to platitudes or appeals to sentimentality.

Four years later, I found myself in the Sudan, in the village of Q'ab, an oasis in the heart of the Nubian Desert long believed to hold the key to a miracle cure for rheumatism. In a run-down schoolroom, the elderly headmaster, Mohammed Ali Hammeto, carefully explained in Arabic that the cure had proven to come from the village sand dune and that each year hundreds of people flock to receive it. They are buried up to their necks in the scorching sand for twenty minutes a day over the course of a week, covered by a little awning to keep the sun off their heads. As their bodies sweat, the mineral deposits in the sand are believed to work miracles. The headmaster said he has seen crippled men walk strong from the village. Throughout the Sudan, this dune at Q'ab is renowned; many have sought its curative powers at other dunes, but to no avail. Q'ab alone holds the secret.

As I prepared to be buried, I addressed the assembled schoolchildren and the villagers, explaining that I was an American, a descendant of slaves, and that I had come to make a film so that Americans and Europeans would know more about the glories of ancient Nubia. A brief silence followed the translation of my speech into Arabic, broken suddenly by a woman who shouted at the top of her voice: "Africa is on your face!" Everyone applauded and laughed. As I looked at the crowd of these multicolored people of Q'ab—their skin medium brown to the silkiest ebony, their hair kinky and tight and soft and straight—it suddenly occurred to me that there are many ways of wearing Africa on our faces, that my daughters wear the great continent's stunning variety in their own ways, while I wear it in still another.

My father and his father, both of whom I knew, and his father's father, whom I did not, were legendary in our family for scorning any sort of wistful romance with Africa. My family and our neighbors and friends thought of Africa and its Africans as extensions of the stereotyped characters that we saw in movies and on television in films such as *Tarzan* and in programs such as *Ramar of the Jungle* and *Sheena, Queen of the Jungle.* Cullen's lamentation of being "three centuries removed

from the scenes his fathers loved" was not in all honesty shared by my father and his father, and practically all of the American Negroes I ever met in the fifties or early sixties.

For as long as I can remember, I have been passionately intrigued by "Africa," by the word itself, by its flora and fauna, its topographical diversity and grandeur; but above all else, by the sheer variety of the colors of its people, from tan and sepia to jet and ebony. I turned ten in 1960, the great year of African independence. Without prompting from my teachers or, Lord knows, from my father, I memorized the names of each independent African country and its new leader, learning to pronounce these polysyllables just as our evening news commentator did on television each night. By the time I was twelve, I had become obsessed with Stanley and Livingstone, with Cecil Rhodes's unfulfilled quest to create a republic from the Cape to Cairo (suitable, he was quick to add, for the comfortable existence of any white man, a part I chose to ignore), and the painstaking persistence of the Leakeys in looking for evidence of the origins of the human family among fragments of bone and tools and utensils sifted from the East African soil. Could I have been the only black person who wanted to throw a party every time the Leakeys identified still another toe bone that lent credence to their claim that *all* of humanity had its birth in darkest Africa? Peking Man and Cro-Magnon be damned! Such was my passion for "Africa," a place I knew primarily through the words and pictures of my geography books.

My father's feeling—shared, I feared, by my two daughters on that sweltering afternoon on the Zambian train—of complete and apparently unambivalent disconnection from Africa has a painfully long history among "African Americans" (many of whom, if truth be told, have never grown comfortable with calling ourselves "black," let alone "African"). Phillis Wheatley, the very first African to publish poetry in the English language, gave voice to this anxiety as early as 1773, even before it occurred to her to use her powerful pen to indict slavery and European racism: "'Twas mercy brought me from my *Pagan* land," she wrote, a land, most probably in Gambia or Senegal, from which she was abducted when she was six or seven. In an earlier poem, Wheatley had called Africa "The land of errors and Egyptian gloom," thanking the "Father of mercy" for bringing "me in safety from those dark abodes" that were the Africa not of her memory but of the Enlightenment imagination of eighteenth-century Europe and America.[1]

"Thank God for slavery," Richard Pryor would outrageously exclaim more than 200 years later, at the end of a devastatingly humorous account of his first visit to Africa. He unwittingly summarized one persistent view among African Americans that no amount of wishful thinking or "political correctness" can seem to wash away entirely, perhaps because its pedigree includes far too many distinguished black intellectuals. Even the redoubtable Frederick Douglass, who as early as 1854 ventured that the liberation of the American Negro slave was inextricably intertwined with the "liberation" of knowledge about ancient African civilization, especially the sub-Saharan "Negroid" origins of Egyptian civilization and what he called the fundamental unity of all Negro peoples—even he preferred to embrace "Africa" more as an imaginative construct than as an actual place, full of tens of millions of black human beings. In fact, in 1872, Douglass wondered aloud "why anyone should leave this land of progress and enlightenment and seek a home amid the death-dealing malaria of a barbarous continent."[2] The Western stereotype of Africa and its black citizens as devoid of reason and, therefore, subhuman was often shared by white master and black ex-slave

alike. Writing early in the nineteenth century, a group of free blacks in Philadelphia adopted the following resolution:

> Resolved that, without art, without science, without a proper knowledge of government, to cast into the savage wilds of Africa the free people of color seems to us the circuitous route through which they must return to perpetual bondage.[3]

Douglass would give voice to still another cause for anxiety among African Americans toward their ancestral kinsmen: slavery, and its complex historical causes, including black African complicity in its origins. "Depend upon it," Douglass wrote,

> the savage chiefs of the western coasts of Africa, who for ages have been accustomed to selling their captives into bondage, and pocketing the ready cash for them will not more readily accept our moral and economical ideas than the slave traders of Maryland and Virginia. We are, therefore, less inclined to go to Africa to work against the slave-trade than to stay here to work against it.[4]

The relation between the descendants of the slaves and their African forebears, Douglass argues, had long been severed by the latter's willing participation in the commodification of their own brothers and sisters. The Negro American was sui generis, not an extension of a noble past filled with black gods and kings, but a new being, shaped on the American continent just as surely as his neighbors of European descent had been. He was urged to forget his putative African past and create a future as an American; as Cullen would put it in "Heritage,"

"Slave catchers": The relation between the descendants of slaves and their African forebears was severed, Frederick Douglass wrote, by the latter's participation in the slave trade.

What is last year's snow to me,
Last year's anything? The tree
Budding yearly must forget
How its past arose or set—

To acknowledge that attitudes such as these run deep and wide in African American culture (assuring my father and my daughters a vast and distinguished company) is not to deny the contrary view, of Africa's and Africans' long and distinguished traditions. The 3,000 black men who crowded into Bishop Allen's church in Philadelphia in 1817 felt compelled to protest colonization because several black leaders such as Paul Cuffe, James Forten, and Allen himself were quite enthusiastic about it. However, Douglass contemporaries Martin R. Delany, Henry Highland Garnet, Alexander Crummell, and Edward Wilmot Blyden, among many others, celebrated the connections they believed to exist between American Negroes and the African continent. For Blyden, Africa was "the negro's home." "Your place," Blyden advised his fellow American Negroes, "has been assigned

you in the universe as African, and there is no room for you as anything else." Nor was there a geographical locale in the world more appropriate and suitable for the Negro than Africa:

Africa is his, if he will. He may ignore it. He may consider that he is divested of any right to it; but this will not alter his relations to that country, or impair the integrity of his title. He may be content to fight against the fearful odds in this country; but he is the proprietor of a vast domain. He is entitled to a whole continent by his constitution and antecedents.[5]

For Blyden, the future itself belonged to Africa and the Africans, because "Africa may yet prove to be the spiritual conservatory of the world . . . it may be that [Europeans] may have to resort to Africa to recover some of the simple elements of faith."[6] In a gesture that must have struck his colleagues as quite bold if not outrageous, Blyden declared that the Dark Continent, with its millions of supposedly benighted Africans, would be the salvation of a decaying and decadent Western civilization.

Like his friend and colleague Alexander Crummell, Blyden believed that it was incumbent upon the American Negro, perhaps out of reciprocity, to serve as the vanguard in the reclamation of "the continent" and "the race"; Crummell maintained that "both our positions and our circumstances make us the guardians, the protectors, and the teachers of our heathen tribes."[7] It is, however, worth noting that even Pan-African nationalism was sometimes infected with a certain ambivalence and condescension toward its African brothers and sisters, the very same condescension felt by those who longed to leave Africa far, far behind in the historical past. As James McCune Smith, a black American physician educated at Edinburgh and friend of Frederick Douglass put it in the middle of the nineteenth century, the American Negroes' identification with Africa, and their habit of calling themselves "African," waned as the Civil War approached:

> The terms by which orators addressed their leaders on [the day the African Slave Trade was abolished in 1808] was universally "Beloved Africans!" The people in those days rejoiced in their nationality and hesitated not to call each other "Africans" or "descendants of Africa." In after years the term "Africa" fell into disuse and finally discredit.[8]

Still, the ardent desire to honor and reclaim the Negro's link to Africa—by color, by history, by culture, by "blood"—never entirely disappeared, even among those who refused to romanticize the American Negro's return to the Continent. Instead, for those so inclined, Africa became a metaphor for an ancestral greatness, for roots, for spirituality, in which American Negroes could share. Mary McLeod Bethune, the great black activist and educator, identified herself as "my Mother's daughter," and claimed that the "drums of Africa still beat in my heart."[9] Frederick Douglass, echoing a belief voiced by John Stuart Mill in 1850, railed in 1854 against "the fashion of American writers to deny the Egyptians were Negroes and claim that they are the same race as themselves. This has . . . been largely due to a wish to deprive the Negro of the moral support of the Ancient greatness and to appropriate the same to the white man."[10] Alain Locke confessed in 1925 that Negro Americans had shared a "missionary condescension . . . in their attitudes toward Africa," which was "a pious but sad mistake. In taking it, we have fallen into the snare of our enemies and have given offense to our brothers." Locke went on to say

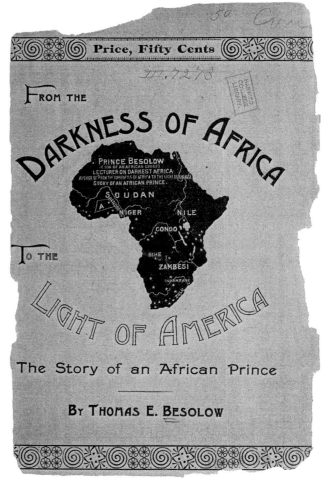

From the Darkness of Africa to the Light of America: *Thomas Besolow's 1891 book typifies the condescension toward Africa among many African Americans.*

that "Africa is not only our mother, but in light of most recent science is beginning to appear as the mother of civilization."[11]

Among black scholars, then, the role of Africa was hotly disputed. As the historian Carter G. Woodson put it: "[T]he contemporary school of thought which taught that the American Negro had been torn completely from his African roots in the process of enslavement had done incalculable harm, especially in the education and training of younger Negro scholars."[12]

In part, this dispute stemmed from the absence of "African Civilization" in the college curriculum. W.E.B. Du Bois himself—the greatest American Negro intellectual in the twentieth century and an ardent Pan-Africanist who would emigrate to Ghana, where he died in 1963 editing the *Encyclopedia Africana*—even he once confessed that he had no idea of the depth of the history of African civilization until the German-born anthropologist Franz Boas revealed this to him in a lecture at Atlanta University in 1906. Moreover, Paul Robeson had to attend the School of Oriental and African Studies in London in the early thirties to learn "that along with the towering achievements of the cultures of ancient Greece and China there stood the culture of Africa, unseen and denied by the looters of Africa's material wealth." "I am a Negro with every drop of blood and every stir of my soul," Robeson declared. "I want to be more African."[13] The effect of the West's systematic ignorance of African history was to treat it as if it had slept for millennia, even as the rest of the world's civilizations erupted. Marcus Garvey, for example, the most passionate Pan-Africanist of his generation (the one preceding Robeson's) and the father of the modern "Back to Africa" migration movement, argued that "when Europe was inhabited by a race of cannibals, a race of savage men, heathens and pagans, Africa was peopled with a race of cultured black men who were masters in art, science, and literature." Nevertheless, "You do not know Africa," precisely because "Africa has been sleeping for centuries—not dead, only sleeping." Garvey demanded that Africans take charge of their own destiny: "Wake up, Ethiopia! Wake up, Africa! Let us work towards the one glorious end of a free, redeemed, and mighty nation. Let Africa be a bright star

W.E.B. Du Bois, who emigrated to Ghana and died there in 1963

among the constellation of nations. Africa for the Africans at home and abroad."[14]

Garvey's popular movement, which struck a certain spiritual chord with working-class blacks in Harlem in the late teens and early twenties, resonated powerfully, if sometimes ironically, with American Negro intellectuals as well, in the form of a primitivistic embrace of "Africa" that was just as unrelated to African reality, in its way, as its opposite—racist stereotyping. The literary movement of the twenties known as the Harlem Renaissance, along with its cousin, the Francophone movement known as "Négritude" (born in Paris in 1934), were based in large

The Pan-Africanist Marcus Garvey: "Africa for the Africans at home and abroad"

part on a primitivistic romance with an "Africa" that never was. These lines from the Senegalese poet Leopold Senghor could be the epigraph of the Négritude movement: "Bare woman, black woman / clad in your color which is life, in your form which is beauty."[15] A poem by the Jamaican Claude McKay, who moved to Harlem and was a pivotal figure in the Harlem Renaissance, is typical of the American version of the romantic re-creation of a misty African past. Its title, "Outcast," reveals the sense of alienation and loss the poet feels, isolated from the haven against racism that Mother Africa once was to black people:

For the dim regions whence my fathers came
My spirit, bondaged by the body, longs.
Words felt, but never heard, my lips would frame;
My soul would sing forgotten jungle songs.
I would go back to darkness and to peace,
But the great western world holds me in fee,
And I may never hope for full release
While to its alien gods, I bend my knee.
Something in me is lost, forever lost,
Some vital thing has gone out of my heart,
And I must walk the way of life a ghost
Among the sons of earth, a thing apart.
For I was born, far from my native clime,
Under the white man's menace, out of time.[16]

Africa, the ultimate source of our identity, Africa, the paradise lost by slavery, is the home for which we are destined to search, yet never retrieve:

Subdued and time-lost
Are the drums—and yet
Through some vast mist of race
There comes this song
I do not understand,
This song of atavistic land,
Of bitter yearnings lost
Without a place—
So long,
So far away
Is Africa's
Dark face.[17]

Africa, for these poets, is the proverbial grail, the definitive sign of identity and authenticity desperately sought, yet never to be recovered. This seeking, without ever finding, is the mark of the American Negro's alienation, the fate of black people living in a majority white culture far removed from Africa's maternal embrace.

Despite the popularity of Marcus Garvey's "Back to Africa" movement and the romantic yearnings of the Harlem Renaissance in the twenties, many African American intellectuals remained ambivalent, at best, about their putative relation to Africa throughout most of the twentieth century—at least until the advent of the Black Power and the Black Studies movements in the late sixties. The novelist Richard Wright's attitude is typical: "I could not feel anything African about myself," in part because Africans "had sold their people into slavery," he

The novelist Richard Wright: "I could not feel anything African about myself."

wrote in 1954. After a sojourn in Ghana in the early fifties, he concluded, "I had understood nothing. I was black and they were black, but my blackness did not help me."[18] European slavery and colonialism, in the end, had been good for Africa, he argued outrageously, because their vengeance had forced Africans to sever themselves from "irrational ties of religion and custom and tradition"—in other words, all of the hallmarks of traditional African civilization. Sounding a still all-too-familiar note, he told a conference in Paris two years later, "I do say 'Bravo!' to the consequences of Western plundering, a plundering that created the conditions of the possible rise of rational societies for the greater majority of mankind. . . ."[19] So much for the Harlem Renaissance writer's attempt to transform Africa's image for American Negroes through primitivism. As Alain Locke had warned at the time, "Even with all our scientific revaluation, all our 'New Negro' compensation, all our anti-Nordic polemics, a certain disrespect for Africa still persists widely."[20]

One could write a dissertation about the range of African American emotions about Africa, as several scholars have. My point in rehearsing these disparate attitudes, from romantic black nationalism to the disgust and anxiety articulated most clearly by black apologists for slavery and colonization, is that the question that my daughters dared me to answer in 1994 on our 3,000-mile train trip through Zimbabwe, Zambia, and Tanzania has in one form or another vexed fully three centuries of African Americans. In (virtually) dragging them, at the ages of fourteen and twelve, to Africa, I was arranging for them to experience this conundrum of cultural continuity and discontinuity for themselves.

My own initial encounter with Africa had come much later in life than theirs. While an undergraduate at Yale, I spent half a year working in an Anglican mission hospital in the village of Kilimatinde in the center of Tanzania. Toward the end of my stint, I hitchhiked, with a recent Harvard graduate, Lawrence Biddle Weeks, across the equator: We began in Dar es Salaam, went north to Mombasa, on to Nairobi, and from there into Kampala, Uganda, a day following Idi Amin's 1971 coup. At the Congolese border we were denied entry—we were too green to offer the expected "dash," or a small bribe—so it was on down to Kigali, the capital of Rwanda, to get new visas, then back up to Goma on Lake Kivu. On the back of a truck full of empty beer bottles, driven by a kindly Lebanese merchant, Larry and I spent six days slowly making our way through tropical rain forests and the bush before arriving in the city of Kisangani, the major port of the indomitable Congo River, just in time to catch the riverboat as it started its five-day journey to Kinshasha, near that great river's mouth. In two months' time, we traveled from the Indian Ocean to the Atlantic without ever leaving the ground.

My attitudes when I first came to the African Continent in 1970 were as romantic as any; in my sophomore year I had read Du Bois's account of his own first visit to the Continent in 1923, and it certainly had shaped my own expectations:

> When shall I forget the night I set foot on African soil? I am the sixth generation in descent from forefathers who left this land. The moon was at the full and the waters of the Atlantic lay like a lake. All the long slow afternoon as the sun robed herself in her western scarlet with veils of misty cloud, I had seen Africa afar . . . The spell of Africa is upon me. The ancient witchery of her medicine is burning my drowsy, dreamy blood. This is not a country, it is a world, a universe of itself and for itself, a thing Dif-

ferent, Immense, Menacing, Alluring. It is a great black bosom where the spirit longs to die. It is life so burning, so fire encircled that one bursts with terrible soul inflaming life. One longs to leap against the sun and then calls, like some great hand of fate, the slow, silent, crushing power of almighty sleep—of Silence, of immovable Power beyond, within, around. Then comes the calm. The dreamless boat of midday stillness at dusk, at dawn, at noon, always. Things move—black shiny bodies, perfect bodies, bodies of sleek unearthly poise and beauty. Eyes languish, black eyes—slow eyes, lovely and tender eyes in great formless faces . . .[21]

Upon arriving in the village, I had written to a black classmate back at Yale, "I am nursing at the breast of Mother Africa." Six weeks or so later, his reply arrived: "Dear Skip—I have been nursing at a few breasts myself. Get a grip, my brother!" By then, I was quite embarrassed by and already disabused of my romantic pretensions. My very first night was spent in tears, wondering what could have possessed me to pledge to live in a village of 500 people, with no electricity, telephones, television, or running water, and where the "express" bus (which delivered both telegrams and the mail) passed through just twice each week. *Please* write to me, I begged my friends, because I *love* to read. After half a year assisting the delivery of anesthesia alongside a band of Australian missionaries, my most naive fantasies about the immediacy of my African heritage were cured. The Wagogo villagers and surrounding peasant farmers and the neighboring Masai herdsmen were not simple extensions of my putative African family but peoples with their own discrete histories and their own unique cultures.

* * *

Opposite: Baobab tree, Mali
Above: Friday Mosque, Shela, Kenya

I would return to Africa many times after that first extended stay in 1970–1971, but it was on the trip I made, in the company of my reluctant family, to film the episode of the *Great Railway Journeys* series that I got the idea for a film series and book about ancient African civilizations and its lost wonders, which I thought of as an African version of "The Seven Wonders of the World."

To compile a list of these wonders, I invited the suggestions of several scholars of African Studies, from Africa, Europe, and America. I collated their responses and arrived at two dozen, including the familiar and less familiar: the Nile, Niger, and Congo Rivers; the Sphinx; the Great Pyramid of Cheops and the Valley of the Kings; the Asante Kingdom and Yorubaland; Dahomey and the slave castles in West Africa; Great Zimbabwe; the Great Mosque at Djenne; the Sankoré Mosque at Timbuktu; the Dogon people; and several others. Since the items on this list conveniently, mercifully, clustered (no fewer than four—the Niger, Djenne, Timbuktu, and the Dogon—are in Mali, for example), I realized that I could encompass most of them in six journeys. My quest to encounter the glories of Africa's past would be a journey of discovery, for the readers and viewers, of course, but for me as well.

Traveling by Land Cruiser, camel, and dhow, interviewing kings and peasants, priests and prophets, renowned archaeologists and local taxi drivers, market women and Imams, I sought in these travels, not so much to answer directly my daughters' questions about what African Americans today bore in common with their African ancestors, but to discover who, indeed, "the African people" were and what, in fact, they had contributed to civilization—especially before the Europeans arrived to enslave many of them, colonize their land, and exploit its natural resources. I knew that any meaningful explanation of what Africa was to me would depend on discovering what Africa was, and is, both to Africans and to all of us, to the world's great family of questing peoples. What was the legacy of art and cultures to which they gave birth? I sought to answer these questions not only on behalf of my own children, but on behalf of all of us who believe that the world's collective civilization cannot be fully understood without our awareness of its historically suppressed or discarded parts. Through this book and its accompanying film series I hope to contribute in a small way to restoring those parts to their full glory for a shared appreciation, critique, and understanding.

Why do I believe this to be necessary? Are the achievements of Africa really so fully suppressed? Let's face it squarely: When most of us think of Africa, the images that come to mind are of poverty, flies, famine, war, disease, and limitless acres of savannah inhabited only by majestic game. How many culturally literate Americans know anything at all about the truly great ancient civilizations of Africa, which in their day were just as complex and just as splendid as any on the face of the earth? Who among us is uninfluenced by the images of Africa perpetuated early in this century by the stories of Tarzan: twenty-three novels, sixteen movies, and a syndicated comic strip, each depicting the inevitable, natural dominance of the scion of a titled English family over Africa's flora, fauna, and its half-witted denizens? (So popular had Tarzan become by 1929 that the New Orleans *Times-Picayune* only half-jokingly suggested that if Tarzan were to run for president in 1929, he would receive as many votes as incumbent president Herbert Hoover!)[22]

Europeans have since the early days of their own civilization been fascinated, if not obsessed, with both Africans and the African continent; but the West has been content more often to use Africa for the projection

"DR LIVINGSTONE, I PRESUME."

"YOU DROP THAT—I'LL SHOOT YOU" (MR. STANLEY'S DESPATCH-BOX IN DANGER).

Henry Stanley's famed search for the lost missionary, David Livingstone, was a fertile source of popular images of Africa. Here is the Stanley we know and a less familiar version.

another. The very name Africa, Ali Mazrui asserts, illustrates how Europe and Western ideology began to shape attitudes about African culture and history.

The etymology of the word "Africa" is uncertain. Adrian Room maintains, "The name derives directly from Latin *Africa* or Greek *Aphrike,* and was applied not to the whole continent but to a region that originally corresponded to modern Tunisia."[23] Valetin Mudimbe points out that "Aethiops" was "the proper name of Vulcan's son in Greek mythology," and "is the generic qualification of any dark-skinned person." By the time of Isidorus, "Aethiopia" "qualifies the continent": "the land or the continent is called Aethiopia because of . . . the heat (*calore*) or the color (*colore*) of the people living near the sun that burns them." By the first century AD, Africa had been subdivided by geographers into three regions: Egypt, Libya, and Aethiopia, "the last corresponding more or less to sub-Saharan Africa."[24] Indeed, many scholars believe that "Ethiopia" in ancient Greek writings

of fantasies from its collective unconscious than to acknowledge it as an actual place to be encountered and analyzed dispassionately, where human beings have forged their own individual identities and collective histories. While this huge continent is the birthplace of humankind, its history of systematic victimization mocks its numerous contributions to the development of civilization. From the very beginnings of documented contact with Europeans, Africa and its peoples have often been misinterpreted to justify one European interest or

"A Meeting of Connoisseurs" by John Boyne. This eighteenth-century watercolor illustrates the West's impulse to project its fears and fantasies by constructing its own images of Africa.

AFRICA IN HOMER'S TIME

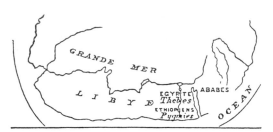

HEKATÆUS'S AFRICA. 500 BC

Notions of Africa's geography, from Homer's time to the twelfth century AD

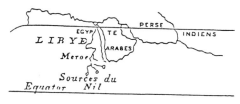

HIPPARCHUS. 100 BC

EDRISI'S CENTRAL AFRICA. 1154 AD

PTOLEMY'S MAP. 150 AD

more often than not refers to the civilizations of Kush and Meroë in present-day Sudan; a word—like "Zanzibar," "Ghana," and "Abyssinia" (derived from Arabic roots)—that refers to the black or brown colors of its inhabitants.

So, the word "Africa" has Greco-Roman origins: "*Africa*" in Latin means "sunny," and "*Aphrike*" in Greek means "without cold." But what the Greeks and Romans used to designate its northern regions, Europeans would soon use to refer to the entire continent. And by declar-

ing the whole region to be Africa, Europe defined a homogeneous population, understood to be black. Thus, the term "African" came to hold racial as well as geographical meanings. Ali Mazrui maintains that consequently, academics, in an effort to reclaim African history as *valuable* and "*African*," have endlessly attempted to prove that our African ancestors were all "negroid." Mazrui argues that "[t]o insist that nothing is African unless it is Black is to fall into the white man's fallacy." Likewise, to make overgenerous claims about the African past has been a pronounced tendency of scholars and commentators eager to refute racist claims about Africa's supposed "primitivism" and "barbarity." The result is that much of African history has been suffocated between two extremes of ideological interpretation.[25]

Scholars such as Frank Snowden, Jr., have observed that the earliest recorded contacts between Europeans and black Africans were not informed by the sort of Western chauvinism that would finally define this relationship. For example, Ethiopia, as the ancients called all of black Africa, occupies a prominent place in Homeric poems, and Ethiopians are mentioned with more kindness than Homer's kindred tribesmen. In the *Iliad*, the poet locates Ethiopia near the warm rim of the inhabited earth—"On the warm limits of the farthest main"—and in the *Odyssey*, he divides the people and the land into two parts, one toward the sunrise and the other toward the sunset. The Ethiopians were Homer's "blameless race," and Memnon was held to be amongst the noblest of men: "to Troy no hero came of nobler line / or if nobler Memnon it was thine."[26] According to Mudimbe, Memnon was "the black son of Eos and a descendent of Tros and Dardanos," and "an ancestor of Ethiopian Kings." Hesiod called him the "King of Ethiopians." And again in characterizing the black-skinned and frizzy-haired Eurybates, who was both Odysseus's herald and close companion, Homer likened him to the great wanderer himself: "For it was in Eurybates['s] large soul alone, Odysseus viewed an image of his own." Emphasis was placed on the justice and magnanimity of these individual Ethiopians, and, by extension, of their entire people. Diodorus Siculus, a first-century BC Roman historian, said that "Memnon led to Troy, 2000 soldiers and 200 chariots and signaled his valor and reputation with the death and destruction of many Greeks till he was slain by an ambush lain for him by the Thessalonians."[27]

Fifteenth-century Flemish tapestry depicting black soldiers in the Trojan War

Moreover, Greek dramatists made Ethiopians central figures in some of their plays: Sophocles and Euripides each wrote a drama entitled *Andromeda*, though neither version survives. These plays were constructed around the experiences of the Ethiopian princess Andromeda, the beloved daughter of Cepheus and his queen Cassiopea. Homeric traditions also associated Olympian divinities with Ethiopian religious festivals. The poet tells us that on the occasion of a meeting of the council of divinities held in the interest of the long-suffering Odysseus, Poseidon was absent, having gone to receive a sacrifice of bulls and rams from the Ethiopians.

Greek pottery (late fifth or early fourth century BC) depicts the hero Odysseus, propped up by staffs, bending to receive a magic potion from a black Circe.

But now Poseidon had gone to visit the Ethiopians
    worlds away,
Ethiopians off at the farthest limits of mankind,
a people split in two, one part where the Sungod
    sets
and part where the Sungod rises. There Poseidon
    went
to receive an offering, bulls and rams by the
    hundred—
far away at the feast the Sea-lord sat and took his
    pleasure.[28]

Likewise, when Iris, goddess of the rainbow, went as messenger to Boreas and Zephyrus "to ask for their assistance in the funeral rites of Patroclus, she was invited by the denizens of the wind to join them in a feast they were celebrating." Iris refused by saying:

not now; for I must again make my way
over the ocean currents to the land
Where dwell the Ethiopians, who adore
The Gods with hectacombs, to take my share of
    sacrifice.[29]

Diodorus relates that when he went to Egypt, the priests told him of the Greeks who had been there and included Homer. They also told him that each year Egyptians carried tabernacles of certain of their gods to Ethiopia and after certain celebrations there, brought the shrines back to Egypt—"as if the Gods had returned out of Ethiopia: The Ethiopians say that the Egyptians are settlers from among themselves. . . . The customs of the Egyptians, they say, are for the most part Ethiopian, the settlers having preserved their old traditions. Considering the kings gods, paying the great attention to funeral rites . . . these are Ethiopian practices; also the style of their statues and the form of their writing are Ethiopian." With the conquest of Egypt by Alexander in 332 BC and the Roman occupation soon after, firsthand accounts of sub-Saharan Africa accumulated dramatically.

No doubt in part because of these occupations, it was not long before contrary attitudes toward Africa begin to find expression in classical literature. Long before this, however, Herodotus, for example, had written that Africans had "speech that resembles the shrieking of a Bat rather than the Language of Men," lacked "individual names," were "dog-headed humans," and even "headless beings."[30] In the first century AD, even after direct Roman contact with black Africans, the Roman scholar Pliny the Elder would confirm that "by report [Africans] have no heads but mouth and eies in their breasts." As Mudimbe observes:

Pliny's geography of monstrosity faithfully mirrors Herodotus's description, albeit in a more detailed way. To Herodotus's general geographic frame of monsters—dog-headed and headless peoples (IV, 191)—living in the eastern region of Libya, Pliny opposes a curious table of "tribes" inhabiting a vague area around the *Nigri fluvio eadem natura quae Nilo* ["the river Black which has the same nature as the Nile"]: the Atlas peoples, who have no names; the cave-dwellers, who have no language and live on the flesh of snakes; the Garamantes, who do not practice marriage; the Blemmyae, who are headless and, as already indicated by Herodotus, have their mouths and eyes attached to their chests; the Satyrs; and the Strapfoots.[31]

What is important about the coexistence of the negative and positive descriptions of black Africans by the ancient Greeks is that by the fifth century BC "Africa" was already a veritable tabula rasa on which Europeans would inscribe their deepest fears and anxieties about the human condition, as well as their most ardent and highest aspirations for human civilization. And, despite even more frequent contact through the first century AD, these attitudes persisted. To recall Sir Thomas Browne's pregnant observation: "[W]e carry within us the wonders we seek without us: there is all Africa and her prodigies in us."[32] But it was the centuries of the European slave trade, and the subsequent "scramble for Africa" at the turn of the century, that led to Africa's almost total demonization as the opposite of all that humanity aspired to be.

The twentieth century both inherited, and contributed to, the generally shared opinion that Africa is a benighted place completely lacking in civilization. The view that Africa lacks "history" (and therefore memory and reason) is most closely associated with the Enlighten-

ment. The claim was standardized by Hegel's *The Philosophy of History,* published in 1790, according to which the peoples of the world are divided into those who have an active historical presence and influence and those who do not, who are passive, without creative powers, and therefore condemned to be conquered and led. Hegel states that Africa "is not a historical continent: it shows neither change nor development." Its people are "capable of neither development nor education. As we see them today, so they have always been," ignorant, static, deracinated. And whatever good Hegel could find in Africa, he attributed it to other peoples.

> Historical movement in [Africa]—that is in its Northern part belongs to the Asiatic or European world. Carthage displayed there an important transitory phase of civilization, but as a Phoenician colony, it belongs to Asia. Egypt will be considered in reference to the passage of the human mind from the Eastern to the Western phase, but it does not belong to African Spirit. What we properly understand by Africa is the Unhistorical and Underdeveloped spirit, still involved in the conditions of mere nature, and which had to be presented here only as the threshold of World's History.[33]

The European custom of crediting non-Africans with African achievements has remained remarkably vigorous since Hegel's day. In 1930, C. G. Seligman, a famous English historian, articulated the Hamite theory, which holds that whites were responsible for African civilization. He writes bluntly: "The civilizations of Africa are the civilizations of the Hamites, its history the record of these peoples and of their interaction with the two other African stocks, the Negro and the Bushman." He then asserts that the two other "stocks" are inferior, and any advances in civilization they have made are due to the extent to which they have been subject to "Hamitic" influence.[34] Seligman's work typified the imperialist and racist assumptions that have structured and infected the formal study of African history. As Basil Davidson asserts: "Time and again the achievement of men in Africa—men of Africa—have been laid at the door of some mysterious but otherwise unexplained 'people outside of Africa' . . . over the past fifty years or so, whenever anything remarkable or inexplicable has turned up in Africa, a whole galaxy of non-African peoples are dragged in to explain it."[35] Even as late as the sixties, the Oxford historian Hugh Trevor-Roper was arguing that the African past was nothing more than the "unrewarding gyrations of barbarous tribes in picturesque but irrelevant corners of the globe. . . . History is essentially a form of movement, and purposive movement too. . . . Perhaps, in the future, there will be some African history . . . but at present there is none. There is only the history of Europeans in Africa."[36]

If theorists such as Seligman proved especially useful in justifying the systematic exploitation of a continent and its inhabitants during the Age of Imperialism, the same sort of thinking, in a more contemporary guise, has come to serve those who would deny the persuasive archaeological evidence that Africa is the birthplace of humankind.

The discovery in the seventies in Hadar, Ethiopia, of the skeleton of "Lucy," the hominid who lived approximately 3.2 million years ago and who has been identified as the human family's common ancestor; along with the discovery in 1979, in the Kibish region of Laetoli, Tanzania, of a 165-foot-long trail of the earliest hominid footprints, have left little doubt that, in the words of paleontologist Christopher Stringer, "what unites us is far more significant than what divides us. Our variable

forms mask an essential truth—that under our skins, we are all Africans, the metaphorical sons and daughters of the man from Kibish."[37] The idea that the ancestors of human beings had evolved in Africa was first suggested by Darwin; but despite his authority, and despite the major archaeological findings of scientists such as Raymond Dart and Mary and Louis Leakey (as well as popularizations of their work such as *African Genesis* by Robert Ardrey), many people in the West find this idea shocking and have been passionately resistant to it. There can be little doubt that centuries of representations of Africa as a continent peopled by barbarous savages have contributed enormously to this resistance. When a *Time* magazine cover featuring an artist's depiction of a reconstructed Lucy announced that she was the Ur-mother, the "Eve," of the human family, its readers were incredulous, judging by the letters to the editor and the resulting commentary on television talk shows. It may be some time before a general acceptance of Sir Thomas Browne's inspired speculation that "there is all Africa and her prodigies in us."

Can scientific evidence, and popularizations of the history of African civilizations, help to erase racist depictions of Africans, depictions at least two and a half millennia old? "Africa is at war," Ali Mazrui has written. "It is a war between indigenous Africa and the forces of Western civilization."[38] But the war, in fact, is one over defining and preserving the heritage of African civilizations in the face of systematic denials of the nature and extent of that very heritage. It is, in other words, a war over interpretation and representation. For far too many of us in the West, Africa remains—even at the dawn of the twenty-first century—the vast, unchanging, irredeemable Dark Continent.

Recent historiography has made remarkable progress in defeating the long tradition of pernicious and misleading accounts of African civilization: staple works such as the *Cambridge History of Africa, The UNESCO History of Africa, The Encyclopedia of Africa South of the Sahara, Encarta Africana,* and *Africana: The Encyclopedia of the African and African American Experience* are solid scholarly contributions to establishing the range and the complexity of the African past. More speculative work has forced us to see the historical reconstruction of the past as ideologically tainted. In 1987, for example, a radical view was put forth by Martin Bernal in his controversial work *Black Athena,* in which he asserts that the Greco-Roman past was distorted by Western historians who altered it to fit an "Aryan model," denying its African and Asiatic roots. Bernal, like many scholars, now contends that the growth of Western civilization owes a great deal to Asiatic and African worlds, and that assimilation and influence occurred in both directions, not merely the one traditionally supposed.

While correcting the errors of two millennia of history is critically important, that corrective impulse is not without its own perils. As the historian Caroline Neale shows, reactions to histories such as Trevor-Roper's gave rise to a generation of apologists and cheerleaders for black Africa, who ignored anything that might reflect poorly upon Africa; that is, any history that would even inadvertently reinforce images of, say, illiteracy or lack of technological development. Neale has argued that by doing this, this generation of apologists played into the hands of racist Western historians by implicitly accepting their views of "civilization." So, historically, scholars have challenged the idea of social evolution—that is, a picture of stagnation in precolonial Africa—instead of also critiquing Western ideas of progress. She contends that historians felt pressured to show "not that whatever Africa had had was somehow humanly worthwhile, but that Africans deserved the respect of others, and could respect

themselves, [only] because they had had in their past the things that Europeans valued!"[39]

Finding a way to let the African past speak on its own terms, in its own multiplicity of voices, to an audience of Westerners both black and white is the challenge I faced in writing this book and the series it accompanies. I have tried to do this, always acutely aware of the vast record of both racist and romantic depictions of Africa, of my desire to redress that grievous imbalance, and of the fact that each of us speaks from a specific place in the world, replete with biases and prejudices—and, in my own case, a great deal of wishful thinking on behalf of my African ancestral past. In my heart, I want all of the pharaohs to have been "black." (They were not.) I want the lost Ark of the Covenant to be located in St. Mary's Church in Axum. (Not likely, but the jury is still out.) I want there to have been a great collection of black scholars at the Sankoré Mosque in Timbuktu between the fourteenth and the sixteenth centuries. (There were.) I want so much for the African past and future . . . a past that has

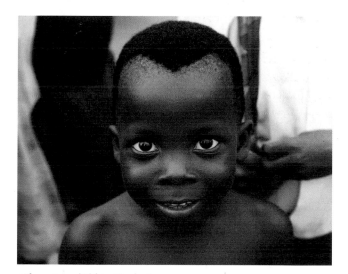

Ghanaian child in Kumasi

23

been denigrated for so very long, and a future that often seems in danger of being stillborn. I want all this—but not at the expense of scholarly evidence and reliable data. To elevate Africa above what height of achievement can be supported by dependable evidence would, in fact, be to demean the heritage that I claim to love so deeply.

It is difficult for most of us even to begin to comprehend the sheer size of the African continent, the second largest in the world. The United States would barely cover the Sahara Desert alone! "In fact," as the writer John Reader notes, "the United States, China, India, and New Zealand could all fit within the African coastline, together with Europe from the Atlantic to Moscow and much of South America."[40] And yet, despite its vast geographical size, the continent's population of 748 million is only slightly larger than Europe's. One hundred thousand years ago, our human ancestors, possibly no more than one hundred, first migrated from the African continent and colonized the remainder of the world, Reader argues, only to return 500 years ago "behaving as though they owned the place." Modern Africa consists of fifty-one countries. Its people speak some 1,500 languages (not counting dialects), yet we often speak about "Africa" as if it were a single country in which people speak one indigenous language. "Say something in African to me," Americans often ask African visitors, not realizing that fully "*one-quarter* of the world's languages are spoken only in Africa," as the Pulitzer Prize–winning scholar Jared Diamond has shown.[41]

In ten months, I visited twelve African countries, and traveled tens of thousands of miles, in run-down trucks and Land Cruisers; dugout canoes, dhows, and diesel barges; by camel and by foot; camped my way across the Sudan's Nubian Desert from Khartoum to Delgo; and navigated the treacherous terrain of the magnificent Ethiopian Highlands in search of the lost Ark of the Covenant. Despite the extent of these travels, Africa remains as endlessly mysterious and fascinating to me as it was when I, at that age of ten, devoted my evenings to memorizing the name of the leader of each new African nation—when Africa was indeed still only a book—and a nightly newscast—to me.

My own attitudes about Africa and my African heritage can best be summed up in an anecdote that Ghanaians like to tell about their African American cousins. In 1957, Kwame Nkrumah became the first president of a newly independent Ghana. Himself a graduate of the historically black Lincoln University, Nkrumah issued a call to black Americans to come to Ghana, claim their patrimony, and help to build the new nation. The first group of black Americans who heeded Nkrumah's call solemnly collected themselves at Labadi Beach in Accra, where they participated under a full moon in a ritual of denunciation of American racism and of their American citizenship. Then they flung their passports as far out to sea as they could.

Late one moonlit night, about a month later, African residents at Labadi Beach noticed strange shadows at the ocean's edge. Curious, they went with their torches to investigate. To their enormous surprise, they discovered that the shadows were those same black Americans, now searching furiously in the low tide for their passports! I'm afraid this anecdote—apocryphal as it may be—defines the arc of my own experience: I love arriving in Africa, almost as much as I love returning home to America.

What else have I learned from my own African journey? I have learned that, contrary to conventional wisdom, the great natural expanses of the Indian and Atlantic Ocean, the Congo, Niger, Limpopo, and Nile Rivers, the Ethiopian Highlands and the Sahara Desert, were not insurmountable barriers for the Africans who lived near to them. Like all civilized peoples, Africans saw such natural wonders as highways, through which to connect with other human beings and civilizations. If trade is the enemy of distance, it is also the godfather of movements among societies that result in the exchange of ideas, languages, and genetic materials, as well as in the barbarity of enslavement. It is the result of one instance of that barbarous practice in the eighteenth century—the enslavement of a woman who came to be called Jane Gates—that I am an American. I have learned that I am neither Fon nor Beninian, Asante nor Ghanaian, Swahili nor Kenyan, Nubian nor Sudanese. Though not a member of any one of these great peoples in particular, I am as a descendant of a West African slave and of ex-slaves, the product of a truly Pan-African new world culture forged out of the crucible of slavery. However deep and abiding my love of the African continent and its people, I am an American, albeit an African American, destined to call this place, and not that unimaginably varied massive continent, my home.

Finally, I have come to understand a truth that may be the only meaningful answer to the daunting question put to me by my daughters on that suffocating train ride through Zimbabwe seven years ago. Africa is not only the cradle of the human community, it is the mother of Civilization itself. All human civilization wears Africa on its face, just as surely as my daughters and I do, as their children's children will, as do we all. And until the West—and the rest of us—knows Africa, we can never truly know ourselves.

2
NUBIA:
BLACK GODS AND KINGS

As between the Egyptians and the Ethiopians, I should not like to say which learned from the other.
—HERODOTUS

It is curious withal, that the earliest known civilization was, we have the strongest reason to believe, a negro civilization. The original Egyptians are inferred, from the evidence of their sculptures, to have been a negro race: it was from negroes, therefore, that the Greeks learnt their first civilization; and to the records and traditions of these negroes did the Greek philosphers to the very end of their career resort (I do not say with much fruit) as a treasury of mysterious wisdom.
—JOHN STUART MILL

If to the race to which we belong mankind can ascribe any glory, the achievements upon which it is founded stretch far away into the past. It is pleasant to know that in color, form, and features, we are related to the first successful tillers of the soil; to the people who taught the world agriculture; that the civilization which made Greece, Rome, and Western Europe illustrious, and even now makes our own land glorious, sprung forth from the bosom of Africa. For, while this vast continent was yet undiscovered by civilized men; while the Briton and the Gallic races wandered like beasts of prey in the forests, the people of Egypt and Ethiopia rejoiced in well cultivated fields and in abundance of corn. I follow only the father of history when I say that the ancient Egyptians were black and their hair woolly. However this may be disputed now, there is no denying that these people more nearly resembled the African type than Caucasian.
—FREDERICK DOUGLASS

Let me understand what this strength of mine is for! [One] prince is in Avaris, another in Nubia, and here I sit associated with an Asiatic and a Kushite! Each man has his slice of Egypt, dividing the land with me.
—PHARAOH KAMOSE

Royal tomb of Meroë, Sudan, third century AD

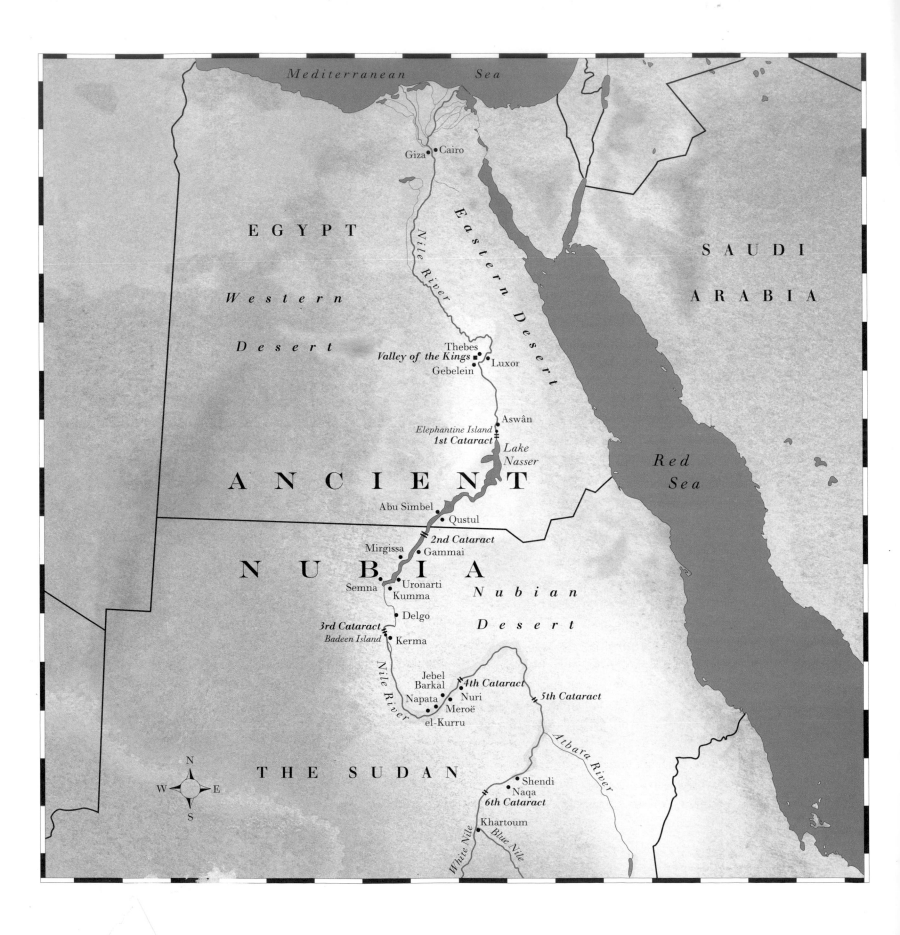

The African Union Society of Newport, Rhode Island, formed before 1787, is thought to be the first institution created by black people in the United States. Its goals included caring for the ill and infirm and burying the dead. But its principal purpose was to return its members to Africa. The society's first secretary was an ex-slave named Salmar, who had been born in Africa and who received his freedom sometime before the American Revolution. When Salmar gained his freedom, he was allowed to select a surname. The name he chose was Nubia.[1] "Nubia"—the word, and all the majesty and mystery it connotes—has a hold on the contemporary black American cultural imagination like no other word in the African lexicon. For our generation of African Americans, "Nubian" has become a synonym for "black" ("black African," in particular), but it is more than that. Uttered like some talismanic Ur-word or text, it seems intended to grant access to a veiled world of mysterious African kings, their black-skinned gods, and all that was once grand in ancient African civilization, the history of which has been denied to us.

African American businesses called "Nubian" abound. The Manhattan White Pages lists the Nubian Asset Management Company, Nubian Business Enterprises, Nubian Inspirations, and Nubian Services. In Brooklyn, "Nubian" is a favorite name for barbershops and beauty salons; among these, there are three called "Nubian Cuts" (one spelled with a "k"). There are also manicure establishments—for instance, Nubian Nails—not to be confused with Nubian Nails by Andy. Nubian Profiles, Nubian Records, the Nubian Transport Company, and the Nubian Conservatory of Music fill out the ranks in Brooklyn, while the Bronx boasts Nubia's Soul and Seafood House. Surfing the web, we find no fewer than twenty-one listings under "Nubian," ranging from the Nubian Webspot ("the spot on the Web for black gay men to come and chat"), Nubian Porn ("pictures, movie clips, stories, and live video of nude black women"), and Nubian Queens ("chat about the Net's finest women of color"), to the Nubian Eyewear Collection and our very own Nubian Haven ("African American interests, personals, sports, politics, computers and related links"). There is even a website called "Back to Eden," for "natural hair services braids, locs and all Nubian haircare needs." And one rap group calls itself Nubian Foundation. My grandfather was colored, my father a Negro, and I am an African American, but it would not surprise me at all if my daughters' generation one day decides to call itself the neo-Nubians.

Why this passion to self-identify as "Nubian"? It is because "Nubia" today denotes not just the geographical region comprising northern Sudan to southern Egypt. It has come to stand for all that has been lost, or stolen, from the historical record of black African contributions to civilization. The identification of the missing pieces hinges on questions extremely controversial for black Americans about the relation between the Nubian kingdoms of sub-Saharan Africa and ancient Egypt: What was the "ethnic identity" of the ancient Egyptians? What, exactly, did the pharaohs look like? *Was* Cleopatra black?, as a *Time* magazine cover story asked recently.[2] Most broadly, did culture and civilization flow from the hybrid Mediterranean world, of which Egypt was the supreme example, south to sub-Saharan Africa; or rather, did it, like the Nile, flow from black African sources north to the Mediterranean? Arguments about these and related matters have been raging in the American academic world throughout much of this century, but never more fiercely than in the past two decades, when scholars such as the Senegalese physicist Cheikh Anta Diop and the historian Martin Bernal, along with laymen by the dozen, have declared war on Egyptologists and classicists

Egypt remains virtually the only African civilization known and valued by most Westerners. Above: North Pyramid of King Snefru at Dahshur
Opposite: Great Sphinx of King Cheops at Giza

who have by tradition imagined an Egypt somehow apart from Africa.[3]

But far from being a late-twentieth-century controversy, the relation between "Ethiopia" (as the ancient Europeans referred to all Africa below Egypt) and Egypt was already of enormous interest to the Greeks and Romans. In the first century BC, the historian Diodorus Siculus's *Universal History* called the "Ethiopians" the "first of all men"—not only pioneers in the worship of the gods but also the originators of many beliefs and customs of the Egyptians. He even goes so far as to assert the following:

> The Egyptians were a colony from Ethiopia, and Egypt was formed of slime and mud brought down from Ethiopia. The laws of Ethiopia and Egypt are identical, and the writing in use in both countries is the same . . .[4]

Statements such as these have led many scholars, especially in the past two decades, to speculate boldly—and sometimes wildly—over the origins of Egyptian civilization and its relation to Nubia. The resulting commentary is known as the Afrocentric Debate.

Within this debate, there are essentially two lines of argument regarding Egypt and the rest of Africa. One holds that Egyptian culture was a hybrid of European and African peoples and cultures and had a formative influence on the sub-Saharan cultures of Africa. (An extreme form of this viewpoint is that Egypt had little to do with Africa and that Egyptian culture is only incidentally "African," if at all.) The other view is that Egyptian pharaonic culture originated in the south, either in the far south of Egypt, in Nubia, or someplace farther south on the continent. Egypt, in this view, was a black African

civilization. It will take decades of historical analysis to resolve these issues.

Egypt remains virtually the only ancient civilization on the African continent known and valued by most Westerners. Wole Soyinka has pointed out that even many Afrocentrists, preoccupied with proving Egypt's intrinsic African nature, have mirrored the West's obsession with Egypt, to the detriment of Nubia. This is certainly true of a great many ordinary African Americans, who over the past decade have been flocking to the pyramids in unprecedented numbers. Indeed, while filming in Egypt just outside the pyramids of Giza, I bumped into a group. When I asked these travelers, "Who built the pyramids?" they responded, without missing a beat, "Why, black people, of course; people who looked like us." One of them, a retired professor educated at Harvard, confided to me that while he loved his visit to Egypt, his tour guide was "giving us the old interpretation" about the ethnicity of the ancient Egyptians. "She just hasn't received the news yet," he said, laughing.

Though scholars have typically considered it in isolation from the rest of Africa, ancient Egypt did not exist in isolation: Other African civilizations grew alongside it and continuously interacted with it. As we shall see, Kerma in ancient Nubia is the earliest urban civilization yet discovered by archaeology within the African continent south of Egypt—but there may well be others still to be found. In addition, while Kush (or ancient Nubia) did borrow much from Egyptian culture, and was for a long period under Egyptian rule, for most of its long history, Kush was a vast and powerful independent kingdom that rivaled ancient Egypt. For almost a century—between 712 and 664 BC—Kush conquered and ruled Egypt itself; their kings of the 25th dynasty styled themselves in Kushite royal inscriptions as "King of Upper and

Over the past two decades, questions about the ethnicity of the ancient Egyptians have generated fierce controversy and sometimes wild speculation.

Lower Egypt" long after the Kushites had been expelled from Egypt.[5]

First used in the *Geographica* (Book 17) of Strabo, who is thought to have visited Egypt in 29 BC, the name "Nubia" is said to derive from the ancient Egyptian word *nub,* which means "gold."[6] Indeed, Nubia was known throughout the ancient world for its supply of this commodity, as well as ebony, ivory, incense, ostrich feathers and shells of the eggs, copper, carnelian, jasper, amethyst, and—above all else—slaves. But in fact it is only since the early Middle Ages that this region stretching south from Aswân, Egypt, to Khartoum, Sudan, has been called Nubia.

The ancestors of today's Nubians migrated from the west to the Nile Valley some two thousand years ago, where they became subjects of the Kushite Empire. Eventually, the newcomers became the dominant ethnic group in the kingdom and their language overtook the existing Meroitic, which had developed a written form. Before the fall of Meroë in the fourth century AD, those who would come to be called "Noba," or the Nubians, had achieved a political and cultural hegemony in the region.

But as we have said, in order to understand the nature and course of this ancient black civilization, one must consider its relation to Egypt's, as their histories are to a large extent intertwined; for this it will be helpful to take a brief excursion through Egyptian history from pharaonic times, about 3000 BC, to the commencement of Greek rule in 332 BC. First, a helpful reminder of the "paradox" of Upper and Lower Egypt and the flow of the Nile: Upper Egypt is the southern half, Lower Egypt the northern bit—the Nile flows south to north. This rule also applies to Nubia, which can be divided from north to south into Lower, Upper, and Southern Nubia. Lower Nubia, Egyptian Nubia, lies where the Nile flows from Wadi Halfa south of the Egypt-Sudan border to Aswân in the north. In ancient times, this area was in constant threat from the Egyptians; it is the site of the Aswân Dam flooding of this century. Upper Nubia, Sudanese Nubia, extends from Wadi Halfa in the north to Khartoum, the Sudan's present-day capital. The ancient land of Nubia is mostly located within modern-day Sudan's boundaries.

Five thousand years ago, Menes unified Upper and Lower Egypt. Thirty indigenous dynasties would rule the united kingdoms over a period of 2,700 years until Alexander the Great's invasion in the third century BC ushered in the final dynasty of foreign pharaohs, the Macedonian Ptolemies (of whom Ptolemy XV, son of Cleopatra, was the last). Then Egypt passed into the hands of the Roman Empire, and subsequently remained under Byzantine rule until the rise of Islam and the Arab conquest in AD 640.

Under Menes, whose Old Kingdom lasted for approximately 850 years, the power of the pharaoh was absolute, and the country first became a truly organized state capable of erecting monumental pyramids. But this order would not last and by about 2250 BC, Egypt had broken up into warring feudal principalities, with weakened central authority.

Princes from the city of Thebes (present-day Luxor) unified Egypt after a civil war in approximately 2000 BC. Their reign launched what is known as the Middle Kingdom and is marked by extensive ruins of tombs and temples throughout Egypt. Theban power was destroyed by the Hyskos ("princes of the foreign lands"), a people from the northeast who invaded an Egypt weakened by feud-

*A painted box from the tomb of Tutankhamen depicts an Egyptian pharaoh
routing the Nubians. Note, however, that some of his fan-bearers are also Nubians.*

ing among the provincial aristocracy between 1780 and 1660 BC. The Hyskos would rule Egypt for more than a century.

From the Middle Kingdom onward, starting with the reign of Senwosret I (1971–1928 BC), Egyptian texts refer to the powerful independent state based in Upper Nubia—first at Kerma, then at Napata, and finally at Meroë—as the Kingdom of Kush. The ancient Egyptians were long familiar with Lower (northern) Nubia, but the independent land of Kush in the south continued to frustrate and dazzle Egypt in her plans to rule the entire region. Kush played the complex role of commercial middleman between the Mediterranean in the north and sub-Saharan Africa in the south, a role that brought the kingdom enormous prosperity. Its capital, Kerma, "became the greatest cultural center in tropical Africa, with massive brick buildings, arts, and the excellent pottery known among specialists as 'Kerma pottery.' "7 And Egypt struggled henceforth to bring Nubia's trade and economic resources completely under its control.

By about 1550 BC, the Egyptians routed the Hyksos from the north, reunified the country, and established a new power base, first at Thebes, and then at Memphis. This commenced the great imperial age known as the New Kingdom, in which Egypt attained unrivaled power and wealth and became the world's first superpower. For 400 years, from the 18th to the 20th dynasties, Egypt controlled an empire extending from Syria to the Sudan, and it was during this period that both Lower and Upper Nubia came entirely under Egyptian rule, although southern Nubia managed to retain some measure of independence. The pharaohs of the New Kingdom are among those most familiar to us, and their monuments are some of the greatest in Egypt. Tuthmosis I was the first to be buried in the Valley of the Kings at Luxor followed by his daughter Hatshepsut, one of Egypt's few female rulers; Akhenatan and his wife Nefertiti, generally considered the first monotheists; the great pharaoh-generals, Ramses I, Ramses II, and Ramses III. Egyptian kings appointed loyal Nubian governors and built massive forts in Lower Nubia. The Egyptian art of this period is full of "xenophobic motifs depicting invasion after invasion against the Nubians."[8]

Once they had driven the Hyskos out of Egypt, the pharaohs turned their armies southward to break the potentially troublesome power of their neighbor Kush, largely because Kush had enjoyed good relations with the Hyskos kingdom during the Second Intermediate Period. Tuthmosis I first invaded the Kushite kingdom, and advanced as far south as the Fourth Cataract. Under his grandson, Tuthmosis III, the capital Kerma was sacked and destroyed, and came under Egyptian domination. This same pharaoh founded an entirely new town, Napata, beneath the cliffs of Jebel Barkal near the Fourth Cataract, with a temple to Amon, chief god of the empire.

From about 1200 BC Egypt was again beset by disunity and increasingly threatened by outsiders, and the pharaohs lost their grip on Nubia, which for the next four centuries is shrouded in a veil of archaeological and historical obscurity. Then, in the eighth century BC, a native Nubian dynasty suddenly appeared at Napata— avidly devoted to the Egyptian gods—and in 712 BC militarily conquered Egypt, establishing the 25th, or "Ethiopian," dynasty. From 600 BC, Nubia, now part of the Meroitic empire, was considered a rival to Egypt. These Nubian pharaohs set themselves as the restorers of proper Egyptian tradition and religion, more Egyptian than the Egyptians, as it were. Right up until the end of the Meroitic kingdom, curiously enough, the royal dynasties preserved many of the pharaonic traditions that had long disappeared in Egypt itself.[9]

If, alas, Cleopatra was not black, the pharaohs of Kush most definitely were, and it was in pursuit of the archaeological ruins of their various kingdoms that I headed north from Khartoum, Sudan, down the Nile and up through the Nubian Desert, toward the Egyptian border.

Because of a terrorist attack in the Valley of the Kings in which several German and Swiss tourists had been murdered, we decided to postpone the rest of our filming in Egypt until April and spend December in the Sudan. The name of this country today is virtually a code word at the U.S. State Department for all the terrorist dangers of sub-Saharan Africa. The American bombing of the pharmaceutical plant in Khartoum in August of 1998 was only the most dramatic manifestation of this perception. A few weeks before I left Boston for Khartoum, Madeleine Albright, the U.S. Secretary of State, warned Americans against traveling to Sudan, citing American and Egyptian intelligence reports that the Sudanese government had stepped up its sponsorship of terrorist activities. Owing to the suspected involvement of the

Gold, panther skins, and ostrich hides are among the riches offered by Nubians as tribute to Ramses II, "Lord of the Two Lands."

Sudanese in an assassination attempt on Egyptian president Hosni Mubarak, the border between Egypt and the Sudan had been closed. Whatever the historical connection, relations between the Sudan and Egypt had definitely seen much better days.

Sudan would prove a challenge for me, not least because the government strictly enforces *sharia,* the traditional Islamic law that, among other things, forbids the consumption of alcohol. In addition, since so much of what was once the Kingdom of Nubia lies in the vast Nubian Desert, we would have to camp out in the wilderness for two weeks filming, cooking for ourselves, sleeping in tents, without hot showers or flushing toilets. And then there was the little matter of my being an American—persona non grata. But I have to confess to a hopelessly naive optimism about being warmly received by black Africans. The absence of wine and toilet facilities worried me far more than terrorists!

My journey to the Sudan centered on three main sites, which neatly divide the history of ancient Nubia into three distinct periods:

KERMA: This was the capital city of the earliest empire of Nubian civilization, when the land of Nubia was united under a dynasty of powerful indigenous kings. The extraordinary remains we see there today date from the period 2400 to 1700 BC, but recent excavations by Charles Bonnet suggest that it was the site of a major settlement even throughout the fourth millennium BC. As we shall see, these ruins reveal that Kerma is the oldest city in Africa yet discovered.

NAPATA: Napata, with its temples and pyramids at Jebel Barkal and its painted royal tombs at el-Kurru and Nuri, was the capital and sacred center of the subsequent era of Nubian power. Adopting a deep devotion to the gods venerated by the Egyptians at Jebel Barkal and restoring their temples, the Nubian kings of Napata stepped onto the world stage as the pharaohs of the 25th dynasty, invaded Egypt in a period of political weakness, and made themselves masters of a vast empire that stretched from Palestine in the north to Nubia in the south. It is one of these pharaohs, the great builder Taharqa, whose name appears twice as "Tirhaka" in the Hebrew Bible.

MEROË: Even after Assyrian invaders had pushed Tanutamani, the last Nubian pharaoh of the 25th dynasty, out of Egypt, Nubia thrived for a thousand years, establishing a new capital at Meroë. The city was a hub of a trading network whose spokes stretched to the Mediterranean, Central Africa, the Middle East, and West Africa. A curious hybrid culture arose here that merged Egyptian traditions long since extinct with distinctly sub-Saharan religious elements; it also produced a script that remains undeciphered.

THE ROAD TO KERMA

We landed in Khartoum late in the evening, only to endure the most meticulous customs inspection of our twelve-country journey through Africa. I had taken very seriously the warning that the penalty for bringing alcohol into the Sudan is flogging. But the customs officials inspected even our shampoo bottles. It took four hours—twice as long as our flight from Cairo. We checked into the Hilton at 1:30 A.M., exhausted and a bit concerned about security. The next morning, we met our "communication conduit," the man to see in Khartoum for faxes, working telephones, and travel accommodations: a Greek expatriate named George. He had arranged for the crew and me to be ferried around the Nubian Desert for the next fourteen days by an Italian named Michele, who drove one of our three Land Cruis-

The Nile and its cataract—a huge dam project of the Sudanese government promises to flood surrounding Nubian villages.

ers, cooked our meals, and whose sense of direction through flat, unchanging, unpaved desert terrain proved nothing short of astonishing.

We flew in a tiny plane from Khartoum—a flying casket, it seemed, with eight passengers squeezed into seven seats—to the city of Dongola, where we met Michele and his two Sudanese drivers, Kale and Amir. Also on hand were our guide and "fixer," Ahmed Osman, a Nubian who had received his PhD in Economics from Harvard; and Abdullahi, a representative of Sudan's Ministry of Culture. We boarded the Land Cruisers that would be our homes for the next fortnight and drove through the desert for the next twelve hours. Our destination? Delgo, a village on the Nile north of the Third Cataract—I had been invited there to participate in a traditional Nubian wedding, an invitation procured by George.

Since by custom the ceremonies would not begin until the early afternoon, we drove to the village of Kajbar, at the northern end of the Third Cataract. The Cataracts are stupendous clusters of boulders and stone formations in the Nile River that create intense rapids and make continuous navigation impossible. We stood on a hill, in the middle of a sixth-century Christian ruin, looking down at several small villages spread along the curving river. Unfortunately, these settlements will soon be lost forever if the Sudanese government goes forward with the planned Kajbar Dam. Though it will not be nearly as vast as the Aswân High Dam—which in the early 1960s created a 125-mile lake that flooded most of Lower Nubia—it still threatens not only to displace thousands of Nubians but also to continue the systematic destruction of their ancient civilization.

Most Nubians are opposed to the dam, especially after the experience of those forced out by the Aswân Dam. Many were resettled in areas far from their homeland, resulting in the loss of their distinct culture and language. Many feel that this will happen again, and that it is no coincidence.

They believe that the effacement of a distinct Nubian people is the current Islamic government's ultimate goal. Many Nubians are keenly aware of having a long history that predates Islam by centuries, if not millennia; some say their history is unwelcome in a republic that likes to portray itself as strictly Islamic and Arab. Somewhat depressed at the prospect of so much destruction, we drove to Delgo to film the wedding of Doctor Abu Zar.

Dr. Abu Zar was educated in Khartoum and has gone back to practice in his family's village. This is Abu Zar's first marriage. Although as Muslims they are allowed to take up to four wives, it is quite rare for Nubian men to marry more than once. Monogamy is probably one of the many customs that survive from the time, before the fifteenth century, when all Nubians were Christian. Though most of his immediate family now live in Khartoum, Zar felt a three-day village wedding would be more traditional, more Nubian. A wedding, the most important ceremony in Nubian culture, is the occasion for Nubians to reassert their distinct ethnic identity, their sense of all being part of one big family.

On the evening before, the bride's and groom's families and friends get together. In the heavily incensed air, the women have their hands and feet elaborately painted with henna; the men stain their fingers with the dye as a sign of friendship or kinship. In both households, the histories of the families are recited.

Early the next morning, bulls and sheep are slaughtered for the celebratory feast. The bride is attended by an intimate group of women, who in a time-honored rite decorate her skin with henna. At the same time, the groom undergoes the *jertik,* a preparatory ritual in which his forehead is adorned with a gold crescent while family members and villagers give advice and tell stories. Lunch follows for the groom's family and friends.

We talked to Zar, who speaks a little English, about his wedding, his village, and his sense of what it means to be Nubian, as we drank tea with the male members of the family. All of us were dressed in the traditional *jellabia,* stark white textured cotton gowns and embroidered caps.

The ceremony begins with the women presenting the groom with a sword wrapped in red silk; he waves it in the air as they dance around him. Then they tie a ribbon bearing the image of a serpent around his forehead. His hands are covered with henna, his nails painted, his eyes rimmed with kohl.

The sharp, clean detail of the henna lines on the women's hands and feet is astonishing. They wear long, brightly colored gowns with matching mules. We all dance to the high-pitched wailing of Fathi Mohammed Dawood, Nubia's foremost traditional singer. We celebrate for hours in the desert heat. At about 10 P.M., the

The wedding of Dr. Abu Zar

bride and groom and their guests proceed to the town's concert hall; a parade of cars, a crazy array of lights, and loud horns. Then the couple is presented to the crowd and seated on the stage on makeshift thrones. Late into the night, traditional dancing: the men in one long line, the women in another, each moving toward the other, almost touching, then backing away. Resting between songs, I happened to sit next to another doctor from Khartoum who also practiced in Delgo. "You love to dance," he said, "and our women are very beautiful. But has it occurred to you that virtually every woman you have seen today has been circumcised? Even the well-educated ones? This is a nightmare for our society, and it is not likely to change any time soon." His comments were devastatingly chilling to me. Before this, I thought of female circumcision as primarily the plight of rural, uneducated women. I had no idea that it affected the urban middle class as well.

The following morning witnessed the final stage of the wedding: The bride and groom walk through the date palms down to the banks of the Nile, step into the river, and wash their faces. The groom with his sword then "cuts" into the Nile the sign of a cross. This detail is obviously Christian, but the ritual washing in the Nile on the occasions of birth, marriage, and death is said to date back at least to pharaonic times and clearly reflects the symbolic importance of the river to the people of Nubia.[10] Following a late breakfast of meat stews and a paper-thin bread, we headed off to Mashakela.

Mashakela is a typically picturesque Nubian village just south of Kajbar. White mud-brick homes with beautifully painted doors are arresting against the bright blue sky. The designs and colors are reminiscent of the artifacts of ancient Nubia. It would be easy to forget the modern world except for one thing: This place is sure to be drowned when the dam is built. While the villagers hope they will be resettled fairly, no one knows exactly what the authorities are planning. Weekly meetings take place to discuss the dam. I visited a *madrassa* (Koranic school), where thirty or so women dressed in brightly colored *tobes* were learning and reciting the holy book of Islam. This is the oldest *madrassa* in the whole of Sudan, famous across Nubia.

Sheikh Abdallah Oshi, one of the two brothers who now run the school, is a striking figure, his aubergine-colored skin glistening against the starched whiteness of his *jellabia*. Having spent much of his life outside Nubia, Sheikh Oshi is rather atypical for a villager. I asked him how he feels about the new dam. His family built the school 350 years ago, and he knows it will be washed away. The sheikh reflects the fear and uncertainty of his neighbors: He allowed himself to be interviewed but would not talk freely in front of our guide from the Sudanese Antiquities Department because he is in an extremely awkward position. As a respected sheikh (teacher) he is much favored by the current Islamic

Christian past: stucco painting from the great cathedral at Faras shows Nubian bishop Petros under the protection of the apostle Peter.

regime, and sometimes fellow Nubians think he is in the government's pocket. At the same time it is government policy that threatens to deprive him of everything he holds dear. Such an ambivalent relation with the regime is not uncommon for Nubians; the reasons are rooted in their religious history.

While most Nubians today are Muslims, few espouse the fundamentalist line of the government. Many I spoke to preferred to emphasize tolerance and peacefulness, qualities they attribute to their Christian past. In the sixth century, polytheistic Nubia adopted Christianity. Judging by recorded changes in burial practices and the consecration of Nubian temples as churches, it was a rapid process. The reasons were mainly political. At the turn of the sixth century, the Dyophysite and Monophysite sects were vying for control of the church. Each side looked for help to the Nubians, still famous for their skills as warriors. For their part, the Nubians saw conversion as a way of strengthening their links with Egypt and Byzantium. Like Egypt, Nubia would become a Monophysite stronghold whose citizens adhered to the dogma of the Coptic church.[11]

The kingdom enjoyed more than 600 years of uninterrupted peace, something of a golden age characterized, in particular, by exceptional ecclesiastical architecture. But in the Middle Ages, Nubia was overrun by invading Muslims and soon became impoverished. The state collapsed, as did organized religion and foreign trade: Writing and formal education disappeared entirely, along with a variety of Nubian artistic traditions. On all practical levels the country reverted to a tribal society. It was into this vacuum that Islamic teachers stepped. Conversion came quickly, again perhaps more as a practical than a religious matter. With such a varied religious past, the Nubians have always been renowned for their tolerance—much to the annoyance of the fundamentalist Islamic authorities.

I discussed Nubia's culture, and the new dam, with a figure who is renowned for her controversial opinions and outspokenness. Soad Ibrahim is a sixty-year-old Nubian communist with wavy gray hair and a magnetism and fortitude that belie her years. Her home is frequently raided by security forces, but she will never give up her struggle against the regime. After a few minutes with her, I could see why. "They do not need a dam. It will not benefit our people. They just want to wipe us out. We will not move, we will die here. We are proud black people who have an ancient history—but the government wants to pretend there is nothing before Islam. Rubbish!" She continued, "Look at the history of the great black pharaohs, Piankhi and Taharqa, etcetera. The Nubians will not have our land taken from us a second time. Over our dead bodies," she declared. Soad's resentment of government religious fundamentalism is equally forceful on women's issues: "What has Islam to offer me as a woman? Men go to heaven and will be surrounded by as many women or young boys as they choose. What will a Muslim heaven offer a woman?"

I left Soad inspired by her strength and love for this people who have fought for so long for the survival of their culture. But I was also somewhat worried about how her outspokenness would be answered.

KERMA

It took several hours to wind our way from Mashakela through the cappuccino-colored sands of the Nubian Desert to Kerma, the center of Nubian civilization from 2500 to 1500 BC. We arrived at 8:00 P.M. and joined the renowned Swiss archaeologist Charles Bonnet for a splendid dinner at the house where he has lived for three months a year for the past thirty years. Behind it is a large farm, where we camped. Bonnet keeps his honorary degree from the University of Khartoum hanging on the wall of his home to fend off the secret police, who often harass him for digging at Kerma. He told me that while there are more than 2,000 excavation sites in Egypt, there are only twenty in the Sudan—explaining perhaps why so much about Nubia remains to be discovered. Bonnet's research has revolutionized our understanding of the nature, extent, and antiquity of Nubia, carrying scholarship far beyond the dismissive early work of George Reisner.

Ancient Kerma consisted of a walled enclosure of 10 hectares (one hectare equals 2.47 acres), with an additional 15 hectares of surrounding settlements. At the heart of the city was a temple, an audience hall, and a palace, as well as some 200 houses. The size suggests that it was the center of a powerful and wealthy African state, controlling the flow of luxury goods from the south that the Egyptians so passionately desired. Archaeological evidence has established that, at its zenith 3,700 years ago, the empire of Kerma stretched as far north as the First Cataract, near Aswân in modern Egypt.[12]

A few years ago the discovery of an urban society 4,500 years old at Kerma transformed all conceptions about early civilization in the Sudan, but in the last seasons of excavating, Bonnet has found remains of extensive town sites beneath the Kerma settlement that carry us back another 2,000 years. The emerging picture is of a complex urban society that evolved here perhaps already

Detail of a model of Kerma, showing the city's center, including the round palace

by 5000 BC. It is the oldest urban site we yet know of in Africa.

The Western Deffufa is the mud-brick structure that rises from the plain like a mud termite mound. As I approached it with Bonnet, its immense facade resolved to individual bricks; I was astonished that it could have survived more than 4,000 years. Bonnet's work has overturned the assumptions of previous archaeologists: While they thought it the fortified palace of an Egyptian governor, he has shown it to be a temple constructed in at least twelve stages.

All around the Western Deffufa are the remnants of what seems to have been the royal city known to the Egyptians about 2200 BC as Yam. What it was later called we don't yet know, but it became the capital of a kingdom called Kush. The name first appears in Egyptian texts around 2000 BC and becomes familiar to us through the Old Testament. In an area of some 30 to 50 hectares are the ruins of two fortified palaces: an older model, which is round and reminiscent of central African models of the ninteenth century (yet its date can be placed at about 2200 BC), and a later model incorporating Egyptian features, dating from around 1600 BC. The earlier round palace had been used for several centuries and had been rebuilt several times on the same spot.

The Eastern Deffufa, thought to be a funerary chapel, is a similar, if slightly smaller temple found on the other side of the modern village of Kerma. It is surrounded by a vast cemetery whose burial mounds are the size of football fields. The kings interred here must have been immensely powerful; they were probably considered divine. I examined the site of one of the largest royal tombs at Kerma, now covered by sand, which measures 295 feet in diameter, and whose occupant was interred with almost 400 human sacrifices, dressed in beaded leather and linen loincloths and outfitted with bows,

Surrounded by vast burial grounds, the upper, or Eastern, Deffufa was most likely a mortuary chapel.

Nearly 65 feet tall, the lower, or Western, Deffufa was Kerma's main religious structure.

bronze mirrors, ostrich-feather fans, ceramic jewelry, semiprecious stones, ivory, and bone. (The presence of archery should not surprise us; after all, the Egyptians referred to Nubia as "The Land of the Bow.")[13]

Egyptian records tell us that the king of Kush (almost certainly at Kerma) had shown himself hostile to the Theban rulers and sided with their rivals, the Asiatic Hyskos kings in the north in the seventeenth century BC. When the Thebans expelled the Hyskos and reunited Egypt, their armies turned south to punish Kush and seek her riches. Under successive pharaohs of the 18th dynasty, the kingdom of Kush was overrun in about 1580 BC. For the next 400 years, Egypt ruled Nubia as a colony as far south as the Fourth Cataract. Its imprint is seen now in the ruins of towns and temples strewn across northern Nubia, reaching as far south as Jebel Barkal. After about 1100 BC, however, the Egyptians withdrew from Nubia, leaving it to local powers yet unknown to history. Only in about 750 BC, when historical documents again became available to us, do we see that Nubia had become reunited under a ruling family of native sons, with their capital at Napata, beneath the 300-foot

cliff of Jebel Barkal. The next leg of my journey through the desert took me there, which was the center of the next phase of the civilization that the Kerma kings had created. It was in this phase that Kush would bring all of Egypt into its own empire, and in which its kings would bring renown on themselves and their race as "the most pious, most just of men" and "whose offerings the gods most preferred."

But just before heading south—*up* the Nile—I met a businessman who runs a large date plantation near Kerma, on Badeen Island. Over a meal of foule (the local staple made of fava beans), Mohammed Sherif explained how little modern Nubians living around Kerma know of their illustrious ancient history. Sherif had lived his whole life next to the Deffufa assuming it was an old Egyptian fortress. He'd been absolutely astonished to learn he had been raised in the oldest city of Africa, the seat of the earliest Nubian kings—a discovery made only when he attended a lecture given by a British archaeologist in Khartoum. When Sherif wanted to set up a new company, he proudly chose the name "Kush," until he realized that no one in Kerma had ever heard of the word!

On the island of Argo, the semi-ruined palace of one of Nubia's last kings

To him, it's small wonder so few people in the outside world know about ancient Nubian civilization, given that so few Nubians do. He admitted sadly that many residents used to use the Deffufa as a public toilet!

We drove on to Argo, an island in the Nile not far from Kerma. Here I met Abdullah al-Melek, a very kind and gentle man who speaks some English, and who took me to explore the beautiful semi-ruined palace on a bluff overlooking the Nile that used to be the home of his grandfa-

ther, one of the last of the Nubian kings. When the old Christian empire fell apart around 1500, Arab conquerors came into Nubia and carved out new principalities. They settled down, intermarried with the local population, and soon became Nubians themselves. The Nubian Meks, or Meleks, were the last royal family in Nubia. Al-Melek pointed out the arcaded terraces where his grandfather would receive his guests, and the harem where his grandfather's ten or eleven wives lived. His family kept their position even under the colonial regimes of the nineteenth century, their power coming to an end with Sudan's independence. They remain, however, the principal landowners in the region, and are still addressed respectfully as "*melek*" or Mek—"king"—by the local people.

That night, Abdullah al-Melek and his cousins honored my crew and Charles Bonnet's archaeological team with a great feast. It was the first time I had dined with kings—*and* eaten like one! I was impressed with the effortlessly regal demeanor of the family, and sad at the faded splendor of their lives. Whatever the discomforts of traveling in the Sudan, my initial fears about encountering hostility among its people were foolish and absolutely unwarranted. Nubian hospitality was, if anything, a bit overwhelming. ("Why *can't* you stay with us for a week?") The Sudan is a study in contrasts: While the civil war rages in the south, sleeping among the sand dunes in a tent one could not feel safer.

THE KINGDOM OF NAPATA: JEBEL BARKAL AND EL-KURRU

I could not wait to see Jebel Barkal, the spiritual heart of the ancient city of Napata. A bold outcrop of rock lifted high above the Nile and the modern market of Karima, it had been the base from which the black pharaohs asserted themselves as the most powerful rulers in the world. By the eighth century BC, the Egyptian empire had splintered into several weak principalities. Upper Egypt was dominated by the priesthood of Amon at Thebes; Lower Egypt by jointly ruling Libyan princes. Far to the south, the Nubian princes of Napata also began to worship the Theban god Amon, whom the ancient pharaohs of the New Kingdom had believed also dwelled within the rock at Jebel Barkal. Thus, at Jebel Barkal and the nearby cemetery of el-Kurru, I confronted the moment when the Nubian princes of Napata assumed power as a new line of pharaohs.

The mountain has a distinctive pinnacle that rises 270 feet above the temple. Timothy Kendall, leading a Boston Museum of Fine Arts expedition, recently discovered at the very peak a monument cut into the rock, inscribed with the name of Taharqa, the greatest Nubian pharaoh.

The king's engineers scaled the rock needle and had sheathed its summit in gold. Kendall has discovered that the pinnacle was seen as a natural statue of a rearing ureas, the sacred cobra-head symbol of Amon and Egyptian royalty that was adopted by the rulers of Kush. Thus they believed it to be the source of their kingship.

Napata came to prominence during the Egyptian occupation. In the thirteenth century BC, Pharaoh Ramses II built the Temple of Amon close to the base of Jebel Barkal. Many Egyptian priests settled there and the whole area became sacred to the great god, who was thought to have been born on the mountain. Successive pharaohs added to the temple, which after Karnak is the most important site in the Egyptian religion. Since the all-powerful Amon had in later centuries sanctified Jebel Barkal and Napata, the city at its foot, the Nubian kings of Napata would come to see themselves as the authentic

THE KUSHITE DYNASTY[14]

c. 1000–850 BC	Rise of a chiefdom centered at Napata
c. 785–780 BC	"Chief" Alara unites Upper Nubia
c. 760 BC	Kashta unites all Nubia; calls himself king (son of Ra) of Upper and Lower Egypt
c. 747–716 BC	King Piye (Piankhi) establishes sovereignty over Upper Egypt
	Wars against the kings and princes of Lower Egypt
716–656 BC	25th dynasty; Kushites establish capital in Egypt
716–702 BC	King Shabako (uncle of Piye)
702–690 BC	King Shabitko (son of Piye)
690–664 BC	King Taharqa
664–656 BC	King Tanutamani
	Kushites expelled from Egypt by Assyrians
	End of control over Egypt

Jebel Barkal, spiritual heart of ancient Napata

sons of Amon and therefore the rightful heirs of the Egyptian pharaohs.

The Napatan king Kashta seized the reins of power in Kush, wresting Lower Nubia (the area now under Lake Nasser) from the Egyptians and moving even into Upper Egypt, then ruled by the priests of Amon at Thebes. He may even have reached Thebes and installed a Nubian princess as the chief priestess of the Temple of Amon at Karnak, the center of Egypt's divine kings. Kashta claimed the title of the pharaohs "King of Upper and Lower Egypt" and founded the line of Nubian pharaohs known to history as the 25th dynasty, though he does not seem to have governed much of Egypt during his life.

The Kushites' fluency in the culture, life, and language of Egypt faciliated their conquest. Piye (also known as Piankhi) would ultimately finish what Kashta had begun. Around 730 BC he conquered the rest of Egypt, adding it to the kingdom of Kush. The new empire stretched more than 1,200 miles from the Mediterranean to beyond the Sixth Cataract of the Nile.[15] Piye was politically savvy: He permitted local Egyptian princes to remain in charge of their own districts and installed his sister as a high priestess in the Temple of Amon at Karnak with the title

"God's wife of Amon." In another gesture of self-legitimation, Piye crowned himself.

With his extensive mastery of the land's rituals and culture, Piye cemented his full pharaonic power by affecting to be more Egyptian than the Egyptians—and he began a few traditions of his own: For instance, he was the first to build pyramids in Kush. Among his other projects was a restoration of the great temple of Jebel Barkal, including the erection of a granite stela upon which is inscribed the oldest and most extensively detailed surviving ancient Egyptian text. The 159 lines of hieroglyphs describe the workings of Piye's palace: his mercy, his love of horses, and his campaigns against Libyan princes. (Piye's love of horses was manifest at the end of his relatively short reign: Decorated with beads and jewels, his horses were buried with him.)[16]

In 716 BC, Piye was succeeded by his uncle Shabako. Shabako invaded Egypt and reconquered it. He named Memphis the new capital to facilitate his governance and he removed disloyal governors. At this time the building of pyramids was expanded, and eventually more royal pyramids existed in Nubia than in all of Egypt. But the pyramids built by these kings around Napata and near Meroë are smaller than the Egyptian ones, and were to me more lovely. The pharaohs from Kush did not see themselves as usurpers but rather as the rightful heirs to the glory that was Egypt's during the Old and Middle periods, and they sought to embrace and restore it.

While the neo-Assyrians were consolidating their empire in the Near East (Phoenicia, Israel, Judah, and Philistia), Shabako maintained a position of noninterference. But Shabitko, the son of Piye who succeeded his uncle Shabako in 690 BC, adopted a more aggressive stand. He provided military support to a rebellious Judah and Philistia, thereby placing Egypt and Kush in direct conflict with Assyria. Though the conflict with Assyria

In the temple of Mut, friezes depict Tanutamani (664–656 BC), last of the Nubian pharaohs, as he is led to the afterlife in the Egyptian style.

into captivity; her young children were dashed in pieces at the top of all the street; and they cast lots for her honorable men, and all her great men were bound in chains.[17]

In 593 BC, the Saite King Psamtik II invaded and defeated Nubia, and afterward he erased the names of the Nubian pharaohs from Egyptian monuments. Up until that point the Saite kings had felt insecure about their control of Upper Egypt, since the kings of Napata still called themselves "King of Upper and Lower Egypt." With the Egyptian sack of Napata in 591 BC, and the retreat of the Kushite court southward, they felt justified and secure "altering" the Kushite mounuments in Egypt, chiseling out names and inserting their own, altering the form of the crowns or mutilating faces.[18]

After the Kushites were pushed out of Egypt, their his-

persisted, he nevertheless built extensively in Memphis and Thebes, especially at the Temple of Amon at Karnak.

Eventually, the Assyrian menace in the north caught up with Taharqa. He defeated the invaders in 674 BC, but in 671 BC he lost control of Memphis and died in Nubia in 664 BC. The Napatan empire began, once again, to shift southward. Yet the Assyrian attack definitely played a prominent role in the relocation of Kush. Following Taharqa's death, his nephew Tanutamani took the throne. He tried to reconquer Lower Egypt, but was defeated and lost Upper Egypt as well. He was pushed back to Napata while Thebes was brutally pillaged and destroyed by the Assyrians in 663 BC. The event is recorded in the Bible: The prophet Nahum, in warning Nineveh, the capital of Assyria, of the town's eventual fate, said:

Art thou better than Ne-amn [Thebes] . . . that was situate among the canals and had the Nile around it for a rampart and wall? Kush and Egypt were her strength . . . Yet she was carried away, and she went

Royal lion cub [Nubian] devouring a Kushite

tory is difficult to determine. The capital remained at Jebel Barkal for some time before it was transferred to Meroë, following Napata's capture in 591 BC by an Egyptian expedition strengthened with Greek mercenaries. Despite the move to Meroë, Napata remained the religious capital of the kingdom, and many monarchs continued to be buried at Nuri (the royal burial ground) through the fourth century,[19] a total of twenty kings and fifty-three queens.

Nubian dominion over Egypt lasted less than a century, but left a profound mark on Nubian culture, particularly among the ruling elite. Napata's art, hieroglyphics, and architecture bear distinctive Egyptian influences, signs that the culture retained pharaonic customs and continued to worship Egyptian gods. They may no longer have ruled Egypt, but Napatan kings were addressed as kings of Upper and Lower Egypt, and were buried under pyramids at Nuri and el-Kurru. Indeed, the upper class as a whole enthusiastically embraced their adopted Egyptian culture with a purity they claimed the "decadent" Egyptians to the north had long lost. Unfortunately, little is yet known of life among the more ordinary Nubians at this time, but what has been recovered so far suggests that there is a real continuum between the general culture of the Kerma period and that of the Napatan.

For one all too brief but glorious moment, Nubia, if not more powerful than Assyria, at least had the largest empire in the world—one ruled by black men and women. Stanley Burstein's summary of their legacy bears quoting at length:

During the approximately half century they ruled Egypt, the Kushite kings of the Twenty-fifth dynasty reunited the country and sponsored a renaissance of culture that resulted in the creation of some of the greatest works of Egyptian art, and whose effects continued to be felt throughout the remainder of the history of ancient Egypt. They also made Egypt an active and significant player on the international scene again for the first time in almost two centuries and helped delay, albeit only briefly, the conquest by the Assyrians of the smaller peoples of the eastern Mediterranean basin such as the Jews and Phoenicians. Even after their retreat from Egypt, the Kushites continued to influence Egypt in various ways. They protected Egypt's southern border against raids by the nomadic peoples who inhabited the Nubian deserts, while providing Egypt with needed imports from the interior of Africa. Equally important, Egyptian rebels against foreign rule—Persian and Macedonian—took inspiration from the existence of a powerful independent state in Nubia.[20]

With the Italian archaeologist Irene Liverani, I visited the Temple of Mut, built by Taharqa underground in the

Shawabtis of King Taharqa (690–664 BC). Intended as servants of the deceased in the afterlife, these figures typify Nubian appropriation of Pharaonic style.

48

Gold mask of Queen Malakaye, early sixth century BC, from Nuri

base of Jebel Barkal. Unlike the tourist temples in Egypt, it has not been cleared and neatened up; Indiana Jones came to mind as I squeezed my way between boulders to enter. The rusted iron roof leaked shafts of sunlight across the gloom to reveal exquisitely carved and painted friezes depicting gods and kings.

As we walked throught the ruins, Liverani explained to me how Piankhi appropriated and reversed the traditional symbolism of Nubia in Egyptian art, representing himself as a legitimate heir of the pharaohs and depicting himself with black features. The role of queens in official art grew in accordance with Nubian custom, as did Kushite customs "such as facial scarring and the deliberate deformation of the horns of cattle."[21] Traditional Kushite burial procedures replaced mummification, and "the lion-headed war god Apedemak gained prominence at the expense of Egyptian gods."[22]

There is no evidence of a sudden end to Napata. It seems to have continued for generations as a royal and religious seat, where kings were anointed by the priests of the Temple of Amon, and where they were buried. But it is clear that the city's importance as an economic and administrative center declined in favor of Meroë, far to the south, away from direct Egyptian interference. At some time between the sixth and fourth centuries BC, Meroë became the royal capital of ancient Nubia. The next stage of my journey took me there.

MEROË

Meroë at sunset was a still life of clustered pyramids tinted by fading light. Here were the remains of an indigenous civilization that had survived more than a thousand continuous years, outlasting ancient Egypt. During the final stage of its history, beginning in 300 BC when the Nubian rulers transferred their cemetery to Meroë from Napata, the kingdom stretched along the whole of the Nile valley from just south of Aswân to 185 miles south of where I stood. Meroitic culture shows definite departures from the heavy Egyptian influences of the preceding Napatan phase with the new art and architecture bearing the marks of the Greco-Roman and Eastern worlds. Indigenous black African (i.e., sub-Saharan) gods, too, came to rival those of the Egyptian pantheon in importance. Nevertheless the pharaonic culture of ancient Egypt was in many ways preserved by the Meroitic kings for centuries after it died out in Egypt.

Positioned between the Fifth and Sixth Cataracts, Meroë was blessed with abundant water and fertile soil. Alexander the Great invaded Egypt at the beginning of the reign of the Meroitic king Nastasen (335–315 BC).

When he died, his empire was divided among his generals, and Egypt went to Ptolemy. The Ptolemies in Egypt and the Meroites in Sudan both thrived, separated by a "semi-neutral zone" known as "the *Dodekaschoinos*" (the twelve-mile strip).[23]

When Octavius Augustus defeated Cleopatra in 30 BC, making Egypt a Roman province, the Romans attempted to colonize Meroë for its gold and its strategic access to trade with sub-Saharan Africa. As we shall see, battles ensued between forces led by Kandake (Queen) Amanirenas and the Roman general Petronius (24–21 BC). Initially victorious as far north as Aswân, Philae, and Elephantine, the Romans counterattacked and chased the Meroites south to Napata. Nubia was divided into the Lower (Roman) and the Upper (Meroitic), and the two kingdoms developed a thriving trade.[24] Meroë reached its height of prosperity in the first century AD. The city may have covered an area up to a mile square, but most of it remains unexcavated, and we have no idea of its layout. There were stone tombs and temples, but other more important buildings were made of red bricks; the humbler structures were almost certainly built of mud bricks. Within Meroë are traces of a royal palace and a large bath complex, clearly inspired by the baths of the Roman world. Outside the walls of the palace is a temple to Amon, the largest Meroitic temple known.

THE PYRAMIDS
OF MEROË

Two to three miles from the ancient city of Meroë lie the remains of forty generations of Nubian royalty. When we arrived at the North cemetery (which, like its southern

Kalabasha temple, built during the Meroitic period in Lower Nubia

counterpart, has an impressive grouping of pyramids that overlook the plain from ridges), we encountered an architect from the former East German Academy of Sciences, Dr. Friederich W. Hinkel, who was hard at work rebuilding one of the pyramids on a new foundation. The North is a royal cemetery that contains forty-four tombs of monarchs and a single crown prince; in 1833, it was "excavated" by an Italian treasure hunter named Giuseppi Ferlini, a medical doctor who came to Meroë with the Turko-Egyptian forces of Mohammed Ali Pasha. Because he believed that the contents of the tombs lay inside the pyramids, he tried to dismantle them from the top, destroying the largest and badly damaging the others. Nonetheless, he found a fabulous treasure in one, which is now divided between the Berlin and Munich museums. Our architect was hard at work repairing the damage, a project that has taken him decades.

Though every royal Nubian tomb is housed in a chamber beneath the pyramid, cut from the bedrock and accessed by a stairway, we should note that the structures depart significantly from their Egyptian models. The largest Nubian pyramid is that of Taharqa at Nuri: It is only 170 feet at the base, compared with 750 feet for the pyramid of Cheops at Giza. The Nubian pyramids are built of small stone blocks and pitched more steeply.

The uncapped pyramid of Natakamani, King of Kush in the early first century AD, Meroë, North Cemetery

Above: "Bent pyramid" at Dashur: unique in that the angle changes halfway up
Opposite: Meroitic royal pyramids in the south knoll at Meroë, third century BC

Early examples are solid masonry, but the later manage only a facade of stone over rubble. They lack the internal passages and chambers found in Egypt, and the royal remains were interred in a few small chambers cut into the bedrock beneath the monuments. However, most of the Nubian pyramids have a chapel attached to the eastern face, and it is in the more opulent of these that we find the relief work and inscriptions that are the most important traces of Meroë's culture. Since, unlike the Egyptian, the Meroitic pyramid was itself not a tomb but only a monument that lay above the tomb, it had to be built after burial. A king had to rely on his successor to build his monument, so it is possible that the building of pyramids figured in the legitimacy of a new monarch.

The second century BC marks the earliest appearance in Meroë of inscriptions in a distinct indigenous alphabetic script. Contrary to Hegel's view that Africans had never developed—indeed, could not develop—their own written language, Meroitic, clearly, served as one for government administration and daily life. But no one has been able to decipher the script, and until a Nubian Rosetta stone appears we are left to conjecture. Employed into the fifth century, Meroitic was displaced eventually by Old Nubian written in a Greek-based script that incorporated three of its symbols. Its wide use on monuments suggests that a significant percentage of the population was able to read it. Some of the longest such inscriptions tantalize scholars with the hint that they are extensive narratives of Meroë's enigmatic history.

Meroë had extensive contact with Egypt, or rather her Roman rulers. In 23 BC, a Roman governor, Gaius Petronius, raided Napata because the Kushites had sacked his frontier at Syene (Aswân) and taken a statue of the Emperor Octavius Augustus, which had been set up in the marketplace. Eventually, the Kushites were forced to submit and sue for peace. Roman historians recorded

Without a Nubian Rosetta stone, Meroitic script remains undeciphered.

that the ruler of the Kushites was a queen called "Candace" or "Kandace," who is also named in the Book of Acts. The name was evidently derived from the Meroitic queenly "Kandke" or "Kedeke," which probably had the meaning "queen mother." Her real name was Amwirenas or Amanirenas.[25] A particularity of Meroitic royal culture worth noting is the prevalence of powerful queens, some of whom ruled in their own right. In joint reigns, the queen was not a consort but a coruler. There are two Meroitic tablets that mention this Amanirenas, both linked with the general in charge. During archaeological excavations, a splendid bronze head of Augustus was found buried underneath a temple doorway, as if placed so that all who entered and departed the building would step on it. It is now in the British Museum.

Meroë was abandoned between AD 300 and 350 during the collapse of the Nubian empire. Its iron industry and agricultural base had deteriorated, in large part due to environmental abuse. Mounds of waste-slag suggest the scale of a smelting industry that consumed huge amounts of charcoal. Trees were cut down faster than new ones could grow, leading to erosion and loss of topsoil. Soon the land lost its fertility. Trade suffered when Meroë's principal market, Roman Egypt, saw its wealth decline and with it the demand for Meroë's goods.

By the fourth century AD, Meroë was being racked from within by two desert tribes, the Blemmyes and the Noba, whom the Romans played off against each other. Even more important, a powerful rival, the new kingdom of Axum in northern Ethiopia, had begun to emerge. Soon it became the largest commercial center in East Africa. The Axumites built a port (Adulia) on the Red Sea, which attracted Roman trade with Africa, Arabia, and India. Meroë thus lost a vital source of income.[26] In AD 350, Ezana, the first Christian king of Axum, vanquished Meroë at the confluence of the White Nile and the Atbara Rivers.

Perhaps the most judicious assessment of this black kingdom belongs to Jean Leclant:

Whatever the importance of this penetration of Meroitic influences through the rest of Africa, the role of Kush should never be underestimated: for over a thousand years, first at Napata and then at Meroe, there flourished a strongly original civilization which, beneath an Egyptian-style veneer fairly constantly maintained, remained profoundly African.[27]

I ended my visit to the Sudan at Musawwarat es Sufra— a twelve-hour drive through the desert from Meroë. In many ways, this is one of the most extraordinary sites in Nubia, and remains a bit of a mystery. Professor Ali Osman, chairman of the archaeology department at the University of Khartoum and a classmate of mine at Cam-

Stela of King Tanyizemani found at Jebel Barkal

bridge, showed me around the Great Enclosure, a series of sandstone edifices (whose smooth walls displayed the work of ancient graffiti artists in several languages) surrounding a central temple raised on a platform and accessible only by ramps. The temple dates from around the first century AD, but there were structures here at least six hundred years before that.

The Great Enclosure is a singular structure in Egypt and Nubia. The buildings seem without purpose; there is no town, no cemetery. Perhaps the number of elephants

Ruins of the enigmatic Great Enclosure
of Musawwarat

sculpted at Musawwarat es Sufra, including one remarkable wall, is a clue. The enclosure's large spaces could easily have lent themselves to the training of elephants for military use, and perhaps the ramps were easier given their bulk than steps. However, recent excavations by Humboldt University have shown that the enclosures were filled with gardens of fruit trees and plants fed by an elaborate system of underground irrigation pipes. The site is now generally assumed to be a royal pilgrimage center where seasonal rituals were performed.[28]

The presence of two or three temples indicates the Great Enclosure undoubtedly had a religious function. But we do not know the whole story. Osman even thinks that it was the site of a great university, perhaps the first on the entire African continent. Given Meroë's sophisticated culture, such a hypothesis is not implausible.

A few months later, I resumed my exploration of Nubia by flying to Egypt, then taking a train to Aswân, with a heavily armed military escort to protect us from terrorists. It was at once unnerving and reassuring. As a boy in the Piedmont of West Virginia I had heard about the Aswân Dam because teachers in the nearby Washington public schools had tried to lead a protest against it, arguing that it would destroy "black Egyptian civilization." What in the world can that be? I had wondered.

Over the centuries, Aswân, Egypt's southernmost city, has been a garrison town and a frontier city; the gateway to Nubia and Africa; a prosperous marketplace at the crossroads of the ancient caravan routes; and, more recently, a popular winter resort. In ancient Egyptian times, it was known as Swenet—which also meant "trade." The Copts called it Souan, which also meant the same thing—hence Aswân. The main town of Swenet lay on Elephantine Island—Yebu in ancient Egyptian, which means both "ivory" and "elephant." Swenet was the base for expeditions into Nubia. From here, at the First

Cataract, Egyptian fleets and trading ships sailed up the Nile through Lower Nubia as far as the Second Cataract.

Near the banks of the river, I met Isra Dahab, a smart young Nubian newswoman with Upper Egypt's Channel 8. She presents her own weekly program called *Nubian Treasures* about Nubian life, traditions, and history. As the first program on Egyptian television devoted entirely to Nubian issues, hers is seen as quite an achievement for this minority.

Dahab and I talked about what it means to be Nubian. She described the Nubians as the black people of southern Egypt and Sudan. She's proud of her heritage—and of a black civilization "which is as old as Egypt's," as she frequently notes. Today they consider themselves Egyptian or Sudanese, but first of all they are Nubian. And she admits that, compared to modern Egyptians, they do feel more African. Dahab finds it a pity that she cannot speak the Nubian language properly, as her father and his generation do, because it's a fundamental part of being Nubian. Today Nubians are separated by borders and politics, but they still feel they are one family, one nation, having fought since ancient times to hold on to a distinct cultural identity. We crossed the river on the little public ferry to Gharb Aswân (West Aswân), a sprawling village on the west bank of the Nile opposite the town of Aswân. It remains a traditional Nubian village, set back from green fields along the river.

Each year, the Nile floods and the sediment that washes down from the heart of Africa creates a strip of fertile land that for centuries has sustained people living along the river. The glories of ancient Egypt were built on the waters of the Nile. But these floods were unpredictable; it was to regulate the flow of the river and to provide Egypt with hydroelectric power that the Aswân High Dam was built. This great monument of modern Egypt, eighteen times more massive than the Great Pyra-

Sculpture among the ruins of Musawwarat. The elephant was of religious importance.

mid of Cheops, has forever transformed the landscape, and forever altered what we know about the history of the Nubian people.

The first Aswân dam was built by the British between 1898 and 1902 to bring more land under cultivation and thereby meet the needs of Egypt's growing population. When Colonel Gamal Abdel Nasser came to power in 1952, plans were drawn up to build a colossal new dam 4 miles south of the old one. In 1956, after the United States, the United Kingdom, and the World Bank suddenly refused the financial backing they had offered for the project, Nasser ordered the nationalization of the Suez Canal as a means of raising capital. This move precipitated the Suez Crisis, in which British, French, and Israeli forces attacked Egypt. A year later, largely the result of pressure from the United States, a cease-fire was called and the troops were withdrawn. The Soviet Union then offered the necessary funding and expertise; work began in 1960 and the Aswân High Dam was completed in 1971. As a result, Egypt's cultivable land mass was increased by 30 percent, the hydroelectric station doubled the country's power supply, and a rise in the Sahara's water table has been recorded as far west as Algeria. On the other hand, the fertile silts of the Nile no longer flow into Egypt. It is estimated that in forty years the whole of the lake will be silted up. Also, should the dam ever burst, the whole of Egypt would be washed away into the Mediterranean.

The dam has created the largest man-made lake in the world, Lake Nasser, which stretches 310 miles into the Sudan. The reservoir completely drowned Lower Nubia all the way to the Second Cataract, forcing the relocation of the thousands of Nubian people who lived in fifty settlements along the Nile, including the Old Nubian town of Wadi Halfa. Ballana, a purpose-built concrete village north of Aswân, is now home to the many inhabitants of

Nineteenth-century sketch of the Hypostyle Hall within Abu Simbel. Eight statues of Ramses II, their torsos rising out of the sand, support the roof.

the drowned villages. Here Dahab and I met Fawzeya Gamel Suleiman, a woman who remembers having to leave her home at the age of nine. Fawzeya did not see her home sink, since they were moved well before the waters started to rise. She says that at first they were excited because the government had promised new homes with better facilities. On a single day they gathered all their possessions, and she recalls simply being carted off and dumped in Ballana like animals. At once they began to regret their loss. Fawzeya says that as children they played by the banks of the Nile; the waters provided sustenance and everyone enjoyed excellent health. Now she lives in an unattractive brick village far from the Nile; malaria is prevalent and the children are frequently ill. Far from the river, the villagers have no way to earn a living.

Many ancient monuments were to be drowned as well, but an archaeological rescue mission from the Egyptian Department of Antiquities and UNESCO excavated and saved what it could. Fourteen temples and fortresses were

Abu Simbel

dismantled and removed, but eleven remain buried forever under Lake Nasser.

However, one of the greatest treasures rescued from the lost land is Egyptian, not Nubian. At the colossal temples of Abu Simbel, in the company of Bassam El Shammaa, an Egyptian Egyptologist who lectures in Cairo, I learned a final lesson about the complex relationship between ancient Egypt and Nubia. Under the UNESCO rescue plan, the temple was sawed into more than 2,000 stone blocks (each weighing between 10 and 40 tons) and reconstructed inside a specially built mountain high above the new waterline. The project took more than four years, and cost $40 million.

El Shammaa explained that Ramses II, the great builder whose round colossus of Luxor inspired Shelley's *Ozymandias,* set Abu Simbel in Nubia for various reasons. First, he wanted to show his power over the region. Tour guides sometimes say that Ramses built Abu Simbel as a gesture of love for his wife Nefertari, whom they claim was Nubian—although there is no evidence for this. It is also described as a massive statement of pharaonic power, a warning to any potential troublemakers from the south that here they were entering the domain of the greatest ruler in the world. Although there are warlike reliefs in the temple, it also contains marriage stelae: It was not, in other words, a place that was meant to terrify, but rather to seduce. El Shammaa believes that the image of Ramses II inside the temple paying respect to a huge cobra is an image of him honoring a Nubian god, a god reminiscent of a figure at Jebel Barkal. Abu Simbel was Ramses's way of introducing himself and his family to the Nubians, on a most gigantic scale!

The great temples of Abu Simbel were carved out of a mountain on the west bank of the Nile between 1290 and 1224 BC. There are two: The colossal temple of Ramses was dedicated to the gods Ra-Horakhty, Amun, and

Jeune Nubienne *by Charles Gleyre (1835). "I wish I was your Nubian girlfriend," an old song goes.*

Ptah, and, of course, to the deified pharaoh himself. The smaller temple of Nefertari was dedicated to Hathor, the cow-headed goddess of love. Each of the statues of Ramses on the front of the temple is more than 65 feet high, accompanied by smaller statues of the Queen Mother and Nefertari. Above the doorway stands a figure of the falcon-headed sun-god Ra-Horakhty. Inside, eight statues of Ramses hold up the roof of the Hypostyle Hall; the reliefs on the wall show the pharaoh victorious in various battles. In the next hall, Ramses and Nefertari are shown in front of the gods and the solar barques that will carry them to the underworld. The innermost chamber is the sacred sanctuary, where the gods (including Ramses) sit on their thrones. Every February 22 and October 22 at sunrise, light penetrates the temple and illuminates the faces of these figures.

As I stood before the Aswân Dam, peering out at the grandeur of Lake Nasser, I recalled the history of ambivalence and enmity between Egypt and its ancient kinsman, the kingdom of Nubia. Here were a second Jacob and Esau. If Nubia was the corridor between the upper and lower regions of the Nile—indeed, between the black and brown world of Africa and the white world of Mediterranean Europe—and if the area around Aswân was the meeting point of these worlds, then so very much of what we long to know about the sub-Saharan influences on Egyptian civilization (and vice versa) is buried forever under the waters of Lake Nasser—no doubt along with a massive amount of evidence about the so-called racial identity of the Egyptians themselves.

I wondered if the dam, which undeniably has had wonderful effects on the Egyptian economy, would have been built in lower Egypt. I found myself, as I stared at the lake, recalling Hegel's definition of tragedy: the war, not between good and evil, but between two goods.

Scholars will long continue to debate the "blackness" of the Egyptians. But no one can debate the blackness of the Nubians, or the Axumites who defeated them in the fourth century AD. As we drove away from Aswân, I could not help but think of my friends and neighbors back home in West Virginia, when I was growing up. They believed that many of the major figures in world history had in fact been black, ranging from Moses's wife and the Queen of Sheba, to all the pharaohs of Egypt and Cleopatra, on down to Beethoven. But here, at the northern end of what was the ancient kingdom of Kush, I had seen the evidence myself— the pharaohs of Egypt's 25th dynasty were black men, who most probably had a hair texture and skin color not all that different from my own. I could not help but wonder what other revelations lay buried beneath the waters of Lake Nasser . . . indeed, beneath the rubble of a thousand African civilizations yet to be excavated.

3

ETHIOPIA: THE HOLY LAND AND THE LOST ARK OF THE COVENANT

There, the sacred waters of the Erythrayean Sea break upon a bright red strand, and at no great distance from the ocean lies a copper-tinted lake, the lake that is the jewel of Ethiopia, where the all pervading sun returns again and again to plunge his immortal form and finds a solace for his weary round in gentle ripples that are but a warm caress . . .

—AESCHYLUS, Fragment 67

There is a land of sailing ships,
a land beyond the rivers of Cush
which sends its envoys by the Nile,
journeying on the waters in vessels of
reed. Go swift messengers, go to a
people tall and smooth skinned,
to a people dreaded near and far,
a nation strong and proud, whose
land is scoured by rivers.

—ISAIAH 18:1–2

St. George's Church of Lalibela

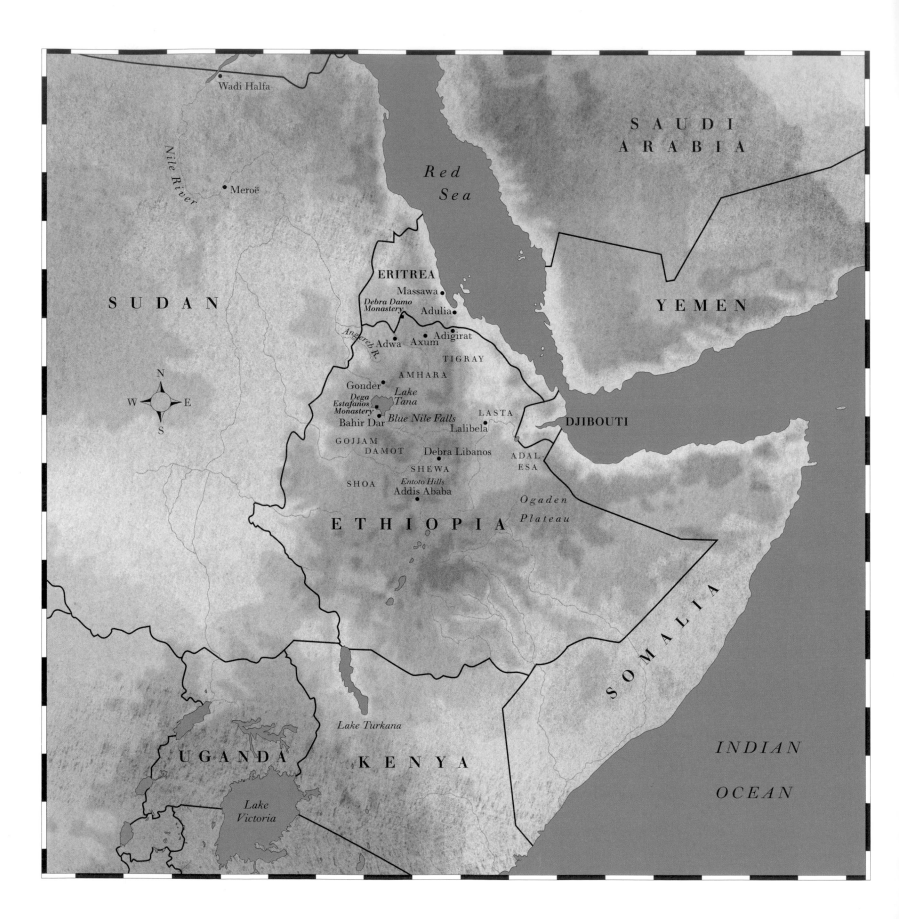

SAUDI
ARABIA

YEMEN

Red
Sea

ERITREA

Nile River

Wadi Halfa

Meroë

SUDAN

Massawa

*Debra Damo
Monastery*

Adulia

Angereb R.

Adwa   Axum

Adigirat

TIGRAY

AMHARA

Gonder

*Dega
Estafanos
Monastery*

*Lake
Tana*

Blue Nile Falls

LASTA

DJIBOUTI

Bahir Dar

Lalibela

GOJJAM

DAMOT

Debra Libanos

ADAL
ESA

SHEWA

SHOA

Entoto Hills
Addis Ababa

*Ogaden
Plateau*

ETHIOPIA

N
W   E
S

SOMALIA

Lake Turkana

UGANDA   KENYA

INDIAN

*Lake
Victoria*

OCEAN

There is a certain pathos in an African American's determination to recognize people from home among the faces of strangers in Africa. As Richard Pryor once put it: When African Americans first visit Africa, they experience the "There goes my Uncle Willie!" phenomenon. In Mali, I met a man, a dealer in artifacts, who looked so much like Michael Jordan I was at once convinced that Michael's ancestry had to be Fulani. I even took his picture and sent it to Michael. This principle can work both ways: The Nubians, Amharic Ethiopians, and the Swahili all tended to address me in their own languages, mistaking me for one of their own kinsmen. And who knows, perhaps I am, by ancestry; yet doomed never to be, on account of culture; and never to know for certain, because of history. There are few emotions more sublime and exhilarating for an African American than to be mistaken for an indigenous African, as a person whose home is "the Continent," as we fondly call it. I think it must be difficult for a white person to understand the rush of emotion engendered in us by being surrounded for the first time by a sea of black faces after a long stint in a desert of whiteness, where white is the default, the baseline standard of "the human." Then again, maybe white people raised in black countries such as Zimbabwe or South Africa experience this feeling when they first visit London or New York. Perhaps this feeling is one reason why I love visiting Africa so very much.

And despite the fact, as I say, that I have had this experience among the Nubians in the Sudan, among the Swahili peoples living along the Kenyan and Tanzanian coasts and on the island of Zanzibar, nowhere in the twelve African countries that I visited was I more consistently mistaken for an African than in the ancient country of Ethiopia, the second most populous in Africa.

*　*　*

For most of us today, "Ethiopia" suggests poverty, famine, and war. And yet, for many black people—especially black Americans and the Rastafarians of Jamaica—Ethiopia has always represented something special, an almost mythically pristine site of blackness untrammeled by white racism or colonialism. Ethiopia's special place in the cultural imagination of African Americans owes much to the importance of Christianity there. Ethiopia is not only the oldest continuous seat of Christianity after the Egyptian church on the Continent, but the second most frequently mentioned African country (after Egypt) in both the Old and New Testaments. In fact, as early as 1844, black historian Robert Benjamin Lewis in his book *Light and Truth* made the bold claim that "Ethiopia (Gen. ii 13) was black, and the first people [Adam, Eve, and their offspring] were Ethiopians, or blacks."[1] While the discovery in Ethiopia of Lucy, or Berkenesh as the Ethiopians call her, the oldest known hominid, and other archaeological evidence support the claim that human beings emerged from sub-Saharan Africa, black people untrained and uneducated have believed this for centuries.

When I was a boy, I attended a church that was 100 percent black. When I was twelve, I was "saved," and decided to "give my life to Christ" and, eventually, become a preacher. But all of our gods and all of our saints were white. It is difficult to imagine today how thrilling Biblical references to Ethiopia were to black Americans desperate for a history to be proud of when I was growing up in the 1950s. I relished the Bible's forty-one references to Ethiopia; I studied them, memorized them, and puzzled over their meanings. There is a well-established and formidable black oral tradition of glossing sacred (and secular) texts, a kind of African American Midrash without the scholarly apparatus. In barbershops, beauty parlors, and other ritualized settings, people would argue for hours about the "secret history" of our people, sifting evidence from a variety of texts and endlessly teasing out their implications for our plight in the Babylon that was America. Since we were devout Christians, no text could possibly be more important to our image of ourselves than the Bible. But we were also black, and "keeping the faith" meant, in part, being aware of, decoding, and nurturing the encrypted revelations about the black presence in even the most obscure places and language, especially the language of the Bible.

In Ethiopia, it seemed, black people had become Christians hundreds of years before Christianity came to England, and a thousand years before Columbus discovered America.[2] What's more, it was whispered, their saints and icons were black! How could we not be fascinated—indeed, obsessed—with this ancient Christian kingdom and its extraordinary history? It was the home of the legendary Christian King Prester John, as well as the Queen of Sheba herself, and her son, Menilek I, who was fathered by the great King Solomon; it was the location of Ophir, where Hiram, the Phoenician king, mined gold for King Solomon; it was ruled, for most of my life, by the Emperor Haile Selassie, a direct descendant of Menilek, and therefore, Solomon, whose title was King of Kings, Lord of Lords, conquering Lion of Judah, and Jah Ras Tafari—for the Rastafarians who worshiped him, God incarnate; it was the home of the Ark of the Covenant; it was home of one of the Lost Tribes of Israel. Little wonder that Marcus Garvey's "Back to Africa" movement argued that Ethiopia was our natural, inevitable homeland, to which we must repatriate. Little wonder, too, that "Ethiopianism" is the name that historians give to one strain of black nationalism that has obsessed African Americans for nearly two centuries.[3]

Perhaps most astonishing to us, not only has Ethiopia been independent for almost 2,000 years, but it has twice

defeated invading Italian armies—once in 1896, under Menilek II (with the help, we were told, of the Ark of the Covenant), and again in 1941, under Haile Selassie, with the more worldly aid of the Allied Forces.

Ethiopia has developed a very strong cultural identity, shaped in part, perhaps, by its unique environmental conditions: While representing only 4 percent of the continent's surface, Ethiopia has 50 percent of the land above 2,000 meters, and almost 80 percent of the land above 3,000 meters.[4] Ethiopia is Africa's Switzerland, its Rocky Mountains. Cut off from the world by its fierce mountain terrain, a protection against would-be invaders, it still managed to have frequent contact with its African neighbors as well as the Near East and India. It is a godly place, being home to indigenous religions as well as Christianity, Judaism, and Islam.

My journey followed the Christian "historic route," beginning in Addis Ababa and traveling through the ages back to the site of the original Christian kingdom in Axum. There, I encountered not only the birthplace of a uniquely African form of Christianity, but also what is now believed to have been one of the last great civilizations of antiquity. Throughout the journey, I followed the trail of a particularly Ethiopian historical mystery: the belief that for three thousand years, Ethiopia has been—and still is—the home of the Ark of the Covenant, the wood-and-gold casket that contains the Ten Commandments.

The route was as follows:

ADDIS ABABA: The country's secular and religious center. Though the city is barely a hundred years old, I could feel its religious passion at the sacred waters of Kedane Mehret.

LAKE TANA: I went to see the monks in their island monasteries, where they have watched over the remains of emperors for centuries. The lake, the source of the

Blue Nile, was the heart of this Christian empire from the fourteenth to the sixteenth century.

GONDAR: We came into Gondar with a resplendent surge of pilgrims dressed to celebrate Epiphany, known in Ethiopia as Timkat. The celebrations of feasts, dances, and baptisms around the palace's pool lasted for two days, during which we were introduced to the central tenet of the Ethiopian church, the veneration of the Ark of the Covenant, which it claims resides at Axum. Gondar is also the home of the Beta Israel, or Ethiopian Jews, most of whom claim that they are the descendants of Hebrews who did not participate in the Exodus.

LALIBELA: A fairy-tale cluster of churches, monasteries, baptismal pools, and secret passages, this mountain village is thought to be the twelfth-century fantasy of King Lalibela, who wanted to build a new Jerusalem in Africa. Legend states that he was aided by a band of angels in the project; even today, every nook seems guarded by a nun or monk.

AXUM: The capital of one of Ethiopia's oldest civilizations, Axum was my final stop. As an article of faith, Ethiopians believe that the Ark of the Covenant resides at Axum, protected constantly by a devoted priest. Their traditions hold that the son of the Queen of Sheba returned from Jerusalem with the Holy of Holies.

As we saw in Chapter 2, the term "Ethiopia" ("burnt-faced") comes from the Greek and was used to refer to all Africa south of Egypt, quickly becoming a powerful metaphor for mystery. We first see the word used specifically to describe the territory of the present country on an ancient stone inscribed with three languages (Greek, Latin, and Ge'ez, the ancient Semitic language of Ethiopia), left by Ezana the great Axumite emperor in AD 327. The territory was generally known

In medieval Europe rumors circulated of a kingdom ruled by a descendant of one of the Magi.

as Abyssinia (from the Arabic word *habesha*—"of mixed race") until the mid-twentieth century. Oral tradition holds that the area around Axum, in northern Ethiopia, was settled by Aethiopis, son of Noah, ancestor of the Queen of Sheba. But of the forty-one references to Ethiopia in the Bible, many refer to Nubians rather than the area known as Ethiopia today. (Not that the Ethiopians admit this.)

Before the arrival of the Portuguese in AD 1520, the country's remoteness cultivated a mystical aura; and in medieval Europe rumors circulated of a land where a great Christian kingdom flourished among barbarians under a ruler called Prester John. This great King John, purportedly a lineal descendant of one of the Magi who

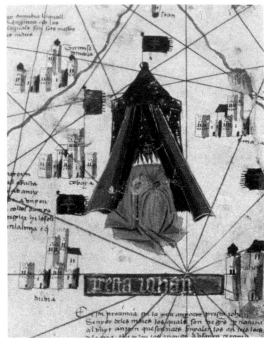

A dreadlocked Prester John imagined on a fifteenth-century Catalan map of the world. The search for the legendary king's riches was a principal inspiration for Portugal's circumnavigation of Africa.

had visited the infant Jesus, supposedly sent a letter in Latin to several European rulers in AD 1165, in which he described his riches and declared his intention to journey to Palestine to defeat the Muslims and regain the Holy Sepulchre. Pope Alexander III was so moved by this promise that he responded by letter in 1177. For the next four centuries, Europeans desperately sought this kingdom, fabled to be the source of King Solomon's gold.

During the Crusades, Europeans believed that they might be able to mobilize this great dominion against the Muslim infidels occupying the Holy Land. The legend of Prester John, however, seems to have puzzled the Ethiopians themselves. In 1441, the Ethiopian mission to Rome brought a message from their emperor: "My name is Zara Yaqob—offspring of the prophet Jacob. My second name is Constantine. Why do Europeans call me Prester John?"⁵

It was the search for Prester John's riches, in part, as well as his fountain of youth, that was a principal motivation for the Portuguese drive to circumnavigate Africa and find a sea route to the East. But it was not only an alliance against the Muslims that Europeans sought; the legend of Prester John's riches persisted, and what a legend it was!

As described in the *Travels of Sir John Mandeville:*

The palace is so wealthy, so noble, so full of delights that it is a marvel to tell of. . . . The steps up which the emperor goes to his throne where he sits at meals are, in turn, onyx, crystal, jasper, amethyst, sardonyx, and coral; and the highest step, which he rests his feet on when at meat, is chrysolite. All the steps are bordered with fine gold, set full of pearls and other precious stones on the sides and edges. The sides of his throne are emerald, edged in fine gold set with precious stones. The pillars in his chamber are of gold set with precious stones, many of which are carbuncles to give light at night.⁶

The first European explorers who finally penetrated the interior of Ethiopia were sorely disappointed. Of course, there was no Prester John to be found. Nevertheless, Ethiopia had become a metaphor for Europeans of wonder and exoticism.

If European views of Ethiopia were mostly informed by the legend of Prester John, no legend has more fundamentally informed Ethiopians' understanding of their own history than that of Solomon and Sheba. And for them, the story is no legend. Their national epic, the *Kebra Nagast* (*Glory of Kings*) narrates the Queen of

Sheba's journey in approximately 1000 BC to meet King Solomon. Ethiopians believe that she returned and bore a son, Menilek I, the patriarch of all Ethiopian emperors.

The Biblical version of her visit is seductively vague. Kings 9:26–10:29 states that the Queen "came to Solomon and communed with him all that was in her heart," and that "Solomon gave unto the Queen of Sheba all she desired. . . ." Though the Bible explains the encounter as her attempt to learn the art of governing from the wise king, it is not surprising that many, with Solomon's rakish reputation in mind, have glossed the passage with a bit of a wink.

Where the Bible is coy, the *Kebra Nagast* is forward. It tells us that Solomon seduced the Queen with the unlikely stratagem of preparing a feast of spicy meat in her honor. When he invited her to pass the night in his chambers, she agreed, with the condition that he promise not to seduce her. But Solomon had terms of his own: She had to swear not to remove anything from the palace. Cunning as he was wise, he placed a pitcher of water near her bed. Parched from the spicy food she had consumed at the feast, Sheba awoke later that night and drank feverishly. The King, who must have been watching for this very moment, exclaimed that she had broken her oath and nullified his in the process. It is not known whether the Queen protested much; suffice it to say that she returned pregnant to Ethiopia and gave birth to his son, Menilek.

After growing up at his mother's court, Menilek went to visit his father in Israel. A genial Solomon took the young boy into his own court and, impressed with his qualities, offered to make him crown prince. Menilek decided, however, to return home, and the King anointed him King of Ethiopia and assigned to him a number of young Israeli aristocrats as his retinue. Ethiopian legend maintains that it was this escort that

absconded with the Ark of the Covenant. It is more certain that the dynasty he is said to have founded ruled Ethiopia almost continuously until 1974, when Haile Selassie, the 237th Solomonic monarch, was deposed.

The Second Article of the 1955 Ethiopian constitution set this legend into law, proclaiming that "the Imperial dignity shall remain perpetually attached to the line . . . [which] descends without interruption from the dynasty of Menilek I, son of the Queen of Ethiopia, the Queen of Sheba, and King Solomon of Jerusalem." Though most

In the Bellifortis *of Conrad Keyser, circa AD 1405 in Bohemia, a dazzling Queen of Sheba is depicted with black skin and golden hair.*

historians take the story with a grain of salt, I remember being taught in childhood that, according to Genesis, Sheba was a descendant of Ham (thought to be our progenitor because of the curse of slavery on his son, Canaan), while the Book of Matthew (12:42) called her "the queen of the South." We all knew what that meant. Sheba was a sister; there could be no doubts about that. For the Ethiopians, however, Sheba was the Founding Mother, Matriarch of their line of Solomonic kings.

If the wisdom of Solomon is thought to have accompanied Sheba to Ethiopia 3,000 years ago, Christianity is said to have arrived in the fourth century in the persons of two shipwrecked Syrian brothers. They were brought to the Emperor at Axum, where Frumentius, the more intelligent of the two, was recognized for his wisdom. After King Elta Amida died, Frumentius began to convert the kingdom, and was eventually consecrated as the first bishop. This event occurred shortly after Constantine I's conversion led to greater acceptance of the faith in the Roman Empire and long before the religion was established in western Europe.

The Axumites may have converted just to establish greater trade with the Hellenic world, but whatever the reasons for the shift, it can be dated by stampings on the coins issued during the rule of Ezana: Early mintings depict the sun and cresent moon; later examples, the cross.

Westerners frequently mistake the Ethiopian Orthodox Church (EOC) for the Coptic Church (which is Egyptian). The two are theologically similar institutions, but the EOC contains aspects imported directly from Judaism: The church adheres to much Jewish law on circumcision, diet, and the restriction of women from religious rites while menstruating. Some have argued that its doctrine includes elements of ancient Egyptian religion as well, since many services also involve dances accompa-

A teacher of theology instructs his students.

nied by drums and sacred rattles. It is a religion seemingly designed to test the commitment of its followers: Priests at Lalibela can spend twelve hours a day in worship. Sunday observances begin at midnight; even throughout the week the devout will pray seven times a day. One hundred and eighty days of the year are given over to fasting, a burden eased somewhat by the fact that this can mean simply avoiding meat until nightfall. At the height of its power, under Emperor Haile Selassie, the EOC had amassed huge wealth, owning 15 percent of the land and collecting rent and taxes from its tenants. The Emperor and the EOC maintained a mutually supportive and reinforcing relationship from the fourteenth century to 1974, the year of the Marxist coup.

The EOC continued to be a powerful institution in Ethiopia even after much of its property was seized in the wake of the coup. Neither the politicization of church fathers nor the country's lean toward atheism during the Marxist regime could excise the EOC from the daily life

*The faithful gather at dawn for prayer at the Church of
St. Mary of Zion of Axum. The church remains central to Ethiopian life.*

of the people, many of whom, though they do not attend services, bow three times when passing a church. Others will stop to kiss the walls. At a church in Addis Ababa, I witnessed crowds of worshipers wearing the *shamma* (a white shroud). Outside the city, the church assumes a more civic role, particularly in its burial societies; it also is often the deciding voice in whether to proceed with public works projects.

But such power can run contrary to the aims of economic development. Not only is the church a strong voice against contraception, it also makes considerable demands on its followers' lives. There are still so many saints' days to be observed that it can be difficult to get the harvest in, or do business with the outside world.

While not everyone is a member of the EOC, religion still plays a central part in the day-to-day life of most Ethiopians. And as we have seen, the country has for more than a millennium been home to three of the world's major religions: There are twenty million Christians in Ethiopia (the EOC claims about thirty-eight million), out of a total population of fifty-nine million. The number of Muslims is similar, though the ratio is always a topic for debate. Only a few Beta Israel (Falasha) remain after "Operation Moses" airlifted them to Israel. Very generally, the northwestern provinces are Christian and the southeastern are Muslim.

Muslims arrived in Ethiopia as refugees during the time of Mohammed when some of his disciples (among them a woman who would be one of his wives) fled to escape persecution in Arabia. The resulting goodwill, embodied in the Prophet's statement that Ethiopia was "a land of righteousness where Allah will give you relief from your suffering," sheltered the land from Muslim attacks until the sixteenth century. Muslims consider the walled city of Harar in eastern Ethiopia central to their faith, much as Christians think of Axum. African deities are worshiped by some eighty different ethnic groups living in the lowland fringes of Ethiopia, though both Christianity and Islam display some influences from their early converts' traditional religious beliefs.

Emperor Haile Selassie's inability to address his country's poverty was the principal motivation behind the overthrow of the monarchy. In September 1974, a group of army officers, calling themselves the *Derg* (the Committee), took power, arresting Haile Selassie, then suffocating him to death. At the height of the terror, Mengistu Haile Mariam, the son of a night watchman, took power. It may not be apocryphal that Mengistu Haile Mariam buried Haile Selassie under his desk to keep him eternally underfoot. With the emperor's execution, a monarchy that claimed roots back to Solomon and Sheba came abruptly to an end, and Ethiopia became a byword for famine and war.

This grand country, with the second largest population in Africa, replete with its long tradition of civilization and literacy, history and myth . . . this Ethiopia of my childhood fantasies of black fathers of the church and black saints, is the land where I searched for the lost Ark of the Covenant.

THE HOLY WATER OF KEDANE MEHRET

The reality of the devotion and faith of the Christian Ethiopian is apparent as soon as you arrive in Addis

Ababa. Kedane Mehret is a church built around a sacred natural spring in the eucalyptus forest of the Entoto hills near Addis Ababa. Each morning, crowds of the old and young, sick and able patiently queue, either to collect the precious water in their plastic containers or to enter the communal showers.

The showers admit groups of ten, women only or men only. I was accompanied by our driver, Gebru, a Christian who speaks fluent English. Inside, a priest in a yellow rubber suit and rubber boots strokes an ancient silver cross across the naked bodies, then holds it over bowed heads to confer a blessing. Some of those showering look desperately ill and are propped up by friends or family members.

Near the showers, another priest exorcises demons in a dingy hut equipped with a tub. The shouts of the possessed make one's skin crawl as devils are wrenched from their bodies. The water is freezing cold. Gebru told me how these waters halted his father's paralysis. "He came here for six months and was cured," he said matter-of-factly.

The pilgrims' stay at the spring can last months. While they seek the cure, they rent rooms or build their own rude shacks. The truly destitute, clad only in their faith, are sheltered by the EOC in makeshift structures by the side of the road. This faith is so strong, so palpable, that I felt a bit guilty about my skepticism. An ancient Ethiopian proverb says "to know Ethiopia, the church is the gate." The reality of the Ethiopians' belief that they are God's chosen people suddenly came alive for me as I wandered the grounds.

The following dawn we set out for Lake Tana, source of the Blue Nile, the great Nile's largest tributary and the home of Ethiopia's island monastery. With the morning

Among the treasures of the remote island monastery of Dega Estafanos are these magnificent murals of the life of St. George.

mist clearing, we mounted the hills behind Addis Ababa. Children, swaddled against the chill, herded horses and donkeys along the shoulder. All around us was a plateau covered by fields of wheat and teff (a grain Ethiopians use to make *injera,* the bread that is the staple of their diet). We drove for hours before the road dived in a series of tortuous switchbacks down canyon walls toward the Blue Nile. The route was spectacular, built by Haile Selassie in 1934 and reengineered by the Italians during their occupation from 1936 to 1941; it remains the most direct way to get to the lake city of Bahir Dar from Addis Ababa. I felt the air grow sticky as we approached the river. Now the road flattened out across the plain that led to Lake Tana, dotted here and there by rusting tanks from the thirty-year civil war that had ended only in 1992. It was an exhausting drive; I was glad to arrive.

Twenty monasteries and churches hide on islands set in Tana's thousand square miles. The lake was a vast moat sheltering Ethiopia's medieval church and government in the tumultuous period between the fall of King Lalibela's dynasty and the establishment of Gondar as a permanent capital. The monasteries are vestiges from that period;

many still hold the art and relics gathered from the rest of the country for safekeeping. Dega Estafanos is the most famous; many of its treasures survived the fire that destroyed the original monastery more than a hundred years ago.

On reaching this island, there is a steep walk uphill through a forest. No females are allowed here, not even hens! Inside the church at the top of the hill, hidden in the forest, are rosewood and silver crowns belonging to illustrious Ethiopian monarchs and a sixteenth-century painting of the Virgin Mary and Jesus. This work is a rare example of the ecclesiastical art of the time, most of which was destroyed in the time of Gragn "the Left-Handed," a Muslim who united eastern Muslims in a holy war against the Christians in the sixteenth century. For a time, the Muslim forces gained most of the kingdom, and Christian Ethiopia was saved only when, at the king's request, a handful of Portuguese troops arrived in the country with guns, including Vasco da Gama's son, Christopher, who was to lose his life in battle here.

It took forty-five minutes to walk to the monastery from our boat, where we were forced to leave the female members of the crew. A boyish-looking monk was our guide. He was twenty-one. At the monastery an elderly monk led me to what looked like a decrepit shack. Opening a creaking door with a huge iron key, he revealed treasures that have been guarded here for centuries. The monk took three ornate crowns and an exquisite silver cross down from a shelf. He showed me a red-and-green parchment book written in Ge'ez, a sixteenth-century hand-written edition of *The Lives of the Saints*. Two paintings of Mary and Jesus, depicted with Ethiopian facial features, hang to the left and the right of the door. I saw a

Late-eighteenth-, early-nineteenth-century Ethiopian Christian iconography

cabinet in which are stored ancient royal robes. In the gloom, we filed into the second chamber and by the flicker of candlelight I was introduced to the past owners of these treasures—the mummified remains of five Ethiopian emperors lie in a stack of glass coffins. Several skeletons were covered with pieces of gray parchmentlike skin. I could not believe my eyes. I was touching glass coffins holding the bodies of five of the Ethiopian kings, who reigned from the thirteenth to the seventeenth century. Dega Estafanos is black Africa's Westminster Abbey.

As I stood there in this holy place, I thought of the dramatic contrast between the peace and solitude of these religious havens hidden in the middle of this great lake and the turmoil of the reigns of the kings whose remains are housed here. The history encompassed by these kings—some later venerated as saints—was a tumultuous period marked by continual conflict with Islam. In 1248, a young monk, Iyasu Moa, opened a small monastic school at the island church of Saint Stephen at Lake Hayqt in Amhara. According to the traditional account of his life, one of his pupils, Yekuno Amlak (1270–1285), became the founder of the Solomonic dynasty.[7] Yekuno Amlak asserted a pristine genealogical link to Menilek, thereby claiming descent from the ancient rulers of Axum and the kings of Israel. As we have seen, Emperor Haile Selassie also laid claim to Solomonic legitimacy.

The Solomonic genealogy reads like a book out of the Old Testament. Who begat whom is always followed by war against the infidel and the construction of the latest church built to honor their faith. In the *Ethiopian Chronicles,* women cry as their men go to war, some to fight the ubiquitous Oromo (Galla), portrayed as the infidels from Hell. Others fight the "real" enemy: Islam. With nomadic kings ruling from roving capitals and camps and no permanent capital, medieval Ethiopia developed little urban culture, except in a few places such as Axum, Harar, Gondar, and some coastal cities.[8]

According to the early-sixteenth-century Florentine trader Andrea Corsali, and the Portuguese Almeida, the army retinue was so large that the monarch could not remain in any one place for longer than four months and

Oromo (Galla) pastoralists migrated to Ethiopia early in the six-teenth century and became an infidel threat, though a minor one compared with Islam.

so destructive he could not return to the same place in less than ten years.[9] The church, along with the nobles, was a mighty arbiter of power, causing kings to rise and fall, while imbuing their reigns with a fanatical hostility against all non-Christians, who were seen as threatening the integrity of the kingdom.

The extensive ecclesiastical population was made up of priests, *dabataras* (lay clerics), monks, nuns, and hermits. There were also several highly influential prelates like the *Abun* (traditionally an Egyptian Copt), the *Aqabe Saat* (an Ethiopian cleric attached to the palace), and the *Echege* (likewise an Ethiopian, who was the country's leading abbot and the administrative head of the church).[10]

Emperor Yekuno Amlak's son, Amda Seyon, "The Pillar of Zion" (1299–1314), built the new kingdom while managing to gain a reputation as a lover (he seduced his father's concubine at an early age) and a warrior.[11] Amda

Seyon's domain was surrounded on all sides by Muslim principalities and confronted early on an invasion by Sabr ad-din, the ruler of Ifat, to the east of Shoa, who burned down many churches and killed many Christians. But finally Amda Seyon not only defeated the Muslim principalities of Ifat and Hayda, but also subjugated Gojjam and Da'mat, and extended a superficial hold over Begmeder. The long-distance trade of this period was based on a network of Muslim towns and villages, many of which were situated in the Christian highlands. The *Gadla Zena Marquos*, a Ge'ez medieval work, states that these traders "did business in India, Egypt, and among the people of Greece with money of the King."¹²

The next ruler, Saifa Ar'ad (or Newaya Krestos) (1344–1372), is remembered for his reprisals against Egyptian merchants for persecutions of Christians in Egypt. He was succeeded by his son Dawit I, who came to the throne in 1380 and reigned for more than thirty years. Emperor Dawit was an unpopular monarch who embroiled himself in conflict with a popular monk, Ewostatewos, whose followers remained faithful to Old Testament edicts, notably the observance of the Saturday Sabbath. Dawit persecuted the Sabbatarians, refusing their ordination and banning them from monasteries and churches. He did not, however, manage to quell the popularity of this movement. It was left to his fourth son, Zara Yaqob ("seed of Jacob"), who became king in 1434, to make peace with the Sabbatarians.

Emperor Zara Yaqob began the practice of coronations at Axum, and in doing so, the Ethiopian scholar Donald E. Crummey argues, invested the crown with the prestige associated with the country's old historical, religious, and political capital.¹³ He was famous for his brutal military success against the Sultan Badlay ibn Sa'ad-Din and the Sidama people, and was praised for his religious and administrative reforms, though these seem to have amounted to an inquisition against non-Christians. Zara Yaqob considered Islam a serious threat to the kingdom and aimed to unify his subjects through force. He replaced existing provincial rulers with his own daughters and other female relatives, and instituted an army of spies to ferret out "idolaters." *The Ethiopian Royal Chronicles* states that "in the reign of Emperor Zara Yaqob there was great terror and fear among all the people of Ethiopia on account of his severe justice and authoritarian rule and above all, the denunciation of those who confessed that they had worshipped Dasek and the devil." Emperor Zara Yaqob may be considered one of the greatest of rulers for his reorganization and consolidation of Ethiopian Christianity, but he was not known for his sense of humor: He is alleged to have put to death his own sons to demonstrate how seriously he took the prohibition of idol worship.¹⁴

When Lebna Dengel (1508–1540) became king, the concept underlying the legend of Prester John—an alliance of Christian kingdoms against Islam—assumed an interesting reality. Lebna Dengel had been unreceptive to a series of Portuguese missions that had arrived in Ethiopia. In 1516, the Ottoman Sultan Selim had conquered Egypt and renewed a jihad against the infidels. Now the Portuguese wished to prevent the Turks from occupying naval bases in the Red Sea, and the Emperor was growing vaguely concerned about the Muslim principalities that were encircling the kingdom. Meanwhile, Muslims in Adal and discontented peoples in the south began to organize against Ethiopia under the Somali Imam Ahmad ibn Ibrahim al-Ghazi, otherwise known as Gragn, "the Left-Handed." Gragn routed the forces of Lebna Dengel in 1529 at the Battle of Shembera Kur, with the help of firearms supplied to him by the Turks. He ruled the Christian highlands from 1531, destroying much of contemporary Ethiopia. *The Chronicles* record:

At this time victory favored the Muslims. . . . They dominated the church of Ethiopia. They were the victors in all fights to the east, west, north and south, and destroyed all the churches whose walls were covered with gold, silver and precious Indian stones; they put to the sword a large number of Christians and led into captivity young men and women and children of both sexes and sold them as slaves. Many of the faithful moreover renounced the faith of the church and embraced the religion of the Muslims; it is doubtful if one in ten retained his faith.[15]

The Somali Muslim Ahmad Gragn ("the Left-Handed") waged war against the Christian kingdom, destroying much of Ethiopia in 1529.

The chroniclers clearly saw this period as the zenith of Muslim aggression and identified their plight with the destruction of the Second Temple in AD 70: "There was . . . a great famine, the like of which had never been since the time of the Kings of Samaria nor at the time of the destruction of the second temple."[16]

Amidst this destruction, Emperor Lebna Dengel remembered the overture of the Portuguese and sent a messenger asking for their assistance against Gragn. Some years later, during the reign of Galawdewos (1540–1559), the Portuguese came to the rescue and Gragn was killed at the Battle of Woyna Weha in 1543.

Despite the alliance formed between the two Christian kingdoms, Portuguese Jesuits attempted to convert the Monophysite kingdom to Catholicism. When he came to the throne, Lebna Dengel's grandson, Susneyos, was courted by the Jesuits who had remained in his country after the war. He converted in 1622 to Roman Catholicism, agreeing to abolish all Jewish-oriented rituals and practices. The resulting upheaval was so swift that Susneyos was forced to abdicate in favor of his son, Fasilidas, who promptly reestablished the union between the Orthodox Church and monarchy and expelled the Jesuits.

As for Susneyos, he is always described as having suffered a sort of lapse of sanity. Perhaps the fact that he was one of the first kings to oppose slavery in Ethiopia accounts to some degree for this reputation. The *Fetha Nagast* (or Laws of the Kings) declared that though all men were born free, as God had created them, the law of war compelled them to become slaves of the victors. The text sanctioned the taking of slaves from among the unbelievers and declared that the children of slaves belonged to the owners of their parents. This of course was a view with Biblical support in Leviticus (35:44–6).[17] Though there were other passages that recommended that masters free their slaves for the love of God, slavery remained a fundamental aspect of the Ethiopian economy from the origins of Axum in the third century BC until it was finally abolished by the Italians in 1936.

Ethiopia is rare among African countries for possessing a recorded history this rich in detail. The preservation and veneration of the remains of the emperors at the monastery of Dega Estafanos in the middle of Lake Tana underscores the role of the church in this achievement. Dega Estafanos consists of three concentric chambers; within the innermost—called "the Holy of Holies"—one finds an object at the heart of Ethiopian Christianity: the *tabot,* which resembles one of the stone tablets that the Ark of the Covenant is said to contain.[18] For the ancient Israelites there was no more sacred artifact than the Ark, virtually the personification of God on earth. The *Kebra Nagast* explains the significance of Menilek I's bringing the Ark to Ethiopia: "Ethiopia was especially chosen by God to be the new home of the spiritual and heavenly Zion, of which his chosen people, the Jews, had become unworthy."[19]

The monks at Dega Estafanos, who range from age 21 to age 98, claim that more than forty *tabots* from churches destroyed by Ahmed Gragn were hidden in their monastery during the sixteenth century. Among these, it is said, was the Ark of the Covenant, which, I was told, was saved when St. Mary of Zion Church at Axum was razed. I could not help experiencing a certain awe at the thought of an African church that has existed for nearly two thousand years! After the monks prayed for our welfare, we descended from the mountain hideaway of the monastery and sailed back to Bahir Dar on Lake Tana.

Fishermen on and around the lake use traditional boats called *tankwas* built from papyrus growing around the lake. Slipping out of Tana, the Nile flows slowly on for twenty miles to pour and stumble over the Tissisat Falls, the spectacular site that James Bruce reached in 1770 and described in his book *Travels to Discover the Source of the Nile:* "It struck me with a kind of stupor, and a total oblivion of where I was, and of every other sublinary

Navigating Lake Tana on a tankwa, *the traditional boat built from papyrus*

concern. It was one of the most magnificent, stupendous sights in creation."[20]

Bruce's sublime encounter may have been a source for Coleridge's "Kubla Khan." The book was a best-seller when published in 1790, and it is known that Coleridge was engrossed by it, though he himself traveled rarely. Coleridge wrote:

> Where Alph, the sacred river ran
> Through caverns measureless to man
> Down to a sunless sea.
>
> A damsel with a dulcimer
> In a vision once I saw
> It was an Abyssinian maid
> And on her dulcimer she played
> Singing of Mount Abora.

One of Africa's most spectacular waterfalls, Tissisat is known in Amharic as Tis Abay ("Smoke of the Nile"). The falls are more than 1,300 feet wide when in flood and

One of Africa's most spectacular waterfalls, Tissisat is known in Amharic as Tis Abay, meaning "Smoke of the Nile."

drop over a sheer chasm more than 145 feet deep, with the waters continuing in an enormous gash through the Egyptian plateau. It was a strenuous climb to the top of the hill. I was guided by three young boys who spoke splendid English. I asked one of them if he had ever had malaria. "No," he replied, "but my brother did. My older brother now lives abroad in Australia. He faxed us a list of all the different medicines that my younger brother could take to cure it." Just then, we passed a young boy playing a homemade wooden flute, like a black version of Pan.

"You have a fax machine?" I asked, incredulous.

"Yes, of course," he responded calmly. "Our entire village docs!"

From a grassy bluff I gazed at the Blue Nile where it left Lake Tana. Next to me stood Haile Selassie's holiday palace, an underwhelming modern affair that seemed a feeble send-off to the river's 2,750 mile journey to the Mediterranean Sea. Almost 80 percent of the waters of the Nile that reach Egypt come from the Blue Nile as it converges with the more languid White Nile in Khartoum.

The next morning I was back on the move, heading to Gondar through small lakeside villages and farmland on a Chinese-built road. Buses passed madly in either direction, half-obscured behind clouds of dust, blaring music as they went. Along the way, we stopped for a rest and found ourselves suddenly surrounded by a swarm of children who pointed at one another and giggled hysterically, intoning over and over, "Black people! . . . All Africans are black." The inexplicable recitation sounded like a school lesson that they had learned by rote. With this

Children of the village of Wolleka

chant ringing in my ears, we returned to our travels on roads that are, in the main, unpaved. Journey by land is hard and perilous. Breakdowns are common—at least, they were for us. Finally, after half a day's journey, dust-covered and exhausted, we arrived at Gondar.

We checked into our hotel, the Foghera, absorbing its well-worn ambiance. It had obviously seen better days as the villa of one of Mussolini's henchmen. Later we drove about 1 ¼ miles out of town to the modest village of Wolleka. A hand-painted sign bearing a Star of David says "Welcome to Beta Israel Village." Until recently, Wolleka was home to several thousand Beta Israel. But during the famine of 1985–1986 and the political crisis of 1991, 70,000 Beta Israel—recognized now as one of the Lost Tribes—were airlifted to Israel in "Operation Moses," fulfilling the Old Testament prophecy that the Jews of Ethiopia would return to Zion. Today, about 3,000 remain. I wandered into one of the tiny huts selling curios and asked the shopkeeper whether he was Jewish. "Yes," came the answer. Why didn't you go to Israel with the others? "I was in the army," he replied. Do you speak Hebrew? "No." Can you read these words? I pointed to the blue T-shirt I was wearing that had "Martha's Vineyard" printed in both English and Hebrew. "No," he replied. He seemed to take some comfort in the fact that I could not read Hebrew either!

I strolled along Wolleka's short main road looking at the few houses. True Beta Israel were not so easy to find. Most of the people here try to survive by pretending to be Jewish, catering to the few tourists drawn to the area by selling amateur sculptures of Solomon and Sheba in a rapturous embrace. Typically they are non-Jewish Ethiopian outcasts who came to live with the Falashas as a last resort.

By the time of the airlift, only a few thousand Beta Israel were left from what once had been an influential segment of Ethiopian society. In this century it became illegal for them to own land, and many turned to handicrafts, for example, a profession scorned by their Amharic and Tigrayan countrymen. Persecuted also as deicides, the Beta Israel came to occupy the lowest rung of Ethiopia's social ladder.

Nevertheless, between the two religions there are striking convergences—even beyond the familiar continuities between other forms of Judaism and Christianity.

But nobody is very clear on how a Jewish people came to Ethiopia in the first place. Tradition holds that the community has been a lost tribe cut off from other Jews for two millennia, which may or may not be supported by the presence in Ethiopia of rituals such as animal sacrifice, abandoned in Israel by AD 70. But could they be the descendants of the Jews who accompanied Menilek I from Israel, bringing the Ark of the Covenant along with them, as they claim? As with so much of Ethiopian history, fact and legend remain inseparably entangled. Still, there are other explanations put forth for the Beta Israel presence.

The fact that the Beta Israel physically resemble their non-Jewish neighbors is often marshaled as evidence that they must have been converted by Jewish travelers. Others have argued that they were Middle Eastern Jews who came to Ethiopia when it ruled Yemen in the fifth and sixth centuries; or perhaps they could have been Egyptians who migrated up the Nile, owing to the similarity in their customs to those of Egyptian Jews. But the determination most important these days to the Beta Israel is that the Israeli Rabbinate has officially recognized them as Jews, giving them the right to emigrate to Israel.

It is Beta Israel tradition that Ezana, the King of Axum, had read the Psalms by the time Frumentius arrived. Many customs in the EOC do suggest a Jewish presence in Ethiopia long before Christianity arrived: circumcision of males, observation of the Sabbath on Saturday, and such dietary laws as the prohibition against pork. These are unique to Ethiopian Christianity—which has been called "antique and ceremonial and imbued with an undercurrent of Judaic practice"—and have provoked criticism from other churches.[21] The scholars Steve Kaplan and Kay Shelemay, to whom no one has been able to offer a serious rebuttal yet, argue that Beta Israel are actually a Judaizing sect of Christianity that emerged under the Solomonic emperors.[22] The history of these religions is extraordinarily intertwined, as evidenced by their shared belief that the Ark of the Covenant resides in Axum. About that fact, neither Christian nor Jew has any doubt.

As we headed back to our vehicles, bound for Gondar in anticipation of Timkat, several trucks suddenly pulled up to the edge of the village, brimming with exhausted passengers. They were UN trucks used for transporting refugees. It turned out that thousands of families fled the Tigray region during the war with Eritrea and went to the Sudan. Now they were being repatriated after a

The next day in Gondar I felt like I'd wandered into an African Camelot of stone castles and fortifications, domed towers, and parapets. I climbed the steps of one tower to behold yet further ruins. This was the stronghold of Fasiladas, one of the kings whose remains I had seen back at the island monastery of Dega Estafanos. The city was built by the emperor in 1635, only a hundred years after Ethiopian Christendom was nearly destroyed by Gragn; it is the sort of miraculous rebirth that reflected a deep religious faith.

Rendering of the King Fasilidas's castle at Gondar, a Camelot in Africa, in 1886

Following the defeat of the Muslims in the seventeenth century, Portuguese Catholic missionaries stayed on in Ethiopia and succeeded in converting Emperor Susneyos, who then decreed death for those who did not follow suit. Most Ethiopians, however, were prepared to risk their lives for their faith, and a bloody civil war raged until Susneyos died. When his son Fasilidas took the throne, he banished the Jesuits from the country. For the previous 300 years (since King Lalibela), Ethiopia had not had a permanent capital, but now to consolidate his power and reunite his orthodox kingdom, Fasilidas established a new capital in Gondar, north of Lake Tana between the Angarb and Qaha rivers. There he built a castle, in which he intended to spend the rainy season. His son, Yohannes I (r. 1667–1682), and grandson, Iyasu I (1682–1706), added to the buildings; and by the late seventeenth century, Gondar had become the capital.

Gondar enjoyed a well-deserved reputation as a thriving urban center of politics, religion, and trade. Goods such as incense, musk, gold, and slaves flowed westward to the Sudan or northward to Massawa.[23] The bishop settled in the Gondar parish of Saint Gabriel. The Cathedral of Axum that had been destroyed in the jihad of the 1530s was rebuilt in Gondarine style. In all, the establish-

seven-year absence. I interviewed two young women who were trying to make their way home, another thousand miles away. They were clad in pink and purple, their heads covered with scarves; one was pregnant and both were holding children. The journey had been very emotional for them both and one began to cry. They had kept in contact with some of their relatives, but it had been a very long time since they'd been in Ethiopia. They had no money and this was the end of the road.

* * *

Fasilidas's castle today

ment of Gondar marked an important turning point in Ethiopian history.

Fasilidas's Castle (or Fasil's Castle) is made of stone and shows a combination of Portuguese, Axumite, and even Indian influences. It is one of the ironies of Ethiopian history that the now-despised Beta Israel provided the stonemasons and other craftsmen who built these monuments to the might of the reemergent Christian Empire. On the wall is the Star of David, the emblem of the Ethiopian royal family after the thirteenth century. Each window from the tower Fasilidas used for prayer overlooks a different church. The Royal Archives building was also built by Fasilidas but was partially destroyed (as were several others) by British bombing during the Second World War when the Italians used the compound as their headquarters. There were also a number of Greek artisans who dwelt at Gondar, signifying how truly cosmopolitan Ethiopia had become by this time, and how extensive trade between black African nations and the rest of the world had become.

Slave trading, particularly on the western frontier, also increased during the reigns of Emperor Fasilidas and Yohannes I, bringing to Gondar chattel from among the Shankalla and Oromo. The English traveler C. T. Beke said that their treatment was "mild" but noted "all the female slaves, without exception, whatever their number, and however tender their age—and many are children of 8 or 9 years at most—are concubines of their master and his servants until they're disposed of to their ultimate possessors."[24]

Despite the Gondarine renaissance, all was not tranquil theologically. The Jesuits stubbornly renewed their efforts to penetrate Ethiopia. The Franciscans smuggled themselves in, reportedly to be stoned on more than one occasion. The emperors had little time for them, or for the Muslims who lived in separate quarters in the city.

But they did involve themselves in disputes that had begun under Susneyos and that were now raging. The principal disagreement concerned the nature of Christ. While Chalcedonian orthodoxy held that Christ had two natures and that it was his human nature that was anointed, the followers of the monk Ewostatewos asserted that Christ's human nature had become perfect through its union with the divine by unction and that the two natures were inseparable—a doctrine called Monophysitism. The theories of the "unctionists" were held by the important monastery of Debra Libanos, but Emperors Fasilidas and Yohannes supported Ewostatewos, who aimed to reform the church, which he considered too secularized.[25] Such rarefied disputes tended to factionalize and paralyze men and wealth; meanwhile, the eastern Oromo virtually overran the royal army in Tigre. It was only in his last years that Yohannes managed to reestablish authority.

Iyasu I (1682–1706) refused to be drawn into the religious controversy. He supported compromise and by 1690 the church was superficially united. Proclaimed by *The Chronicles* as one of the greatest of the Gondarine Emperors, Iyasu reduced the power of the Oromo, who were moving onto the plateau, temporarily conquering Shoa, and the southern Enerea and Sidama principalities.

Following Fasilidas's example, Iyasu built a palace decorated with ivory, gold leaf, and precious stones. A three-room sauna appears serviceable even today, replete with rhino-horn pegs on which to hang your clothes. I visited the Debra Birhan Selassie church, one of the few surviving churches that has Gondarine features, the rest having been destroyed by Sudanese Mahdists in the nineteenth century. Legend has it that a swarm of bees attacked the Mahdists, thus saving this church. The ceiling is a mass of eighty brown, moon-faced cherubs, while the walls are covered top to bottom with frescoes of Biblical scenes,

Gondarine dinner party, evidently one of the tamer ones

including a terrifying black devil and Ethiopia's most revered image of St. Francis of Assisi—who, it is said, wore no clothes because his body was covered with fur!

But according to James Bruce, a Scottish traveler, the kingdom's ungodly side was remarkable as well. He described a dinner where guests would be served slivers of flesh from a cow bellowing as they were cut from its living body. Family members were sometimes murdered to ensure succession; prisoners were cruelly tortured as a matter of course.

James Bruce re-creates an orgiastic atmosphere in which both men and women partook:

> Love lights all its fires, and everything is permitted with absolute freedom. There is no coyness, no delays, no need of appointments or retirement to gratify wishes; there are no rooms, but one, in which they sacrifice both to Bacchus and to Venus.[26]

Apparently Bruce fell in love with the daughter of the Queen Mother, during an extended stay in Gondar. Unable to comprehend his tolerance for deprivation in his wanderings, the Queen Mother responded to his rev-

elation that he was searching for the source of the Blue Nile with the outburst:

> See! see! how every day our life furnishes us with proofs of the perverseness and contradiction of human nature: you are come from Jerusalem, through vile Turkish governments, and hot unwholesome climates, to see a river and a bog, no part of which can you carry away were it ever so valuable, and of which you have in your country a thousand larger, better and cleaner . . . While I, on the other hand, the mother of kings, who have sat upon the throne of this country more than thirty years, have for my only wish, night and day, that after giving up everything in the world, I could be conveyed to the church of the Holy Sepulchre in Jerusalem, and beg for alms for my subsistence all my life after, if I could only be buried at last in the street within sight of the gate of that temple where our blessed Savior once lay.[27]

By the early eighteenth century, Gondar was consumed by intrigues and plots worthy of Renaissance drama, however, and Iyasu was assassinated in 1706 in connection with the Ewostatewos affair. Two years later his son was also murdered. By the mid-eighteenth century, the Gondarine monarchy finally disintegrated. The nobles usurped most of the royal power and the emperors became their puppets. Nevertheless, it beggars the imagination to see these unique castles that served as the homes of royalty from the seventeenth to the nineteenth century here in the heart of an African nation. It is almost as if the legends of Prester John's splendor had finally came to life in Gondar.

* * *

Celebrated on January 19, the festival of Timkat, or Epiphany, is the most spectacular religious occasion of the year, and it is observed most grandly at Gondar. As I walked around the grounds of Fasilidas's castle, I saw a flood of pilgrims flowing into the center of town, all dressed in their white *shammas.* Timkat is a peculiar fusion of elements from the Old and New Testaments: It commemorates John's baptism of Christ in the waters of the River Jordan, but the *tabot* also has a central role and is carried from its sanctum in a procession whose singing, dancing, beating of staffs, and rattling of *sistra* (a cross between a rattle and a tambourine) evoke ancient Biblical scenes:

> David and all Israel danced for joy before the Lord without restraint to the sound of singing, of harps and lutes, of tambourines and castanets and cymbals. (Samuel 6:5).

This is one of the few times of the year that the laity are allowed near the sacred *tabots,* which the priests head-carry on cushions; each *tabot* is covered with heavy brocade cloth to protect the people from its powers. The processions, followed by thousands of people, meet at the town square, then head slowly down to Fasilidas's pool at his palace.

Under dozens of extravagantly colored velvet umbrellas, the head priests wearing white turbans are gorgeously arrayed in heavy deep purple, red, and green velvet embroidery. The young deacons wear cotton robes of green, purple, yellow, and white, with crosses sewn on them and hats resembling Catholic bishops' mitres. They comprise a fabulous spectacle, these thousands of teenagers dancing and screaming, beating large drums to music punctuated by an unearthly combination of chant and traditional ululation. Everyone seemed to be wearing

Commemorating the baptism of Christ, Timkat is the most lavish celebration in Ethiopia.

an ornate silver cross of one style or another. It was the most joyful and colorful Christian ceremony I have ever witnessed. The ecstatic crowd pursued the *tabots* through the gardens surrounding Fasilidas's bathhouse, pushing me into the pool's shrine. As evening fell, the crowd settled down in the garden surrounding the bathhouse to prepare their food and drink *t'ella,* a local barley beer brewed especially for the celebration. Wrapped up warmly for a night out in the open, the crowds sang and danced around the pool, lit by a thousand candles.

Beginning at 5 A.M., thousands gather to receive the blessing at Fasilidas's sacred pool.

At sunrise the next morning, the early mists cleared from around Fasilidas's pool to reveal thousands of people clustered around the edges of the water. The priests began their blessings just after five A.M. Three hours later, amid ever-mounting religious euphoria, they gave the sign, setting a wooden cross of candles afloat on the water, whereupon the pilgrims jumped en masse into the pool, seeking by this leap of faith a cure for infertility, or some other blessing, or a symbolic renewal of their vows to the church. Despite the freezing cold, it was a most joyous baptism for thousands of the faithful. Hours later, priests slowly carry the *tabots* back to their churches, escorted by the crowd.

Early the next day, we headed off on the long drive to the mystical town of Lalibela, the twelfth-century capital of Ethiopia often called the "Eighth Wonder of the World." I could easily see why. It is a weird and wonderful place, built out of the devout dreams and religious fervor of the great eponymous king. The historian Edward Gibbon once wrote: "Encompassed on all sides by the enemies of

their religion the Ethiopians slept near a thousand years, forgetful of the world, by whom they were forgotten."[28] But in fact, the history of Ethiopia during this period was probably more fantastical than even the rumors, and isolated though she may have been—a religious citadel protected by high mountains on all sides—Ethiopia certainly was not sleeping.

The line of Ethiopian kings said to descend from Solomon was broken only at the end of the first millennium when legendary Queen Yodit, possibly Jewish, rallied the Beta Israel and defeated the Christian kingdom at Axum. The tale explains how after her death in the early eleventh century the Zagwe (Agaw) dynasty came to power. By the thirteenth century the Zagwe had converted to Christianity, and were inspired to build one of the wonders of the religion, the city of churches known as Lalibela.

THE ZAGWE DYNASTIC PERIOD (1137–1270)

The Zagwe established their new power base at Roha (now Lalibela), in the Lasta region of Ethiopia, in 1170 and ruled remnants of the old Axumite empire until 1270. The territory included the central and south highlands of Eritrea, Tigre, Wag, Lasta, Angot, and Amhara to the east; the Ethiopian plateau to the north; the Tekeze river to the south; and to the west, the upper waters of the eastern tributaries of the Blue Nile. The exact circumstances of this dynasty's rise to power are difficult to ascertain but it is known that this new elite were called usurpers in the *Kebra Nagast* and by the Amhara nobility who would later constitute the Solomonic line of emper-

ors. Edward Ullendorff calls their short reign "a sinister interregnum between the last Axumite King Del na 'od and Yekuno Amlak."[29] Nevertheless, four of the Zagwe kings—the *Chronicles* say there were eleven in total—are some of the most celebrated saints of Ethiopia.

Among them, the lyrically named Lalibela, is rightfully the most renowned:

> He was perfectly beautiful, without defect from head to foot; his cheeks were as red as the peel of the pomegranate, his eyes were like the morning star . . . Every one who saw him admired his bearing and majesty and foretold his royalty: the bees had also known of this in advance, on the very day of his birth.[30]

His name means "The bees recognize his sovereignity" and was given to the king because it is said after his birth a swarm of bees surrounded his cradle to foretell his kingship. His brother, the then-reigning king, himself seemed to have taken this prophecy seriously, and supposedly plotted for years to have the young Lalibela murdered. In a three-day coma, the result of poisoning by his brother, Lalibela ascended to Heaven and was commanded by God to construct churches, whereupon he woke up and built them in one night with the help of angels.[31] His new Jerusalem consisted of rock-hewn structures that would be invisible to invaders and protect the faith and wealth of the EOC and his empire.

Far-fetched though the story may be, the churches carved out of the volcanic rock do constitute an almost superhuman architectural feat. It must have taken teams of craftsmen dozens of years to complete the intricate work on what are truly among the great architectural wonders of the world, and which, if nothing else, attest to the remarkable effect that Christianity has had on Ethiopia's citizens. Francisco Álvares, a Portuguese friar who was the first Westerner to visit the site, was so awed by the city's splendor that he despaired of his reputation back home: "I weary of writing more about these buildings, because it seems to me that I shall not be believed if I write more, and because regarding what I have already written they may blame me for untruth."[32]

There are eleven churches in all, four of which are completely freestanding. I peered over the edge of a cavernous hole in the ground and saw, in the shape of a cross, a church carved entirely out of rock deeply embedded in the ground. I walked down the hundred stone steps to the courtyard, and was met with an even more bizarre sight: In a tiny cave in the rock face I saw a pair of leathery feet protruding. Taking a closer look, I realized with a start that this was not some elderly hermit taking a nap but a moldering dead body. Samia Salleh Kebire, my guide, a Muslim businesswoman, told me these are the remains of a 300-year-old monk, kept largely intact by the arid climate. In the courtyard surrounding the church are various dens, tiny caves dug into the rock, still inhabited by such monks and nuns.

Many of the churches hold valuable treasures; I was saddened to learn that theft is a problem. Three years before my visit, the country was shocked that the 800-year-old cross of Lalibela had been stolen from the sacristy of Bet Medhane Alem, the largest monolithic rock-hewn church in the world. They were further dismayed when twenty-five priests were arrested for the crime. The ringleader, still imprisoned, allegedly sold the cross to an art dealer. Bet Maryam is rich in artwork, too, though it is visited most by childless women who come to plunge into the algae-filled soup of its fertility pool. Many will return a year later, baby in hand, to give

St. George's Church at Lalibela. Carved entirely out of volcanic stone, it was built in one night with the help of angels, according to legend.

A hermit makes his way through the walls of Bet Medhane Alem.

church. They live off the villagers, unable to sustain themselves in this place "built by God." A hilltop school nearby trains boys in Ge'ez by rote for the priesthood. The complex is dotted with tiny caves housing hermits and tombs. One hermit said he was a carpenter with five children. But now he doesn't see his children, who are grown and live in the city, nor does he know where his wife is. His days are taken up collecting alms and reading the Bible, preparing for the glories of the Kingdom of Heaven.

King Lalibela may have been a practicing priest; and his attempt to create a new Jerusalem in Ethiopia was an inspiration derived from his purported pilgrimage to Israel before becoming emperor. Even today, visitors there can imagine themselves in the Holy Land—the river that flows through the town is the Jordan; the mountain above is the Mount of Olives. King Lalibela was a devout Christian, but it was the Solomonic emperors who forged the strong relationship between the monarchy and the EOC, and until the Derg took power, the kings and rulers of Ethiopia all endorsed Ethiopian orthodoxy as the state religion.

thanks that their prayers were answered. The twin churches of Bet Golgolta and Bet Debra Sina contain stunning artifacts as well. King Lalibela himself lies in the former, renowned also for the spectacular Holy of Holies that contains its *tabot.*

The "Path to Heaven" leads to another cluster of churches, linked by tunnels and bridges. Behind them is a nunnery sunk into a tiny gully. The nuns and hermits live in poverty, having abandoned their families and jobs and traveled vast distances to dedicate themselves to the

We reluctantly left the architectural wonders of Lalibela, setting off through the grand saw-toothed Adwa Mountains in Ethiopia's northernmost province of Tigre. The road to Debra Damo carries one past the battlefield at Adwa, site of the 1896 Italian defeat at the hands of the Ethiopian army. The entire continent then saw Ethiopia as a symbol of independence; it was the only time that an African army had thwarted the colonial designs of a European power. It is said that Menilek II carried a *tabot*— and perhaps even, it is said, the Ark itself—into battle like an Old Testament warrior king. The facts are that on March 1, 1896, 35,000 Italian soldiers naively attempted

Nineteenth-century painting of the battle that won Lalibela the Zagwe throne

to defeat 100,000 well-equipped Ethiopians led by a king the Italians had written off as a barbarian. Hard-pressed through the morning's battle, the Italians retreated at noon with 6,000 killed, 1,428 wounded, and 1,800 captured. On October 26, Menilek II signed the Treaty of Addis Ababa, ensuring Ethiopia's unique independent status during Europe's mad "scramble for Africa"—and enhancing her legend.[33]

The monastery of Debra Damo, the oldest monastery in Ethiopia and one of the oldest on the continent of Africa, sits on the top of a mountain 7,268 feet above sea level and about two and a half hours from Axum (leg-endary home of the lost Ark of the Covenant), just off the road that connects Adwa and Adigrat, in the middle of the Ethiopian highlands. The mountain, or *amba,* on which the monastery sits is an isolated island in the midst of canyons and parched land, connected by roads that wind like snakes through the valleys and what we would call hollows back home in West Virginia. I grew up in mountains like this, but not nearly as high: Ethiopia is the Grand Canyon of Africa. And Debra Damo, a square plateau that juts from the ground with perfectly square edges and ripples of stone up and down its edges, looks like nothing if not a rectangular piece of lasagne sitting

93

alone on a vast valley of a serving platter, in the midst of the Adwa Mountains.

These mountains are famous because they were the site of Italy's ignominious defeat. Following the Conference of Berlin in 1884, European countries established the following colonies: South Africa, Egypt, the Anglo-Egypt Sudan, British East Africa, Nigeria, the Gold Coast, Sierra Leone, and Gambia (Britain); Mozambique, Angola, and Portuguese Guinea (Portugal); Algeria, Morocco, French West Africa, French Equatorial Africa, and Gabon (France); Togoland, Cameroon, South-West Africa, and German East Africa (Germany); Libya, Eritrea, and Somalia (Italy); and the Congo Free State (Belgium). Before 1884, the European presence had been primarily restricted to coastal areas, except for two trading outposts in Senegal. Italy was determined that Ethiopia, an independent kingdom since the fourth century, would become a key part of its African domains.

The effect of Ethiopia's victory, however, was devastating for Italy, leading to a resurgence of impassioned and often hysterical nationalism. The Pizza Margherita, in fact, with its quasi-nationalistic tricolor pattern of tomato, mozzarella, and basil, was created in the aftershocks of despair at the Ethiopians' victory.

The mountains always had a spiritual presence for Ethiopians as well, at least since the monastery at Debra Damo was so mysteriously constructed in the sixth century AD. According to legend, the monastery was founded by Abba Aregawi (Za-Mikael Aregawi), one of the proverbial Nine Saints who spread the doctrine of Christianity from Axum throughout Ethiopia. Abba Aregawi chose the *amba* as his place of worship and meditation, prayer, and penitence. But its inaccessibility, which had attracted the Abba, also presented a major difficulty, for there was absolutely no way to scale its steep cliffs. What to do?

God conveniently commanded a snake that dwelled on the *amba* to wrap the coils of its tail around Za-Mikael, like a rope, and lift him to the *amba's* pinnacle, which is 650 feet above the mountain's perpendicular cliff faces, and 50 feet above the end of a dirt path that winds through the rocky slope at the *amba's* base. God commanded the Archangel Gabriel to stand guard with a drawn sword as the Abba ascended, to make certain that the snake did him no harm. The monk shouted "Halleluya" when he arrived at the mountain's top, giving the monastery one of its bynames, Debra Halleluja.

Za-Mikael's miracle soon attracted the attention of all and sundry, including the great king of Axum, Gabra Masqal. The king ordered that a church be built, at the Abba's request, on the very site where the serpent had deposited him on the top of the *amba*. King Masqal built a ramp to facilitate its construction. When the church was completed, Za-Mikael uttered the word *"dahmemo,"* which means "take it off," referring to the ramp. *"Dahmemo"* was shortened to *"damo,"* which gives the monastery its most common name.

For the past 1,500 years, only a 50-foot plaited leather rope dangling from the monastery's gatehouse at the edge of the cliff's overhang has connected its serene spiritual universe to the secular world below. It was this rope that I had to climb if I was to see the monastery.

I didn't really become frightened until I stood at the base of the cliff after a twenty-minute climb from the end of the dirt road, past huge boulders and exposed twisted roots of prehistoric-looking trees, staring up at a doorlike frame at the top, some 50 feet above my head, a leather rope with a loop at the end swaying gently in the breeze. Fifty feet to the top of that cliff looked like the length of the Empire State Building to me. I asked that the crew

Sketch of Debra Damo, Ethiopia's oldest monastery, during the nineteenth century

Debra Damo's dauntingly steep sides today. Monks descend from this spiritual haven by a frayed leather rope, as they have for the last fifteen hundred years.

stop filming, because I didn't want all that fear to be recorded for posterity. *They must be joking,* I thought, as I also thought about ways to avoid my certain fate.

Somehow, I had allowed myself to be comforted by the thought that I would simply be hoisted up the cliff face in a chairlike structure, slowly, gently, securely. I mean, *that* would have been frightening enough for me, who had never been able to climb the rope in gym class, both because I was fat and had the weakest biceps, and because, truth be told, I was a bit of a coward when it came to heights (with a lot of chicken thrown in for good measure).

Oh, I would have sat in my little chair, strapped cozily—and securely—to a fail-safe rope-and-pulley mechanism, waving to the crew below for a possible publicity photo opportunity, while I narrated my sense of wonder at seeing candelabra euphorbias and spurge from

on high, as I slowly made my way up the cliff, hauled by a robust monk or two.

In fact there was no chair; no harness; no robust monks at the top, waiting to welcome the pilgrim home to Mother Africa; no system of pulleys. Only one elderly monk, about my father's age, pretending that he could pull me up with a leather rope whose age made him look like a baby by comparison, a rope frayed and discolored with use. Apparently this was the monk's sole task: hauling up visitors to the monastery. And judging from the look on his face, he was quite perplexed at my hesitancy. He looked to me like a bronzed elf, as he peered over the edge of the cliff, his snow-white goatee framed by what struck me as the Door to Eternity behind him.

And that is how I found myself paralyzed at the bottom of a cliff in Africa, petrified, as our cameraman kept rolling while he and our director waited for me to react, to say something in a "piece-to-camera," then crawl my way to the summit of the *amba* in my maiden voyage up a rope.

"I don't think so," I managed to mumble, with as much composure as I could muster, knowing that a rolling camera records all. After all, I was "representing the race" here in Mother Africa, making a film about the lost glories of the African past, of which most of us in America are blissfully unaware. I couldn't *not* climb up, after all; too much was riding on it.

Still, it was a *very* long way up that cliff, I found myself thinking. And would be an even longer way coming down.

"Let's try it, slowly," I found myself saying, in a desperate attempt both to stall for time and to salvage any bit of dignity that I had left. The crew was as surprised as I was at the words springing from my lips, as if someone else had uttered them.

The rope—by now I had come to think of the aged leather rope as the noose—was at least as old as the monk's feet, which were all that would anchor him against the fragile wooden frame of the Door to Eternity at the pinnacle of the cliff. It slipped itself over my head, stopping snugly just above my waist. It suddenly went taut, speaking a language of its own.

All of a sudden, I found myself moving up the mountainside, how I had absolutely no idea. Within a second or two, it seemed, I was stumbling my way up the face of this precipice, my feet finding their way into ruts and craggy spaces worn into the face of the cliff. The hoisting bronze elf who with his goatee now seemed an ancient mountain goat apparently did not know that I wanted to stop and discuss my options. He spoke Tigrinya, the language spoken in Tigre Province, the region that had spearheaded the revolution against the Communist dictator, Mengistu.

By rappeling, no doubt without the flair of someone who knows what this ancient art is supposed to look like, I stumbled my way up the first half of the face of the *amba*. To my own astonishment, I had just begun to move up the cliff, walking, sort of, sideways or perpendicular to the sheer sides of the mountain, just like someone wearing anti-gravity shoes in a film. I didn't have time to wonder what happens at the top; in fact, I had little time to think of anything, astonished as I was that I was moving at all.

All of a sudden I stopped moving, as my feet lost their grip and slipped off the side of the mountain. The craggy first half of the climb had been replaced by the far smoother surfaces of the upper half, which were both sheer and slippery. From my ninety-degree stance of an anti-gravity climber, I now found myself face-to-face, as it were, with the side of the mountain, feet extended directly below my body, which was perfectly upright. I was dangling from the ropes like a piece of butchered meat, completely stalled and paralyzed.

Terror, in the face of death, no doubt must be protean in form, assuming as many guises as improvisation to crises allows. Mine assumed two forms: I kept repeating to myself, once that I realized what had happened, that it would be a terrible idea to look down at the crew below filming me, and I began to yell over and over to my sacred lifeline, that wizened monk, to "pull . . . pull . . . pull," please, for God's sake, and my own, pull me up the cliff.

I wondered now if the rope might snap, and whether this holy geezer had the power to pull me against the combined forces of inertia and gravity. Where was that serpent when I needed him?

Slowly, I began to move, inch by inch, haul by haul. Unbeknownst to me, the crew members who had been sent up before me, so that I could "imagine the climb,"

Ascending Debra Damo—the frayed leather rope is still the only way up.

reached out and grabbed it, wondering if the monk could catch my other hand and pull me the two feet further through Eternity's Door. For him to do so, however, I had to let loose of the rope. Suddenly, several hands reached around the monk and, grabbing onto my shirt, arm, and hands, dragged me through the two-foot gap of air that separates the wooden peg from the wooden frame of the open door. Our driver, Gebru, had taken charge.

"You saved my life . . . you saved my life," I gasped pathetically, realizing now how very winded I had been by the grip of the rope around my chest, whose marks took three or four days to wear off.

As I lay there, promising God and myself that I would try to live my life as a better person, wondering what grand act of charity I could embark upon to make things right with the order of the Universe, it occurred to me—in the way that a crisis or a disaster comes into one's consciousness upon awaking from a deep sleep not immediately, but only after a moment or two—that now that I had arrived at the monastery of Debra Damo, I would, in an hour or two, be forced to repeat this hand-to-hand combat with Death on the journey back down.

I wondered how long it would take me to become fluent in Tigrinya.

had begun to assist my modern sacred serpent, standing in a line behind the monk and pulling along with him.

A monk has the legal status of a dead man in Ethiopia. They pay no taxes, they do not appear in censuses, they cannot vote. They are known as "the living dead." They dedicate their lives to going to Heaven—which was where I wondered if this journey up the face of the *amba* might lead . . . if I were lucky.

Miraculously, the wooden stump to which the hand-over-hand rope was knotted came into my view. I

From Debra Damo, we headed to our final destination of Axum, the site of the birth of Christianity in Ethiopia. In so many ways, Axum is the key to Ethiopia's past, as well as being one of the greatest civilizations of antiquity.

Because many of the sites here have not been excavated, we have yet to discover the extent of the Axumite civilization's greatness. Peace came to Ethiopia only in 1991 and now, for the first time since a brief period of digging in the 1970s, archaeologists can start to unravel the roots of the ancient empire. There is reason to think that northern Ethiopia had links with ancient Egypt. In Chapter 2, we examined this question of ancient Egyptian ethnicity, learning that no one has yet provided a fully satisfying answer though some scholars believed the Egyptians to have migrated from another part of Africa. This view dates to the millennium before Christ in Greece, where some historians thought Egyptians had come directly from Ethiopia in 3000 BC.

With or without the departure of the ancient Egyptians, scholars have satisfied themselves through excavation and textual analysis that there was an agricultural civilization in Northern Ethiopia by 1000 BC (the pre-Axumite period). The following half millennium is known as the Sabean period, owing to the extensive trade links Ethiopia developed with the city of Saba, located in what is now Yemen. Some suggest that a migration occurred from South Arabia and that those people then mixed with the indigenous population, contributing some distinctive features to northern Ethiopian culture, especially literacy and the use of the plow.[34]

I believe that Ethiopia's extensive body of medieval myths and legends evolved in a complex process through which later generations sought, both consciously and unconsciously, to retrieve and enshrine the obscured achievements of the great Empire of Axum, which thrived between the third and tenth centuries. With so many Biblical references to Ethiopia, given the long history of Christianity there, and in the absence of a reliable historical narrative, medieval Christian scribes fabricated and codified ancient legends about Solomon and Sheba, angels and arks, and other sacred tales from the Bible itself—the most resonant symbols imaginable for a Christian kingdom. When the British army stole a copy of the *Kebra Nagast* (described by Ullendorff as a gigantic conflation of cycles and tales that defines the importance of Axum to Ethiopians) in the Magdala invasion, the

next emperor, Yohannes IV, petitioned them to return it, saying, "[F]or in my country, my people will not obey my orders without it."[35] It was not without reason that the constitution of 1955 stated that the only legitimate royal line was descended "without interruption from the dynasty of Menilek I, son of King Solomon and the Queen of Ethiopia known as Queen of Sheba."[36] Nearly every Solomonic king and emperor from Zara Yaqob onward attempted to be crowned at Axum in recognition of this legacy, although in reality few emperors were actually tonsured there.

If the efforts of Ethiopian scribes to link sacred history with their own secular history bespeaks a certain audacity, it must be acknowledged nevertheless that the actual heritage they sought to recover—the glory that was Axum—was unmistakably grand and, in many ways, without precedent in sub-Saharan Africa. At its height, in the fourth and fifth centuries, Axum's empire "extended throughout the regions lying south of the Roman Empire, from the fringes of the Sahara in the west, across the Red Sea to the inner Arabian desert of Rub'el Hali in the east."[37] The Axumites developed the written script called Ge'ez, as well as a system of silver, gold, and copper coinage—the first one in sub-Saharan Africa until the tenth century, when Arabian coins were used in East Africa. Already by the first century the city of Axum was described as a "metropolis" in *The Periplus of the Erythrean Sea;* by the sixth century, its population numbered 20,000.

Trade made Axum great and linked the interior of Africa with "commodities from as far afield as India, China, the Black Sea, and Spain."[38] And they traded far and wide—with Egypt, the eastern Mediterranean, and Arabia, through its famed Red Sea port, Adulia. Ivory, rhinoceros horn, hippopotamus hides, slaves, gold dust, frankincense, civet cat musk, and elephants, among other goods, moved from Axum to ports north and east. It was one sign of Axum's power that the Persians counted it among the world's four great civilizations, the other three being Persia, Rome, and "Sileos," which scholars believe to be China.[39] By the third century, "a very complex society, most likely at the state level, was firmly established on the northern Ethiopian plateau, a society that had begun to distinguish itself from influences from the Sabean kingdom in Saudi Arabia."[40] By the first century, these Sabean influences had been "almost entirely subsumed." By the fourth and fifth centuries, Axum was a world power and a Christian kingdom. Axum was the capital of the empire that, as we saw in the last chapter, crushed the Kushites of Nubia in the fourth century.

Archaeological evidence suggests that the arrival of the Sabeans did not represent the beginnings of Ethiopian civilization. For centuries, other peoples had been interacting through trade, warfare, and intermarriage in the Ethiopian region, and by speaking Kushitic and Semitic languages. Semiticized Agaw peoples are thought to have migrated from southeastern Eritrea, possibly as early as 2000 BC, bringing their "proto-Ethiopic" language, the ancestor of Ge'ez, with them. Various stone paintings attest to these early Ethiopians in Eritrea and Tigray. At Matara and Yeha, pottery types similar to Sudanese pottery have been found and Rodolfo Fatovich has suggested that pre-Axumite culture might also owe something to Nubia, specifically the Kerma C-group and later Meroë.[41] Axum was a grand manifestation of several cultures, and scholars date its origins to the third century BC.[42]

In the fourth century AD, when Axum, under King Ezana, became a Christian kingdom, it also conquered Meroë, causing its rulers to flee to the western Sudan. Axum also annexed part of Yemen under King Ella Kaleb in AD 525 and remained in control of the western Red Sea coast down to Zeila until the armies of Islam cut it off in

the seventh century from direct access to their trading partners and thus their allies. And by the ninth century, Axum included the provinces of Amhara, Lasta, Gojjam, and Da'mat. The Zagwe dynasty, following long after the fall of Axum, shifted the capital to Lasta. As we have seen, Axum's glory would be reclaimed by the Solomonic dynasty, which ruled Ethiopia from the thirteenth to the nineteenth century and saw itself as Axum's rightful heir.

An inscription by King Ezana, written in about AD 350 on a large stone slab bearing names and titles, presents a picture of forceful tribal leaders resisting Axumite advances and their reduction to tributary status by the kingdom. It tells us how King Ezana, particularly, gradually incorporated and integrated diverse populations into a single state. The rationale behind the conquest of Meroë is preserved:

By the power of the Lord of Heaven who is mightier than everything which exists on heaven or earth. Ezana, the son of Elta-Amida, of the descent of Halen, King of Axum and of Himar, Raydan, Saba, Salhen, Tseynao, Bega and Khartoum, Kings of Kings . . . and invincible to the enemy. By the might of the Lord of Heaven who has made me lord, who reigns as the perfect one for all eternity . . . By the might of the Lord of All I made war on Noba, for the peoples of Noba had rebelled and made a boast of it . . . And as I have sent warnings to them, and they would not listen to me and refused to stop their [evil] deeds and heaped insults upon me and then took to flight, I made war upon them.[43]

In this way, he built an empire extending over the rich cultivated lands of Ethiopia, Sudan, and southern Arabia, which included all the peoples who inhabited the coun-

Above: At 75 feet, the largest stela in the world
Opposite: Stelae in the holy city of Axum

tries south of the boundaries of the Roman Empire, between the Sahara to the west and the inner Arabian desert of Rub'el Hali. The Axumites were the first of the Ethiopian imperialists, bent on incorporation and expansion.

They also raised great stelae. Some are a hundred feet in height; one is the largest monolithic monument in the ancient world. The inscriptions suggest a complex polytheism, including gods such as Ashtar and chthonic deities such as Beher, Meder, and Mahrem, the dynastic and tribal deity of the Axumites, equated in bilingual inscriptions with Ares, the Greek god of war. It was to him that the early pre-Christian kings of Axum offered sacrifices and consecrated their victories. The *Monumentum Adulitanum* mentions Poseidon, the sea god, who was worshiped at Adulia. We know from the *Odyssey* and the *Iliad* that Homer associated Poseidon with the Ethiopians. Because Axum possessed Adulia, the most famous and widely trafficked port on the Red Sea, it comes as no surprise that one can detect religious influ-

ences from a variety of peoples here. Even little Buddhas have been found, probably brought by merchants from India.[44]

Axumite preeminence was altered irrevocably by the eighth-century rise of Arab power in the Middle East, the Mediterranean, and North Africa. Naval warfare began with the advent of the Umayyads and Mu'awiyya. The Dahlak Islands were annexed and Christians lost control of the coastal trade. The importance of Adulia declined and new ports like Massawa and Zeila became significant. Muslim merchants took over the seaborne trade routes, although Axum managed to secure the mainland. The many revolts, and the weakened defense of its northern frontiers with the Beja people, drove Christians into the interior and southward, as did ecological erosion and dramatic changes of climate affecting annual rainfall.

What happened to the Axumites is uncertain. The *History of Patriarchs* mentions that the king of Ethiopia faced an enemy named Queen of Bani-al Hammwiyya and the country suffered from plague and drought.[45] In the 970s, Ibn Hawqual mentions the country had been ruled for thirty years by a woman, who had killed the king, or "Hadani," and now ruled the Hadani's territory along with previous lands in the south. He also stated later that the king of Yemen sent a zebra that had been received as a gift from the female ruler of el-Habasha to the ruler of Iraq in 969–970.[46] Ethiopian legend identifies this ruler as Gudit, Yodit, or Ewato, who drove the legitimate kings into hiding and preceded the Zagwe, who did not take over for another one hundred years. By the tenth century, however, the glory that was Axum had long faded.

Ancient skyscrapers: The pre-Christian obelisks are reminders of the Axumite Empire that flourished three thousand years ago.

Without a doubt, the most striking monuments surviving at Axum are its towering stelae, built in the third and fourth centuries to serve as markers for the tombs of royalty. Carved with bas-relief doors and windows and giving the impression of ancient skyscrapers, these are the largest decorated stones ever cut by human beings. The tallest still standing is 75 feet high and was taken from a single piece of granite, quarried more than 2 miles from the site where it was erected and carved, constituting a considerable technological achievement. Theories abound as to how they were raised: In Axum (for they are found in a few other towns as well), they believe it may have been through the power of the Ark of the Covenant. The largest of the 140 stelae at Axum now lies shattered on the ground, allegedly a victim of Queen Yodit's campaign against the Solomonic dynasty. Hewn in the form of a thirteen-story building, it was 108 feet high and weighed 700 tons; it is the biggest monolith in the world. By contrast, the largest such stone that survives from prehistoric Europe, the Grand Menhir's Men-er-Hroeg at Locmariaquer in Brittany, is half its size.

As I walked through the towering monoliths with Roderick Grierson, a scholar of early Ethiopian history and the Ark of the Covenant, he directed my attention to the tallest; it resembled a ten-story building and had a false door carved at the base. A similar, but slightly smaller stela, he said, had been removed to a piazza in Rome near the Circus Maximus by Mussolini's army. Negotiations between the two governments have been concluded for its return to Ethiopia. The stelae have an ironic role in modern Ethiopia. Though their construction was stopped after AD 341 when Ethiopia became a Christian kingdom, they now provide the backdrop for the festival of St. Mary of Zion, which marks the arrival of the Ark in Axum.

Just outside Axum, I drove to a farming area that has for centuries been referred to as the Queen of Sheba's palace.

After a recent excavation, a palace with more than fifty rooms was indeed discovered underneath the fields. It seems to have been built in AD 7, rather than the thousand years earlier when Sheba is said to have lived, though the site does contain a field of small stelae that some believe mark the queen's grave.

From Sheba's palace, I drove back to the Church of St. Mary of Zion, the most important Christian site in Ethiopia, though the original church was leveled by Ahmed Gragn, "the Left-Handed." A newer church stands on its foundations, flanked by a modest, green-domed chapel said to house the Ark of the Covenant. The monk who guards the door is the only person in the world permitted to behold the Ark—if, in fact, the relic resides there. His last act before death is to charge a successor with the responsibility not only to protect the relic, but also those who might be tempted to expose themselves to its power:

> When they came to the threshing floor of Nacon, Uzzah stretched his hand out to the Ark of God and steadied it, as the oxen were making it tilt. Then the anger of Yahweh blazed out against Uzzah, and for this crime God struck him down on the spot, and he died there beside the Ark of God.
>
> 2 Samuel 6:34-4

Even the replicas of the Ark, the *tabots,* are removed from the churches only on important religious days such as Timkat and are at all times hidden from view by a draped cover.

The Ethiopians believe that they possess the Ark through the power of its own choice and by the will of God. Outsiders have usually been less ready to accept this claim. The scorn of a nineteenth-century traveler named Dimotheos is typical:

Stupid people like the Abyssinians who blindly accept this stone as the original are basking in a useless glory by possessing it, [for it is] not the true original at all. Those that know the Holy Scriptures do not require any further proof of this; the fact is that the tablets on which the divine laws were inscribed were placed inside the Ark of the Covenant and lost forever.[47]

From the Bible we know that the Ark was the most revered of Jewish artifacts, the manifestation of God on earth. The Ark was housed in the temple built by Solomon after the Jews settled in Jerusalem in 1000 BC, but no one knows what happened to it when the temple was destroyed by Nebuchadnezzar's Babylonian army in 581 BC. The Hebrew Bible is mute on the issue. Perhaps the invaders found the Ark, perhaps it had been removed for safekeeping before the troops arrived. The most important object in the world—mentioned 200 times in the scripture before the appearance of Solomon—simply ceases to figure in the story of God's people, almost overnight.

The Ethiopians believe they have the answer to the mystery: The Ark was not destroyed in the fire set by the Babylonians, it resides in Ethiopia. This second act is recorded in the *Kebra Nagast*, where we learn that the Ark came to Axum with Menilek I in the tenth century BC, a problematic date since historians believe Axum to be a thousand years younger.

If scholars were allowed to examine what is so scrupulously guarded at Axum, it should in theory be possible to determine its authenticity. The Bible gives us two distinct accounts of its creation, one in Exodus and the other in Deuteronomy; the latter gives us a description of a much simpler object. However, God also gave Moses precise instructions on its design and embellishments in the elaborate priestly account in Exodus written centuries after the Ark was created.

> Make an Ark, a chest of acacia-wood, two and a half cubits long, one cubit and a half wide, and one cubit and a half high. Overlay it with pure gold both inside and out, and put a band of gold all around it. Cast four gold rings for it, and fasten them to its four feet, two rings on each side. Make poles of acacia wood and plate them with gold, and insert the poles in the rings at the sides of the Ark to lift it. The poles shall remain in the rings at the side of the Ark, and never be removed. Put into the Ark the tokens of the Covenant which I shall give you. Make a cover of pure gold, two and a half cubits long and one cubit and a half wide. Make two gold Cherubim of beaten work at the ends of the cover, one at each end: make each cherub of one piece with the cover. They shall be made with wings outspread and spreading upwards, and shall screen the cover with their wings. . . .
>
> Exodus 25 10:22

The point is that it would not be easy to use the Bible to determine what is preserved at Axum, assuming that anyone was ever allowed to look at it. But it is highly unlikely that the EOC will ever submit their most sacred relic to such scrutiny, as I learned when I asked Abuna Paulos, the head of the church, if he would consider it. He accused me of being a seeker of fame, and not devout enough!

In their new book about the Ark at Axum, Roderick Grierson and Stuart Munro-Hay contend that the example at Axum is probably only one of any number of arks that were known to the ancient world; it is highly possible that one of those did arrive at St. Mary from South

According to legend, Sheba is said to have lived here, though the fifty-room palace discovered beneath this site was probably built in AD 7—a thousand years after she lived.

Pilgrims at the Church of St. Mary of Zion of Axum

Nineteenth-century rendering of the old St. Mary of Zion, Ethiopia's most sacred site. Its walls were said to contain the Ark of the Covenant.

Arabia. Such arks housed the sacred objects of their respective cults. The modern-day practice that permits replication of the *tabots* provides us some insight into the practice. And, as Grierson and Munro-Hay point out, an ark similar to the Biblical description above was found in Tutenkhamen's tomb, though empty of the Commandments.

As I stood there in front of St. Mary of Zion, I could not help admiring the sheer audacity of this African nation, isolated for centuries by its mountain ranges and highlands, laying claim to the most sacred object in the Hebrew tradition! I then remembered that during this journey through Ethiopia, I happened to encounter three religious leaders: Minister Louis Farrakhan, head of the Nation of Islam; Dr. George Leonard Carey, the Archbishop of Canterbury; and Abuna Paulos, Patriarch of the EOC. Each propounds a widely subscribed truth not entirely, or even primarily, based on reason. The first

teaches that a mad geneticist created a mutant, malignant form of the human species and exiled it to Europe. The second holds that a virgin gave birth to a child who died and was resurrected, and that there is life for all after death. The third maintains that the son of Solomon and the Queen of Sheba carried the Ark of the Covenant from Jerusalem to Ethiopia almost 3,000 years ago. Whatever I myself may believe, it is clear to me that among these three narratives, the one about the Ark least strains credulity.[48] Until Vendyl Jones, the archaeologist who was the model for Indiana Jones, proves the Ethiopians wrong (as I write, Vendyl is searching for the Ark in Israel), I prefer to give the benefit of the doubt to the Ethiopians, those "most blameless of men," as Homer called them.

So many of Africa's genuine contributions have been denied or appropriated by non-Africans that many of us who love the continent and its cultures have a tendency to err on the side of optimism, or even wishful thinking, making dispassionate scholarly assessment difficult if not impossible at times. Let me make clear that the odds of the Ark being housed in the Sanctuary of the Tablet at St. Mary's Church at Axum are overwhelmingly against the Ethiopians. Nevertheless, I must confess I am haunted by the claim, and I started this journey hoping most ardently that it would turn out to be true. If it remains frustratingly impossible to know for certain, I did at least end my journey with an even fuller realization of another truth: the overwhelming importance of this symbol to Ethiopia's traditional Jewish and Christian communities. The profound faith that the Ethiopians share in the tangible presence of the Ark in their country inspires a sense of cultural heritage that is incomparably galvanizing. It is in itself something of a wonder.

4

SALT, GOLD, AND BOOKS: THE ROAD TO TIMBUKTU

I am apt to suspect the Negroes and in general all the other species of men (for there are four or five different kinds) to be naturally inferior to the whites. There never was a civilized nation of any other complexion than white, nor even any individual eminent either in action or speculation. No ingenious manufacturers amongst them, no arts, no sciences.

—DAVID HUME

Timbuktu is a city unsullied by the worship of idols, where none has prostrated save to God the Compassionate, a refuge of scholarly and righteous folk, a haunt of saints and ascetics, and a meeting place of caravans and boats.

—AL-SA'DI

In Africa (a quarter of the world)
men's skin are black, their hair is crisp and curled;
And somewhere there, unknown to public view,
A mighty city lies called Timbuktu.

—WILLIAM THACKERAY

The Great Mosque at Djenne

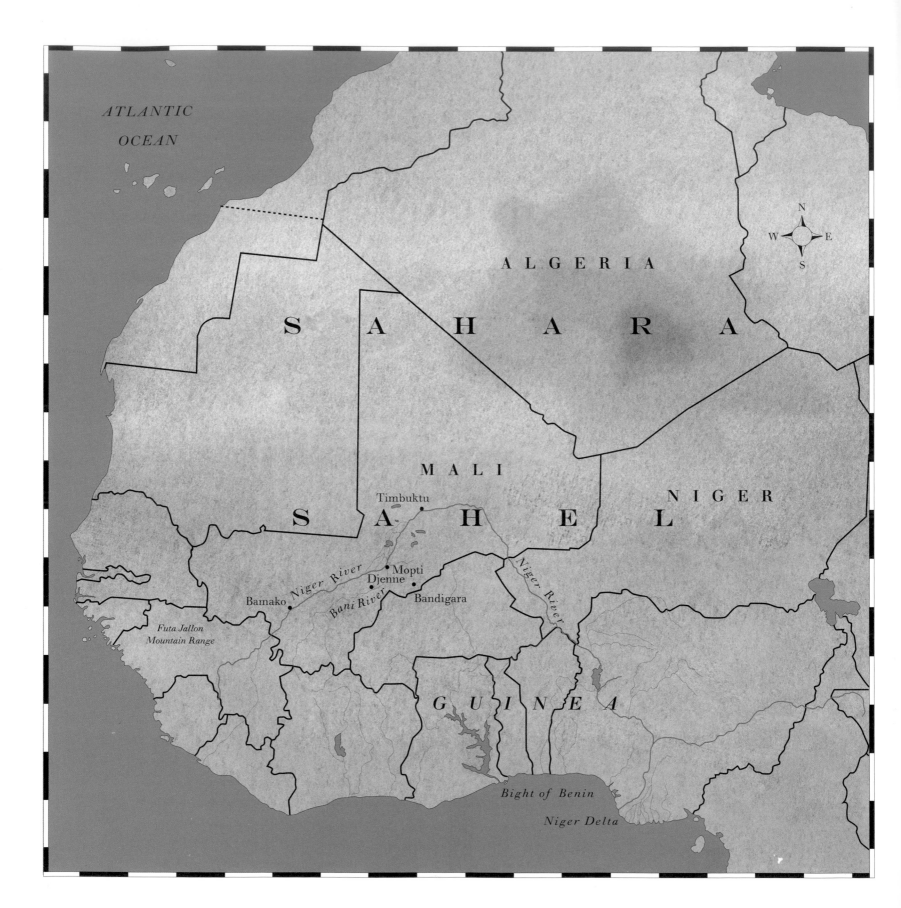

Two poets, Robert Browning and Ogden Nash, arrive at the Pearly Gates. To prove their worthiness, Saint Peter requires them to compose a poem on the spot; there is only one condition: The poem must start with "As" and end with "Timbuktu." Robert Browning goes first:

> As I was standing on the shore,
> I heard the ocean loudly roar,
> A sailing ship was passing through,
> Destination, Timbuctou!

Then it is Odgen Nash's turn:

> As Tim and I awalkin' went,
> We spied three ladies in a tent,
> Since they were three and we were two,
> I bucked one and Tim bucked two![1]

When I was a boy, we used to threaten, "I'm gonna knock you clear to Timbuktu!" Of course, none of us knew if there was a Timbuktu, let alone where. Even as an adult, I tended to dismiss stories of a magnificent library and university as yet another contribution of the "Beethoven is Black" school of history. Still less did it ever occur to me that I would one day visit Timbuktu. But I was wrong on several counts. Timbuktu did exist, and still does, nestled in the southernmost tip of northern Africa and the northernmost tip of sub-Saharan Africa. It was the almost mythical conduit through which Africa, Arabia, and Europe sometimes collided, sometimes fused; and in the late Middle Ages it was the site of black Africa's most important center of scholarship and learning before the twentieth century, rivaling Europe's emerging universities.

At the height of its glory, in the fifteenth and sixteenth centuries, Timbuktu was widely known as "the gateway to the Sahara Desert" and "the most distant place on earth." It was, in particular, the publication in 1525 of the *History and Description of Africa* by a Moroccan traveler named Leo Africanus that catapulted Timbuktu into the European imagination. Born al-Hasan ibn Muhammed al-Wazzan al-Zaiyati, in Granada, Spain, Africanus traveled throughout northern Africa and the western Sudan in the early years of the sixteenth century. (The Sudan was then the name for much of sub-Saharan Africa between the Atlantic Ocean and the Red Sea.) On a mission from the sheriff of Fez, "where his uncle owned land,"[2] he was captured by pirates in 1518, and then presented as a slave to Pope Leo X. The Pope baptized him "Johannis Leo," and urged him to write about his travels. *Della Descrizione dell' Africa* was published in Rome in 1525; an extremely popular English edition appeared in 1600.

As we might expect, the city's gold hugely intrigued Africanus. "The rich king," he wrote, "possesses great treasure in coin and gold ingots. One of these ingots weighs 1,300 pounds . . . The royal court is very well organized and magnificent. . . . The king has some three thousand cavalry, and a huge number of infantry armed with bows made of wild fennel. They fire poisoned arrows." Yet the city's reverence for learning, its passion for knowledge, and its valuation of books struck Africanus as forcefully as its fabulous wealth: "In Timbuktu there are numerous judges, scholars and priests, all well paid by the king, who show great respect to men of learning. Many manuscript books coming from Barbary are sold. Such sales are more profitable than any other goods."[3]

Notwithstanding the usual hyperbole of travelogues at this time, this was an essentially accurate account. Timbuktu, the crossroad where sub-Saharan Africa and the

Mediterranean confronted each other, was not only magnificently rich, it was also a world-class center of arts and letters. The historian Elias Saad writes in his *Social History of Timbuctou* that it was "a whole society [that] came to be characterized by the status and role of its scholars."[4] For half a millennium, fables of Timbuktu's glory as a center of learning have been greeted skeptically in the West. But these, it turns out, were true. As the English historian P. E. H. Hair observed recently:

> In Timbuctou, scholarly disputations were held between individuals from all levels of society and almost all occupations, and concerned the practical structure and operation of the local society, which their thinking both reflected and molded, as much as they concerned the abstract problems of Islamic ethics and the universal dispensations of God. Philosophers were kings; or, at least, scholars were also notables, officials, merchants, and family heads; and their descendants held in memory the intellectual triumphs and questionings of their forebears.[5]

Although it is difficult for us to imagine this today, in Timbuktu, books were valued as much as salt—and salt, being then a rare commodity and difficult to obtain, was valued as much as gold.

As a boy in West Virginia, I first heard of Timbuktu reading the Sunday papers. I think it must have been in "Ripley's Believe or Not!" There they were: black-skinned, turbaned men, elegantly tall and gaunt, draped in flowing white gowns, moroccan leather volumes under their arms, gliding into the library at the University of Timbuktu. Believe it or not, indeed.

To appreciate just how improbable this image appeared to me then, you must consider the context of the early sixties, the great moment of African indepen-

At the barber's in Djenne—a world away from Combie Carroll's shop

dence, and how it looked to us in America. Despite centuries of the deepest ambivalence about their relation to Africa and Africans, many Negroes in America in the late fifties and early sixties took a keen interest in the end of colonialism and the coming of independence to black African nations, perceiving this movement somehow to be fundamentally related to their own civil rights struggles at home. Especially curious and puzzling to us was the fact that Africans, often darker and more "negroid" than their American kinsmen, were sometimes exempted from the strictures of racial segregation. The black Africans in that picture, carrying books and wearing gowns, were vaguely reminiscent of the popular "Punjab of Javapour" episode of *The Amos and Andy Show* television series, in which Kingfish and Andy anticipate the dress and demeanor that some American Negroes would affect in the late fifties and early sixties in an attempt to trick white racists into allowing them to patronize segregated restaurants and hotels. Dressed as "Africans," they would gain entry only to unmask themselves just outside the establishment after the ruse had proven successful.

But these guys in "Ripley's" were no "Punjabs of Javapour." They were some serious brothers, strutting like Oxbridge dons.

I was not the only one to be impressed. The older men, many of them my father's coworkers on the loaders' platform at the paper mill, who gathered on Saturdays down at Mr. Combie Carroll's Barber Shop whether or not they needed a haircut, must have seen the same item, because that's all they wanted to talk about—that is, when they weren't talking about trying to get some booty or who was spotted in the backseat of whose car, on the way up to the colored cemetery to "park." On the day that item appeared in the funny papers, this image of black scholars was on everybody's minds. After the lively conversation had died down, it was the role of the proprietor to break the silence:

"There's shit buried deep in books," Mr. Combie Carroll almost whispered in his most conspiratorial tone, "that the white man don't even want us to see." I began to wonder what other things lurked in this forbidden region of knowledge about our past.

"That's right," Mr. Nate responded, slapping Mr. Carroll a low five. "Black Africans, too . . . coal black." Nappy minds had suddenly been roused by awe in this ritual communal setting on a packed and hot Saturday afternoon, the men huddled around Combie's lone barber chair, his gas stove at one end, an old fashioned red "sliding" Coke machine at the other.

I didn't know what the humid silence of the grown men meant exactly, but the vision of black men, skin gleaming under a Saharan sun, speaking Arabic and God-only-knew what other unpronounceable African languages, fired my imagination even more than did the weekly tales of male conquest. Huddled there, in the warmth of Combie Carroll's Saturday circle, peppered with visions of black men writing books—in Arabic, of

The Eastern Letter Writer, *by William J. Muller (1812–1845): Such images fueled the daydreams of my youth.*

all things—books about astronomy and cosmology, medicine and the practical arts, treatises on the eternal conundrum of human existence . . . I felt a curious kind of pride. It was what I'd felt the day Willie Mays made his famous over-the-shoulder catch of Vic Wertz's drive in the 1954 World Series or when Jackie Robinson's heroics had won a World Series game. Granted, Timbuktu was a long way from Piedmont, but the notion of black men writing books was as heady to me that day as was the scent of Old Spice that Mr. Carroll splashed with unusual abandon on the napes of the necks of his all-colored clientele.

After Leo Africanus's text, it seemed that everyone in Europe wanted to be the first white man to trek across the desert to capture the gold buried at Timbuktu. Not since the desperate quest in the high Middle Ages to find the mythical black Ethiopian Christian king, Prester John, had Europeans so passionately sought to bridge the distance that separated them from black Africa. John II and John III of Portugal had visions of ships transporting gold direct from Timbuktu to Lisbon. An official attempt to reach the city was made in 1565 by one Diogo Carreiro. For three centuries, until 1853, no fewer than forty-three Europeans set out across the Sahara to find Timbuktu. Only four succeeded. In 1826, Gordon Laing became the first European in 300 years to arrive at Timbuktu, but failed to return home. Laing reached Timbuktu in 1826, arriving with terrible injuries from an attack by Tuareg robbers. He was warmly received by a nomadic sheikh in the desert, but the Fulani sultan who had just conquered Timbuktu, learning that Laing was a Christian, ordered him banished. On his way back, his guide had him murdered a couple of days' journey from Timbuktu. One of Laing's servants managed to return to Tripoli two years later to report this unhappy story.

Ironically, by the time that Leo Africanus's book was translated into English, Timbuktu's glory had already begun to fade. In 1824, the Geographical Society of Paris offered 10,000 francs for the first European who could reach Timbuktu and return to tell the tale. It wasn't until four years later that René Caillié, an Arabic-speaking French explorer disguised as an Egyptian, claimed the prize. Rather than the splendid city whose legend fueled 200 years of fevered pursuit, Caillié found a town whose glory had faded. A year later, nineteen-year-old student Alfred Tennyson of Trinity College, Cambridge, would win the Chancellor's Prize for a poem that compared Timbuktu with the legendary lost civilizations of Atlantis and El Dorado:

> Wide Afric, doth thy sun
> Lighten, thy hills enfold a City as fair
> As those which starr'd the night o' the elder World?
> Or is the rumour of thy Timbuctou
> A dream as frail as those of ancient Time?

As Tennyson's lines suggested ("Low-built, mud-wall'd barbarian settlements"), the city was showing the effects of neglectful occupation by the Moroccans, who had conquered it in 1591, and the ensuing plundering by the nomadic Tuareg, the pastoral people who originally founded Timbuktu as a summer camp around AD 1100. The Moroccans valued Timbuktu mainly for its position as an entrepôt to the "great salt road" that connected gold and slaves from the south with equally valuable salt that the Tuareg and their slaves, the Bella, mined in the bowels of the desert, fifteen days by camel from Timbuktu. The conquerers had little time for culture and learning. In 1593, the invaders rounded up and deported the leading intellectuals and plundered their houses and their libraries. Soon the Tuareg began to harass the city; at times over the coming centuries, they had it wholly within their grip.

By 1897, later visitors such as the explorer Felix Dubois mocked the city that had once transfixed Europe: "And this is the great Timbuctou, the metropolis of the Sudan and the Sahara, with its boasted wealth and commerce," he wrote in *Timbuctou the Mysterious*. "This is Timbuctou the holy, the learned, that light of the Niger, of which it was written 'We shall one day correct the texts of our

Greek and Latin classics by the manuscripts that are preserved here,' and I have not even seen one of the open-air schools which were so numerous at Jenne. These ruins, this rubbish, this wreck of a town, is this the secret of Timbuctou the mysterious?"[6]

In the course of seeing Timbuktu for myself, I wanted to encounter some of Mali's wide variety of ethnic groups. The largest is the Bambara; it is their language that is the lingua franca for trade in Mali. The Bozo are fishermen who make their living from the Niger, living in such proximity that they must flee their houses when the water rises. The Dogon live on the firmer ground of the plateau near the border with Burkina Faso. The Malinke and Sarakole live in the southwestern part of the country, while the Peul (or Fulani) are widespread throughout Mali. In the northern desert live the Tuareg. Nomadic and brown-skinned, they travel in camel caravans; serving the Tuareg as servants, in a relationship that remains perilously close to that of master-slave, are the darker Bella. I also hoped to meet the Songhai, a people of great learning who live near Timbuktu. These peoples, each with especially rich cultural heritages and histories, have created or live in proximity to no fewer than five of the "wonders" of the African world that my colleagues and I compiled at the beginning of this project: the Sahara Desert and the River Niger, the Dogon culture, the mammoth mud-brick mosque at Djenne, and Timbuktu itself. In addition, these peoples are the descendants of three of the most sophisticated and legendary civilizations of medieval Africa: Ghana, Mali, and Songhai. It was under the domination of the latter two that Timbuktu grew into Africa's most glorious city.

Today Mali is a democracy, slowly pulling itself out of the depths of generations of poverty, drought, and illiteracy, but many forget this was once the seat of the trans-Saharan trade that shaped the old kingdoms of Ghana, Mali, and Songhai and enabled their hegemony in western Africa. There is considerable debate about the movements and formations of peoples that shaped the beginnings of these empires: Ghana, or Wagadu (circa 300/500–1076), Mali (circa 1240–1546), and Songhai (circa 1450–1591). But no one doubts that their reach was extensive: As Mamadou Diawara puts it, at its height, Mali "included most of the area of modern Mali as well as Senegal, Gambia, and parts of Mauritania," while "Songhay . . . extended its reach throughout most of present-day Mali and also into what is now Niger and Burkina Faso." Diawara continues, "All three empires . . . exploited slavery to an extent previously unknown in western Africa."[7] The empires of Ghana, Mali, and Songhai revolved around the movement of trade and the resources of gold and salt.

By the time that Europeans had become obsessed with finding Timbuktu's wealth, the glory of these empires had long faded. My journey begins on the banks of the mighty Niger, in Bamako, the capital of Mali: I would travel the old trade routes, following in the footsteps of those first European explorers. Journeying 700 miles northeast down the Niger, from the gold fields in the forests south of Bamako, through to Dogon country, and then by boat to the thriving port of Mopti, the Muslim religious center of Djenne, and ultimately to Timbuktu, once described as "the most distant place on earth," the port on the sea of sand, black Africa's great center of learning on the southernmost edge of the Sahara Desert.

Since so much of Mali's history was shaped by her huge gold reserves, I wanted first to see the present-day goldfields. A route extending from the Atlantic across the

Sahara to the Mediterranean permitted the exchange for goods from the north. It was the flow of this wealth that inspired Europeans in the eighteenth and nineteenth centuries to seek out the legendary city of Timbuktu. The Malian empires were built on the Islamic world's and then Europe's lust for gold, but also the southern world's urgent need for salt. At its peak in the fourteenth century, the Malian empire was one of the greatest states in the world, covering an enormous area from the forests toward the Atlantic to the farthest stretch of the Niger River in the Sahara desert. With gold mines in the south and salt mines in the north, Mali was abundantly endowed in two sources of great wealth, which at that time were equally valued ounce for ounce. The entire region was known as the western Sudan. As Nehmiah Levtzion puts it, "Until the discovery of America, the Sudan was the principal source of gold both for the Muslim world and for Europe." By the fourteenth century,

"two-thirds of the world's production of gold came from the Sudan to replenish the raw materials needed for the European mints."[8]

We set off at 7:00 A.M. from Bamako on a three-hour drive south to the goldfields in the village of Kokoyan, near Tambola, a few miles from the Guinea border. The very narrow footpaths leading to the goldfields are hidden by long, thick grasses that are common here. We inched our way across a natural log bridge to reach a large reddish brown field.

This was not the goldfield of my imagination but a huge stretch of open desert, covered with mounds and wells, a few feet from a river. There were perhaps fifty such mines, each dug thirty feet deep into the mud. Early in the morning, men of the village slide down into these holes to dig out the earth in horizontal tunnels up to ninety feet long. The women wait above to receive buckets of mud that the men haul up using pulleys; then they pound the mud with a long wooden mallet. Many do this work carrying babies on their backs in a kanga sling: a cloth that covers the baby and is wound around the mother's body across the breasts. The infants seem remarkably comfortable, though the arrangement strikes me as unstable. Standing in shallow water holes, the women swish the pulverized gravel around in large trays, searching for gold nuggets.

I chatted with Dantoume Magassouba, the leader of a group working one of the mines. He said that his forefathers used to work for the king, but that he mines to support his family. Magassouba told me that the work was dangerous—the week before my visit a young man had died, buried in the thick mud. He gestured to a black rag tied to a stake next to one of the mines: "That was where it happened." But the two days it took to dig him

Gold merchants of Mali: Before the discovery of America, the empire was the chief source of gold for Europe and the Muslim world.

out was valuable time lost, since any find makes a significant impact on their lives.

I called out to the women panning for gold, Found any today? Not really; they shrugged, lifting their mud-filled pans for my inspection. I could just make out the unmistakable sparkle of gold dust on the side of the pan. What's the biggest piece ever found here? I asked. The answer was depressing: a chunk weighing about 1 gram retrieved the previous year, worth about one dollar.

The methods employed by the villagers probably differ little from those of 500 years ago, but while Mali was one of the world's richest nations in the fifteenth century, it is now among the five poorest. And while the land still has enormous gold reserves, there is little commercial exploitation of these resources. These villagers barely eke out a subsistence income. Women often move to the village to escape the men in their family, and thereby keep their own earnings. They are then considered outcasts by their families, so they assimilate into the mining community, abandoning their kin and ethnic groups.

Back in Bamako, I went to a small club, reminiscent of a juke joint in the American South or a funky blues club on the South Side of Chicago. Bubakar Traore was playing this night, to a crowd numbering perhaps one hundred at the most. When Traore, one of Africa's best-known musicians, plays in Europe or America his audience consists of thousands. I couldn't believe my good fortune. His guitar style evokes B. B. King's to me for some reason, despite the enormous differences in the sound of their music. Traore admitted that he admired American blues very much, and that it influenced him. The crowd seemed, if not indifferent to Traore initially, certainly cool—until, that is, he began to sing the traditional epic of Mali's great king, Sundiata. As he did, his audience erupted, clapping, cheering, and dancing. It was as though someone had played "The Star-Spangled

Gold mining techniques have changed little in the 500 years since Mali was one of the world's richest nations. Today it is among the poorest.

Banner" with the same affect, let's say, of Wilson Pickett's "In the Midnight Hour." But once I understood Sundiata's exploits, it was easier to understand the electricity that Traore generated in the bar.

The great Empire of Mali began in 1240 when the legendary hunter king, Sundiata Keita, fought the Soso King Sumanquru at the Battle of Kirina. Before this, though, the Malinke kingdoms in the Niger interior, or delta, united and formed an extensive commercial, political, and military network that would be employed in the formation of this new empire. The history of Sundiata's achievement is memorialized in D. T. Niane's transcription of the *Epic of Old Mali*. Here we have the tales, as passed down by the *griots*, or oral historians, of the wanderings of Sundiata—how he gained the respect of the Malinke (or Mandingo) peoples along the Niger, including the aristocratic refugees from the old kingdom of Ghana who now resided there, and how he fought Sumanquru, the Soso king.

According to the *Epic of Old Mali*, Mari-jata, or Sundiata, was the fruit of a prophecy that foretold his coming as the liberator of Mali. He was born at Niane, the first son of the Malinke Nare-Maghan, a Keita king, and his very mysterious wife, Sogolon Djata of Do, described as a hideous hunchback. The Keita clan, the rulers of a chiefdom on the Sankarani River, claimed descent from Bilali Bunama, the black Mu'adhdin (the man who calls for prayer in Islam)[9] of the Prophet. Although Sundiata had an inauspicious beginning—he was born without the use of his legs, managing to walk only at seven years old—he was persecuted by his father's jealous first wife, Sassouna Berete, and her son, Dankaran Touman, who usurped Sundiata's rightful place as heir to the throne. Things got worse: Sassouna Berete attempted to assassinate him. He escaped with his family into exile and began his wandering throughout Mali.

Sundiata eventually stayed in the court of Mema, the new seat of the Soninke kings. There the king took him under his wing in order to train him as a warrior. King Sumaoro of Soso, meanwhile, determined to crush the nascent political power of the Malinke, drove Sundiata's elder half-brother and reigning king, Dankaran Touman, into exile. At this point, all the pro-Sundiata old chiefs and *griots* who were silenced under Touman's reign sought out Sundiata, following his footsteps to Mema. They begged him to return and unite Mali against the Soso tyrant. He gathered his friends—once young princes like himself at the court of Niane, now kings and chiefs of the various Malinke villages—and, united, they fought Sumaoro gloriously at the Battle of Kirina on the Niger River. The *Epic of Old Mali* gloatingly tells us that Sumaoro was killed by Sundiata himself during battle.[10]

The poetry of the *Epic* is densely lyrical and rhythmic. Looking around at the faces in the bar, I could begin to understand the effects that ancient oral literature such as the *Iliad* and the *Odyssey* must have had on the Greeks. Traore's rendition galvanized the crowd; even I began to

dance, swept away by the music although not comprehending the words.

The next day, I set off by car along the banks of the Niger, heading for Mopti, a river port with a waterborne market. The river bustles with heavily loaded boats carrying trade goods, as it has for more than a thousand years. This was the first leg of my long journey to Timbuktu. The land gradually becomes drier as scrub and sagebrush replace trees. This is the Sahel, "the shore of the desert," which every year reaches a little farther south.

At the Mopti market I saw one trader lauding the powers of crocodile heads, goat hooves, and various fetishes. Not far away a competitor with a megaphone advertised medicine for gynecological problems. We moved along to the fish market, near the pier. On sale was the captaine, a delicious meaty white fish seemingly served everywhere. All of the fish were covered with flies. In Mali, flies are everywhere. I have never seen so many in my life; flies in Mali don't alight on your skin, they perch.

The French fashion industry created modern-day Mopti at the turn of the century, when it was little more than a river settlement. Its colorful bird life furnished beautiful feathers that were much in demand for hats in Paris. And so the French built a direct road to the port where the Niger and Bani rivers meet to form the inland delta.

I met Oumar Cisse ("Peace Corps Baba") the next morning in the market. His nickname dates to the sixties when Corps volunteers showed him how to start a business in African art. Oumar is a Moptien and speaks eight languages, including English, French, Bambara (Mali's national language), Arabic, Mossi, Dogon, and Fulani. His trading skills have taken him around the world. Ethnically, he is a mixture of Hausa, Fulani, and Dogon, a

Mali's salt was once as valuable as gold.

good example of the sort of cultural hybridity that occurs in centers of trade. Piles of large bricks stacked in front of the stalls caught my eye, so I stopped to examine one, taking note of its sand and crystal composition. "What is this?" I asked. "Timbuktu salt," he explained, smiling at the newcomer who had never seen unrefined salt, the resource that with gold had been the foundation of Mali's wealth and power.

In the medieval world, boats would travel the Niger carrying a variety of goods from the south to trade with merchants from the north: honey, cotton, cloth, millet, rice, soap, preserved foodstuffs, allspice, dried fish, and kola nuts—all exchanged for salt from the north. But the most important of all came downriver from Timbuktu— salt. I had never before understood its importance. The long gray blocks are a foot or so wide, bound together five or six feet high, and have a rough, grainy texture. A trader explained to me that the salt comes in several grades, ranging from 1 to 4. He gave me a piece of grade 1, an extremely kind gesture, considering its value. He also claimed to have twenty-five wives. The man was a Tuareg, dressed in their traditional white gown with a

bold indigo turban. With him was another man, very dark, dressed in an indigo gown, who performed all the menial tasks for the Tuareg tradesman. When we had passed them, Oumar told me that the Bella man was a slave. The word "slave" is not used but is the only one that accurately describes the traditional relationship between these two peoples. I was astonished. This is as close to slavery as I ever hope to get.

Throughout the sixteenth century, the Songhai *askias* of the Gao Empire rarely intervened in the affairs of the city, which was run instead by aristocratic families. The Tuareg were masters of Timbuktu in the mid-fifteenth century, and in the seventeenth and eighteenth centuries they often controlled its affairs. As the trans-Saharan trade began to decline, the Tuareg had recaptured the town in 1433. These days they find themselves wandering the desert around Timbuktu. Many were forced into refugee camps after their animals died in recent droughts, or having lost their jobs on account of their role in a Libyan-sponsored rebellion in the early 1990s.

Nineteenth-century drawing of Tuareg nomads tending their flocks. The Tuareg founded Timbuktu as a summer camp in the eleventh century, but today dwell mainly in the surrounding deserts.

Above: Mosque of Mopti: In this century the town was resuscitated by French fashion.
Opposite: Mud structure housing an institute of herbal studies

But it would seem that even the most destitute can own slaves: The Tuareg have maintained their relationship with the Bella for so long that the Bella are now incapable of leaving, though nominally "free."

Bella men accompany the Tuareg camel caravans on foot, setting camp and cooking every night on the road to the salt mines, a trip of about sixteen days. At the mines it is the Bella who do the work, in exchange for the most meager wages, or simply for food and drink. On the return trip each camel carries four bars of salt, worth approximately eight dollars each in the market of Timbuktu. The Tuareg and the Bella are caught in an economic anachronism. Their way of life has not changed substantially for centuries, despite the fact that the world has turned now to more accessible deposits of salt; what was once worth its weight in gold is today a common commodity.[II]

We ended our day at Oumar's art gallery, where I purchased an antique Dogon door for my African art collection at Oumar's "Mali price" as opposed to his "Senegalese price," a considerable savings. The Dogon are as renowned for their art as they are for their hermetic culture, and I was eager to meet them. Few of the philosophical systems of African people have been written about as extensively as the Dogon's has. In fact there is a joke commonly heard in Mali: how many people are there in a Dogon family? Five: two parents, two children, and a French anthropologist.

THE DOGON

The next morning, we set out in search of the ancestors of the Malian empire's legendary reclusive people: the Dogon. Dogon country consists of an imposing rock escarpment that rises out of a flat scrubby plain. Here these cliff-dwelling farmers incredibly grow crops among rocks in soil that is seldom more than six inches deep. Having arrived in the thirteenth century, the Dogon today number around 300,000 and live in several hundred villages scattered over an area of 5,000 square miles, east of Mopti and Djenne. There are about thirty-five spoken Dogon dialects.

Famous for their complex religious beliefs, their artwork, their nomadic traditions, and their knowledge of the stars, the Dogon have lived along the Niger River since their arrival in southeast Mali, where they fled to escape forced conversion to Islam. Today they are battling for their livelihood. Year after year, the Sahara devours more arable land, leaving less and less for herding or cultivation. In an effort to save themselves, the Dogon have allowed a bit of a coming out, sharing their communities with tourists and other strangers. The surrounding cliffs have always protected them from the outside world, and it was not until the French ethnographer Marcel Griaule's extensive field research among the Dogon in the 1930s that their art and culture began to be discovered and understood. Griaule also introduced the onion; and today Dogon onions are available throughout Mali and in great demand in neighboring countries as well.

The Dogon maintain a complex religion and continue to worship their ancestors, though approximately 35 percent are Muslim. A first-time visitor to a Dogon community might not notice the settlement's layout in the shape of the human body. At the head is a men's meeting house, from which women are excluded. Granaries, too, are divided into compartments that represent the parts of the cosmos. They stand on stilts to protect the crops from mice. The *hogon,* or spiritual leader of the village, lives in a house decorated with figures and religious symbols.

A stand of massive baobab trees outside Dogon village

Above: Dogon village granary
Opposite: Carvings on a Dogon door allude to mythical and
historical ancestors.

Trying to get around a Dogon village without a local guide is almost certain to offend, since there are ritually correct ways of walking past the many sacred sites.

According to Dogon myth, the creator god Amma had intercourse with the female Earth, producing the primordial couple who themselves brought forth eight children. Often the original couple is portrayed in figurines, seated together upon the flat circular earth, which is upheld by the tree of life. The geometry of their faces reflects the couple's complementarity: The man has a beard jutting from his chin, while the woman has a lip plug. The representation of mythical or historical figures is not uncommon in Dogon art. On granaries of the *hogon,* for instance, relief carvings frequently allude to the original forty-four families who migrated to the Niger River from their homeland in central Mali.[12]

The Dogon's most important rite is that of the *sigui,* a dance performed only once every sixty years to renew their myth of origin. In it they use a 33-foot-high mask to represent their first ancestor, who at death assumed the form of Lebe, a snake. They believe that Lebe not only delivered them to their homeland, but also taught them speech, a mixed blessing that introduced death as well. Dances are also performed at funerals to assist the deceased's spirit as it seeks another home. The body is carried aloft on a stretcher and run through the streets of the village by men wearing masks bearing the three main symbols of Dogon mythology: the serpent, the tortoise, and the crocodile. The corpse is then hauled up the escarpment cliffs on ropes made from baobab bark and laid to repose in the caves.

As we drove into the village of Gongo, Dogon men and boys, standing on rocks and boulders lining the road, began firing their rifles in the air as they performed the

Yanna Goy: "women go out"

djancombo; the two-step hop is a form of welcoming dance, accompanied by swords and guns. The guns sounded like firecrackers; they were the old-fashioned kind that use powder and ramrods, made by a Dogon blacksmith—decorated with silver buttons along the sides. The men used them to hunt monkeys and cheetahs. Following the welcome dance, we were led to the top of a cliff outside Gongo and to the upper village of Gongo Sinou. Surrounded by huge rock escarpments we saw in the valley the magnificent fields of Dogon onions, green and bright against the rocky background of the encampment.

At Gongo Sinou, the men performed a very special dance they would normally never do for outsiders; it is called *Yanna Goy,* which means "women go out." All the men wear female face and breast masks, so that women, who are denied physical access, may be represented and "spiritually" present. We made a donation so that the women in our film crew could attend the ceremony, since afterward the priests would have to bless the place and offer a sacrifice to purify it. Some of the men were on stilts, five or more feet above the ground. Their masks varied in size and shape—some covered in conch shells and beads; others starkly geometrical, with triangles painted on them and rectangular cutouts for eyes, nose, and mouth. Some wore masks adorned with another popular Dogon symbol, that of two arms reaching for the heavens interlocked with two arms reaching for the earth. Such masks are kept in a secret cave and retrieved only for ceremonies. They are buried when they are too worn to use. The breastplates were also adorned with shells and beads, and tassels dyed red, blue, and yellow twirled furiously as the men danced.

We visited another village to see the famous paintings on the walls of its circumcision cave, high above the settlements. There the ritual is performed every three years, often in a mass ceremony. "This year sixty-one boys between the ages of ten and thirteen were circumcised here," a Dogon guide explained to me as we entered. It is believed the serpent Lebe comes down to the cave from the mountain during the ceremony, lured by a sacrificial chicken. An elder who leads the rite warns the children that if they cry, the serpent will eat not only the chicken, but them as well. When asked if they really saw the serpent during their circumcision ceremony, the Dogon boys insist they did.[13]

But circumcision here is not just for boys: While Mali may brag of its advances in the rights of women, it still has the highest rate of female circumcision in the world, obviously a matter of much controversy in the West. Nevertheless, it is an ancient and traditional rite among many West and East African peoples, as we have seen in Nubia and Ethiopia, and for the Dogon, it is thought to be vital to the identity of the individual being. According to the tradition the "fundamental law of creation is twinship; at birth, each infant is 'twin'—doubled, equipped with twin souls of different sex. In the girl, the masculine

side resides in the clitoris, which is considered her male organ. In the male, removal of the prepuce, in which the female soul resides, confirms the boy in the sex for which he was destined. Excision, which ablates the clitoris, rids the girl of the male element."

Once the circumcisions have taken place, "[t]he person will find his twinned unity again only at the time of marriage. It is the man's duty to go after his lost femininity and find it again in his wife. And the woman who was freed from her masculinity at the time of excision finds it again in the person of her husband."[14] The union of husband and wife is thought to accomplish the ideal union of twins. But a woman cannot marry a man circumcised the same year as she. The fact that female circumcision, unlike male, is a bodily mutilation that invariably results in physical dysfunction does not alter their belief in its necessity. Typically girls are circumcised at age three or four, ostensibly so they won't remember the pain later. Those from poorer families may have to wait until they are older, when their parents can afford the rite. Despite its role in traditional beliefs, controversy over its barbarity has increased in recent years.

Circumcision caves: The serpent Lebe is said to descend during the ceremony, lured by a chicken.

At the cave entrance, we were stopped and told that Judi, our sound engineer and a dark-complexioned black Briton, could not enter the sacred place. No African women are allowed to see the paintings done by the newly circumcised young men. A huge argument ensued when we protested, pointing out that she was not African but British. Berte, our fixer, after failing to convince our guide, went himself to see the chief. It was a hopeless mission: He returned to ask Judi to leave. After we had reluctantly filmed, I asked the guide if African American tourists come here. He answered yes. "But they are lighter than she is," he said.

The wall paintings are a stunning interplay of abstract shapes and animal representations in red, black, and white. The serpent Lebe in white and black takes center stage. The rock where the boys are circumcised is stained the color of charcoal from centuries of blood. I felt like crossing my legs.

We left with everyone sulking a bit—Judi because the Dogon would not let her work at the site, Berte because he could not convince Judi of their rationale, and the crew who, due to the delay from the quarrel, had missed filming in the best light. Berte, who felt compelled to explain his rebuff, informed us that the chief had told him that the last three black women who had visited the sacred paintings had all died. Asked by the chief whether he felt he could protect Judi's life, Berte was persuaded to desist. I was angered by the Dogon's distinction between white women and black women. If Judi had been lighter, I was told, she could have remained because "white" women do not figure in their cosmology.

That evening, we returned to Mopti to attend a concert given by one of the traditional oral poets. The *griot's* song reflects the Malian veneration of the past and is often based on one particular element of a larger historical epic. As I had learned in Bamako, the epic of Sundiata

Keita is an especially popular source. *Griots* are both historians and journalists, interpreting events of the present and the past. While the civil servants in government ministries have supplanted the diplomatic, recordkeeping, and communications functions of the scribes that once prospered in Mali, the *griots* (generally but not exclusively women) continue to perform many of these traditional functions. The role of *griots* has been romanticized in African American culture. But in Mali the *griots,* while essential, are not necessarily beloved. Raymond Maunay defines them as "a despised but feared caste of musician-genealogist-sorcerer parasites."[15] Ibn Battuta provides probably the earliest account of them:

> They stand before the sultan in that ridiculous attire and recite their poetry. . . . So do good, that good will be recounted after you. . . . I was informed that this performance is old among them: they continued it from before Islam.[16]

Griots were hired at all weddings and other important occasions to sing the praises of their patron, who was obliged to provide for them and live up to their words. A *griot* is still necessary at a wedding, where the guests and family will shower money on her for exalting those present. And while royal engagements are no longer available, today's praise-singers will perform for thousands in the Palais de Culture, where they extol the virtues not of the king but of the businessman sponsoring the concert, perhaps the owner of a leading company in Mali, or even of the occasional visitor and his film crew.

As seen in the lyrics of Mandou Louyate, the *griot* is very often self-referential about her position:

> We are vessels of speech, we are the repositories which harbor secrets many centuries old . . . with-

out us the names of kings would vanish into oblivion, we are the memory of mankind; by the spoken word we bring to life the deeds and exploits of kings for younger generations.

Indeed, without the centuries of *griot* oral tradition a great deal of African history would have been lost. Historians have begun to value, and utilize, their records as historical evidence.

We arose at 5:00 A.M., and drove toward Djenne, site of the most famous mosque in all of Africa. The *Tarikh al-Soudan* states: "This blessed city of Djenne is the reason why caravans came to Timbuktu from all quarters—north, south, east and west."[17] Djenne was founded in the twelfth century, though oral tradition claims the eighth. Djenne was eventually overtaken by Malian kings and came to rival Timbuktu as a center of trade and scholarship.

Analyzing the oral traditions, two American archaeologists, Roderick and Susan MacIntosh, became convinced that alongside Djenne there existed the remains of an even older town, dating to the third century BC.[18] Excavations here confirmed the presence of a city that began as an average-sized fishing camp, and grew by ca. AD 900, if one includes Djenne, to a size equal to medieval London. The population engaged in ironwork and trade and had apparently reached a peak of 10,000 as early as AD 800. These discoveries are rewriting the history of West Africa, which had been previously assumed to lack civilization before the coming of the Arabs. Old Djenne (Djenne-Jeno) has attracted more study than any other site in West Africa; archaeologists can now trace Mali's later kingdoms continuously from the third century BC.

Nineteenth-century Djenne

Djenne-Jeno is covered by a thick carpet of broken pottery and accumulated debris 16½ feet deep. From afar, the site seems just so many mounds of red earth. On close inspection, however, the mounds consist of pottery shards, human bones, and fragments of buildings. I could not believe that one could simply lean over and touch the collective remains of more than two millennia of history. Although the inhabitants of old Djenne left to establish Djenne in AD 800, it is thought Djenne-Jeno remained in occupation until at least ca. AD 1400. Some think that the move to Djenne coincided with a conversion to Islam and that the original might have been abandoned in an attempt to escape its pagan past, or there might have been an epidemic that forced people to leave. Whatever the reason, the people of Djenne were forbidden to speak of the earlier town. But the building of the new city came up against a strange problem: According to legend, the walls

Djenne's houses of sun-baked mud were multistoried structures with wooden columns.

kept falling down. An ancient oracle was consulted who declared that if the walls were to stand the most beautiful virgin would have to be buried alive within them. Tapama Djennebo was selected for the honor by her own father, the ruler of the town. She agreed, and after she was immured the walls stayed up and the town prospered. Two hundred years later, the new city had 4,200 scholars and was also a thriving center of commerce, a place for traders to store goods for sale to Timbuktu, then only a clump of Tuareg huts. Today Tapama's tomb in Djenne is preserved as a sacred site where the devout pray and leave coins for her descendants, who act as caretakers.

Djenne figures prominently in Islam's growth in Mali. Though it would ultimately yield pride of place as Mali's center of learning and religion to Timbuktu, for several hundred years Djenne dominated the kingdom's cultural landscape, a dominance that coincided with the apex of Mali's power and glory.

Sundiata was succeeded by his son Mansa Uli, who made a pilgrimage through Egypt during the reign of Mamluk Sultan Baybas. "Mansa Uli," says Ibn Khaldun, "was one of Mali's greatest kings."[19] Under his rule, Mali's territory included parts of the Sahel and took in the trading centers of Walata, Timbuktu, and Gao along the Niger River. By now, the ancient markets of the west, such as Awdagust and Ghana, had ceded to the new ones of the east, such as Walata, nestled in the bend of the Niger River. The Bend had become an intermediary region of some commercial importance. Its double advantage of belonging both to the desert and to the Sudan made it a preeminent commercial area from the thirteenth century onward.

The golden age of the Malian Empire was surely the reign of Mansa Musa, also known as Kankou Moussa (1312–1337), the favorite of Muslim writers Arab and Sudanese: He became their patron in every way. In 1324 he made the pilgrimage to Mecca and on his return encouraged the building of mosques and the pursuit of Islamic learning throughout Mali, but especially in the city of Timbuktu. This pilgrimage—specifically its political as well as spiritual implications—made the western Sudan an integral part of the Islamic world. The journey, called the Hajj, took more than one year and was an expensive venture, but it was a worthwhile investment: Three of the rulers of Mali who went to Mecca—Mansa Uli, Sakura the usurper, and Mansa Musa—are all remembered as powerful kings.

At this time the word "infidel" also assumed a powerful symbolism, and it was applied by the Muslims to Christians and pagans alike with increasing militancy and violence. It was in the Malians' best interest, situated as they were on the border of an increasingly Islamicized and Arabicized Sahel and North Africa, to make pilgrimages and to incorporate Muslims as peacefully as they could into their kingdoms. Traditional African religions predating the Islamic conquest still managed to flourish

Djenne today

and to coexist with Islam (albeit awkwardly), but Muslims held a privileged position in the changing western Sudan. Their literacy was employed in the service of the state, while their business and trade fueled the economy.[20]

The pilgrimage that Musa made to Mecca made a deep impression in southern Europe and the Arab world and was celebrated in the chronicles until the sixteenth century. So great was Musa's renown that his image appeared on two maps in the fourteenth century: Angelino Dulcert's 1339 *Mappa Mundi,* and a map printed in 1375 on which Musa is depicted as holding a huge nugget of gold. He traveled with a retinue of thousands and took camel loads of gold from every province in his kingdom on his journey. While Musa was in Cairo, he was lent a palace to reside in before embarking upon the Hajj. He distributed so much gold by way of presents and alms that the value of gold is said to have decreased in Cairo for several years. In fact, he spent so much that he had to borrow from Egyptian merchants at exorbitant interest. But his motivations were not merely political. It seems that Musa was actually quite pious and took his new religion very seriously. At home he built several mosques, instituted public prayer on Fridays, and attracted to his kingdom the Maliki scholars who would play such an important role in the creation of Timbuktu.

Musa had paused long enough in Cairo to relate a curious tale of his own path to the throne, which the encyclopedist Al-Omari published in 1340:

His predecessor, Abu Bakari II, "the Voyager King," in an act of willfulness and hubris, had determined to discover the other side of the Atlantic Ocean, and set out from the West African coast, probably from the Gambia. He and his 2,000 ships never returned. "He assigned to me his authority and power until such day as he should return," Musa said, "but to this day no one has ever seen

Mali's great king Mansa Musa depicted in the atlas of Spain's Charles V. In the course of his pilgrimages to Mecca he distributed so much gold in presents and alms that the price of the precious metal in Cairo was depressed for years.

him again." Musa, entrusted with the rule of the kingdom until his colleague's return, ascended the throne, transforming Mali into a world power, a thriving, bustling, cosmopolitan kingdom that gave birth to the greatness of Timbuktu.[21]

In the fifteenth century, Mali had to face the invading Mossi and the rebellion of the Songhai, who had become independent of Mali and henceforth rivaled it. The territorial expansion of Songhai, west of the Niger's bend, had begun during the reign of Sunni Silman Dama (d. 1464), who conquered Mema, and reached its peak under Sunni Ali "the Great" (1464–1492), who conquered Djenne in 1473.

Djenne became a great center of Islamic learning.

and bore it to the king. Konboro had it thrown in the Bani River. Next day at market, Ismail's wife brought a large fish. Cutting it open, she found the gold. When Konboro summoned him, Ismail was able to produce the treasure, declaring, "My god sent the fish to protect me." Konboro, deeply impressed, became a Muslim. He asked the *marabout,* "How may I please God?" Ismail replied, "Plant a tree, and for years the people who enjoy its shade will bless you. Dig a well and long after your death people who draw water will bless you. And build a mosque. The people who pray in it will bless your name for centuries." Konboro did all three things. He turned his palace into a large mosque.[23]

To return to Djenne: Before King Koi Konboro converted to Islam there were sixty small mosques in Djenne. When he turned his palace into a place of worship, he was able to put an end to the bickering between the smaller mosques by converting them into child cemeteries, revered to this day. A larger-than-life character, Konboro was the city's twenty-sixth king and its first ruler to become a Muslim. The following legend relates his conversion:[22]

When a Muslim sage, or *marabout,* named Ismail settled in Djenne, Koi Konboro, angry and suspicious, sought an excuse to kill him. A counselor hit on a scheme. Lend Ismail gold, he suggested. I will find and steal it. You ask for it back. When Ismail cannot produce it, you can execute him as a thief. Konboro agreed. He lent Ismail a tobacco box filled with gold dust, which the *marabout* buried for safekeeping. The counselor, posing as a convert, grew friendly with Ismail, who at last revealed where the gold was hidden. The counselor secretly dug it up

Master and pupil: a Madrassa or Koranic school

133

*Believed to be built on the site of the converted palace of Kon-
boro, the city's first ruler, Djenne's great mosque is the continent's
supreme example of mud architecture.*

Today, Djenne remains a center of Islamic learning, concentrating on the earlier stages of education in more than sixty Koranic schools for young boys. I visited the oldest of these, the "School of Three Doors." The students have come here from all of West Africa to absorb the word of the Prophet. They shift for themselves, sleeping wherever they can so as to be able to spend their days reading the Koran on the dirt floor of the school.

The Imam of the Djenne mosque—who is considered roughly equivalent to the Archbishop of Canterbury—is descended from a line of some nineteen Imams. There are only five families in Djenne from whom an Imam may be chosen, and they are considered to be among the holiest men in West Africa. The mosque fell into ruin under the Empire of Masina (1818–1843), according to whose strict branch of Islam it was deemed too elaborate and decorated. Since Islamic law forbids the outright destruction of a mosque, however, the Peul leader, Sekou Amadou, undertook to eliminate it by neglect, cutting off its gutter system to await its eventual decomposition. Early in the twentieth century the mosque was rebuilt, and although the new one shares many of the same design features it is not identical, but it still stands as a monument to the sophistication and splendor of traditional African culture; its huge mud structure with a forest of elaborate parapets and towers suggesting something out of *Star Wars*. Imagine Notre Dame or Chartres, or more particularly Gaudi's Sagrada Familia—such is the status of this mud mosque in the Muslim universe of the Niger's bend. It is considered, without contention, one of the wonders of the African world.

In 1473, Djenne was conquered by the Songhai after a siege that according to tradition, is said to have lasted seven years, seven months, and seven days. A century later, the Moroccans invaded and genuine decline ensued. Once the French built the road to Mopti, Djenne became further isolated. I returned from Djenne to Mopti, where I would find a boat that would take me to Djenne's sister city to the east, Timbuktu.

THE NIGER RIVER AND THE BOAT TO TIMBUKTU

There are two ways to reach Timbuktu: a ninety-day camel caravan across the Sahara's scorching sands, or a boat trip from Mopti. I chose the latter, boarding the promisingly named German steamer *Timbuctou* for a three-day run down the river. The *Timbuctou* was truly public transportation, a sort of floating "mammy wagon," the overcrowded vehicle that provides most of West Africa's transportation. The boat had three decks and pulled a barge alongside where people sleep as space allows. "No. 2," my door announced with the serenely self-confident European elegance that the vessel once possessed, perhaps fifty years ago, as it steamed the Rhine. With the fates of Caillié and Laing never far from my imagination, I entered to find a dirty room graced with a nonflushing toilet. The heat and discomfort would be mitigated only by the splendor of the Niger River, grandly brown and sprawling, flowing west to east.

The powerful Niger runs for 2,600 miles, passing through diverse landscapes. It flows northward from the Futa Jallon mountain range (in present-day Guinea) through the center of Mali and across the Sahel to the borders of the Sahara, and then bends south (through Niger and Nigeria), ultimately emptying into the Bight of Benin. It was formed from two ancient rivers—the upper Niger, known as the Djoliba, which continued northward into the Sahara, and the lower Niger, known as the Kwara, which had its source in the mountains of Ahaggar in the desert.

For centuries, the Niger has been both a route of pilgrimage and a commercial waterway. For the people of Mali, "The Great Water" and its inland delta are an ever-constant and ever-changing source of life. It's the home of the Malian clans and has seen empires rise and fall. It is a region that has always welcomed Islam and yet still managed to sustain its indigenous religions. Each village or stop along the river tells us a story of the Malian hero Sundiata's wanderings, of the first Malinke chiefs, and of the traders who passed through in pirogues (wooden canoes) in search of gold. "Mali is eternal," says the *griot* Mamadou Kouyate, in the *Epic of Old Mali:*

> Go to Krinkoroni near Niassola and you will see a tree which commemorates Sundiata's passing through these parts. Go to Bankoumana on the Niger and you will see Soumaoro's balafon, the balafon which is called Balguintiri. Go to Ka-ba and you will see the clearing of Kouroukan Fougan, where the great assembly took place which gave Sundiata's empire its constitution.[24]

The *Epic of Old Mali* imparts a sense of sacredness to the Niger and the Niger Delta, as the river plays on the *Epic*'s universal themes of exile, separation, and unity. Undeterred by the malaria-carrying mosquito, for which the Niger would be known as the "white man's grave," Arab and European travelers alike tried to find the source of the Niger, just as they sought Timbuktu. For many encountering it, the great river was almost a religious experience. The Scottish explorer Mungo Park wrote:

And looking forwards, I saw with infinite pleasure the object of my mission—the long sought for majestic Niger, glittering in the morning sun, as broad as the Thames at Westminister, and flowing slowly eastward. I hastened to the brink, and having drunk the water, lifted up my fervent thanks in prayer to the Great ruler of all things, for having thus far crowned my endeavors with success.[25]

Along the Niger, cities such as Djenne, Mopti, and Gao emerged, as we have seen, as crucial participants in a long-distance trade in gold, salt, agricultural products, and slaves. During the Malian and Songhai empires the Niger waterway connected the two great trade centers of Timbuktu and Djenne as well as two important overland routes: the salt routes from Taghaza to Timbuktu and the gold route from Djenne to the edge of the forest. It was the river that allowed the region to be the commercial center of the Sudan from the thirteenth century onward.

All along the river are people who depend on our passing for trade. The boat is a floating farmers' market, a moveable feast of grilled ribs, chicken, yams, and plantains exchanged for other goods. Meager islets somehow support the mud-brick villages of the Bozo, a fishing people with an intricate mythology. They run the river in pirogues or pinnaces (canoes with engines), often wearing their traditional conical hats. The Bozo live so close to the water's edge that many of them are forced to maintain second homes for use during flood season; they move back to the banks as soon as the river abandons their waterlogged houses. As we surveyed one village—its men harvesting rice, boys fishing, women scrubbing clothes—Baba Jennebo, a boatman, related the story of Tapama, the virgin immured in the thirteenth century so that Djenne could stand. Baba claimed to be her descen-

The salt trade in Mali looks today much as it did in the nineteenth-century scene pictured at left.

dant, a matter whose details I let pass (descended from a virgin?).

With Timbuktu three days downriver, there was no rush to arrive; the first stop, Youvarou, a lively market town seventy miles upstream, seemed a great excuse for a party. After dinner there was dancing to Malian music, an impromptu celebration fueled by beer from the first-class bar.

The boat was dark that night when I headed up to the bridge to talk to the captain. He explained to me that it was best to pilot by moonlight lest one offend the river spirits. A Bozo, he relied on years of experience to navigate sandbanks. He recalled a time when a crew member had turned on a searchlight, only to send a startled hippo into a rampage against the boat, damaging the engine. Such incidents did not seem uncommon; the boat is often laid up for repairs. "The hippo?" I asked. "Cut in two," he replied.

The next morning I could see that beast's more fortunate brethren in shallows that lapped the edges of dunes; we were encroaching on the desert. I sat on the deck

reading *Travels in the Interior District of Africa:* "Worn down by sickness, exhausted by hunger and fatigue, half naked, and without any article of value by which I might get provisions, clothes or lodging. I felt I should sacrifice my life to no purpose, for my discoveries would perish with me."[26]

Every night, we gathered on the first-class deck and watched African MTV on videotape as well as 1996's Bulls/Jazz game number 5. Michael Jordan excited the Malians just as he does Americans. Even I never tire of watching him pull the game out. Still nothing—not even Michael—could compare to the thrill when, after three days, we finally landed near Timbuktu.

Timbuktu is situated between two very different peoples of West Africa. In the south are the agriculturist and Sudanic black peoples, while in the north are the brown nomadic tribesmen like the Tuareg, who were considered to have founded the city at the end of the fifth Islamic century (AD 1100), mainly using it as a sort of nomadic summer camp. To travelers crossing the empty expanses of the Sahara Desert, Timbuktu was a welcoming port on the sea of sand, for its location also affords the advantage of being the point where the Niger inundations reach farthest north into the Sahara.

The city has often been referred to as the "pearl of the desert," the cultural and intellectual gem of Africa. It boasts of having been one of the greatest centers of learning ever to have existed on the African continent, with more than 180 Koranic schools, numerous other circles of higher learning, and a population that may have reached forty to fifty thousand in the sixteenth century. Yet now, nothing remains but desert, leaving only a fragmented textual record to tell the story of this legendary intellectual Mecca. Timbuktu scholars recorded their history as well as that of their neighbors in the form of chronicles, or *tarikhs,* beginning as early as the sixteenth century. The history of Timbuktu and its adjoining kingdoms is an African culture shaped by Arabian influences.

If the city is to be associated with any one empire, it would be that of Songhai. Although Timbuktu began its formation as an intellectual center under the rule of Mali in the early fourteenth century, its height of success was

Once hailed the "pearl of the desert," Timbuktu today is full of makeshift dwellings—as much a disappointment as it was to the first European explorers.

A pool at the gates of Timbuktu: a welcoming port—if only one could find it—in the Sahara's seemingly endless sea of sand.

under the following empire, the Songhai (1463–1591). In the 1590s, a black Muslim, Mahmoud Kati, wrote *Tarikh al Fettach,* the oldest known historical work written in the Sudan. Kati wrote the following of his hometown:

> In those days Timbuctou did not have its equal . . . from the province of Mali to the extreme limits of the region of the Maghrib for the solidity of its institutions, its political liberties, the purity of its morals, the security of persons, its consideration and compassion towards foreigners, its courtesy toward students and men of learning and the financial assistance which it provided for the latter; the scholars of the period were the most respected among the believers for their generosity, force of the character and their discretion.[27]

Kati was not alone in his admiration for Timbuktu. Al-Sa'di speaks of Timbuktu as "this virtuous, pure, undefiled and proud city, blessed with divine favor, a healthy climate, and commercial activity which is my birthplace and my heart's desire."[28]

But it is Leo Africanus who gives us the fullest description of the wealth of the court. He traveled through Mali and visited Timbuktu at its height during the Songhai Empire:

> There are numerous artisans' workshops, merchants, and in particular, weavers of cotton cloths. The cloths of Europe reach Timbuktu, brought by Barbary merchants. The women of the town still have the custom of veiling their faces, except for the slaves, who sell all the foodstuffs. The inhabitants are very rich, especially the resident strangers, to the extent that the present king has given two of his daughters in marriage to two merchant brothers, because of their wealth. . . . When anyone wants to address the king, he kneels before him, takes a handful of dust and sprinkles it over his head and shoulders. This is how they show respect, but it is only demanded of those who have never addressed the king before, or ambassadors . . . The only horses native to this land are some small hacks. Merchants use them for their travels, and courtiers for moving about town. But the good horses come from Barbary. They arrive with a caravan, and about ten or twelve days later they are brought to the king, who takes as many as he likes and pays accordingly. The people of Timbuktu have a light-hearted nature. It is their habit to wander in the town at night between 10 p.m. and 1 a.m., playing musical instruments and dancing. The citizens have many slaves to serve them, both male and female.[29]

As we have seen, the real expansion of the Empire of the Songhai began when the leader Sunni Ali conquered Timbuktu in 1468 from the Tuareg, who had taken it back from the Mali Empire during its decline. From Djenne eastward, Sunni Ali and his successor Askia al-hajj Muhammed (1493–1528) built up their own empire directed from their capital at the old city of Gao. Sunni Ali was ruthless toward those he considered his enemies, and was especially hard on the holy men of Timbuktu. When he died, Songhai was fought over by his son, who represented the old Songhai values derived from indigenous religion, and the new *askias* led by Askia Muhammed, founder of a new dynasty that stood for Islamic values.

Under the *askias,* the Songhai attacked the northwestern provinces of Mali between the Senegal River and the Upper Niger. In the 1540s the attacks were directed against the capital and the provinces of Mali on the Niger and the Bani rivers. The *askias* never actually conquered Mali but raided the villages and towns until their political authority was no longer viable. Songhai armies also carried out campaigns against the Mossi kingdoms to their south, the Hausa states to their southeast, and the Tuareg Sultanate of Agades due east of Gao.

All of this came to an end in 1591, when the forces of al-Mansur, the Sultan of Morocco, defeated the main forces of the Songhai Empire and took control of Timbuktu. The Moroccans forced many of Timbuktu's scholars into exile, and the great center of learning went into a long and slow decline.

Timbuktu still calls to mind a university town, with its surprisingly wide sand-strewn boulevards, its Tuareg leather and silver craftsmen, its inviting comfort for cosmopolitan transients, the love of learning that still lives among its polyglot citizens. Little effort is required on the part of the contemporary visitor to summon up

Mansa Musa's patronage of Islamic learning led to a proliferation of mosques, including this one in a Dogon village.

images of nests of scholars congregating around the marketplace, where today residents slurp the bittersweet brew called Malian tea, or munch on deep-fried yam *pommes frites,* sprinkled with unprocessed desert salt and wrapped unceremoniously in greasy brown paper.

I wandered along a wide sand-blown central avenue, crumbling houses on either side. Two Tuareg men in sweeping blue robes passed me silently. The heat was oppressive. Of course, Timbuktu had to be a disappointment, as it was for those explorers who eventually reached the city. By the time they arrived its glories had long faded. . . . I walked past the house where the French explorer René Caillié lived while he recovered from scurvy. Caillié had said:

I looked around and found that the sight before me, did not answer my expectations. I had formed a totally different idea of the grandeur and wealth of Timbuctou. The city presented, at first view, nothing but a mass of ill looking houses, built of earth. . . . Timbuctou and its environs present the most monotonous and barren scene I have ever held.[30]

HISTORY OF TIMBUKTU

Circa 800	First Songhai state crystallizes around Kukiya, then Gao.
Circa 1100	Timbuktu is established as a summer camp for nomads.
Circa 1290	The newly established empire of Mali conquers Timbuktu and Gao.
Circa 1300	Timbuktu becomes a meeting place for traders from the Sahara and North Africa and merchants operating along the river Niger. Gold and salt are the principal items of their trade.
1324	Mansa Musa, emperor of Mali, stops in Timbuktu on his way home from the pilgrimage to Mecca. He orders the construction of the Great Mosque.
1350–1450	Large-scale settlement of merchants and scholars in Timbuktu.
1353	World traveler Ibn Battuta visits Mali and describes its great wealth.
1375	Timbuktu is marked for the first time on a European map. A flourishing gold trade with North Africa and Europe is taking place.
1433	Mali, in full decline, abandons Timbuktu to the Sanhaja/Tuareg Saharan nomads.
1468	Sunni Ali, building a Songhai empire, conquers Timbuktu.
1470	Benedetto Dei, businessman of Florence, visits Timbuktu.
1493	Al-Hajj Muhammad Ture of Songhai founds the Askia dynasty, and shows favor to Timbuktu and its scholars.
1530	King John III of Portugal, hearing reports of great wealth, sends missions into Mali, including one to Timbuktu. Only one man—Pero Reinel—survives.
1550	Leo Africanus publishes his account of Timbuktu and Gao, based on two earlier visits, describing a fabulous court. He writes in Italian and an English translation appears in 1600.
1570	The Ortelius map marks Timbuktu as the capital of a huge province of the same name.

I explored Timbuktu with Ali Ould Sidi, an Islamic scholar descended from generations of local residents. There could have been no better guide to the Old Town's narrow streets; he transported me back to the city's glory days as the commercial center of Mali's various empires.

We approached the Sankoré Mosque, once the heart of Timbuktu's scholarly quarter. Mansa Musa encouraged Islamic learning and brought scholars of religious law back with him from his travels. The religious nature of the town grew and the mosques built then were joined by the Sankoré Mosque, erected by an anonymous female patron. There were centers of learning; together with the city's Koranic schools and teaching circles they constituted what has come to be known as the "university" of Timbuktu, which boasted teaching at the highest level of grammar, rhetoric, logic, theology, and law. Students and teachers wrote and illustrated beautiful manuscripts on all of these subjects. Many of these manuscripts still exist in the state-sponsored library, as well as—according to rumors I had heard—in the jumbled collections of old families in Timbuktu.

There is a well-worn adage: "In Timbuktu the salt comes from the North, the gold comes from the South, and money from the Whites. But the stories of God, the

1591	Timbuktu and the Songhai Empire are conquered by a Moroccan army, including many soldiers of European origin.
1593	Timbuktu sacked by the Moroccans, and the cream of its scholars are deported to Marrakesh.
1613	End of Songhai resistance. Moroccan military rule firmly established with headquarters at Timbuktu.
1627	Death of Ahmad Baba, Timbuktu's best-known scholar.
1650	Moroccan rulers of Timbuktu now completely independent of Morocco, begin to marry locally and acquire land. But their state is very weak and is a prey to attacks from the Tuareg, Bambara, and Fulani surrounding them. Timbuktu suffers an economic and intellectual decline.
Circa 1656	Al-Sa'di writes his celebrated chronicle of Timbuktu, *Tarikh al-Sudan*.
1788	In London the Association for Promoting the Discovery of the Interior Parts of Africa is founded. A principal objective is to reach Timbuktu, still thought of as a fabled city of gold.
1806	Scottish traveler Mungo Park sails down to Niger and passes Kabara, the port of Timbuktu. Perceived hostility prevents him from landing.
1826	English officer Major Gordon Laing reaches Timbuktu but is killed on his return journey. The Fulani of Masina take over the city.
1828	Frenchman René Caillié enters Timbuktu in disguise and returns with an account of a city not paved with gold, but crumbling from the effects of a long decline.
1854	Heinrich Barth, German traveler exploring on behalf of the British government, spends six months in Timbuktu under the protection of Shaykh al-Bakkay, a leading religious figure.
1893	French military expedition enters Timbuktu. Beginning of French colonial rule.
1960	Mali becomes an independent country.
1992–1996	Tuareg revolt creates great insecurity and economic hardship.
1999	Internet reaches Timbuktu. Population estimated at 10,000.

knowledge of wisdom, beautiful tales, these we find in Timbuctou." The truth of this saying, at least the last part, was embodied in Ahmed Baba (1556–1627), who was one of the greatest scholars to come from Timbuktu, having studied and then taught here until he was forced into exile by the Moroccans in 1593. The present-day library at Timbuktu is named after him. He himself had a personal library of 1,600 volumes before the invading Moroccans plundered it—and he had, by his own account, the smallest among his contemporaries! When the Moroccans invaded, Baba, along with other members of his clan, was arrested and carried off to the Mediterranean coast. At first he was held in confinement, but his fame as a learned man was so great that his Moroccan captors found themselves under siege to release him, or at least treat him with respect.

Ali Ould Sidi and an ancient Imam escorted me into the Sankoré Mosque, which resembles nothing so much as a mud pincushion stuck with wood needles. They informed me that 500 years ago the number of students in the system centered here was 25,000, more than double Timbuktu's present population. They came to Sankoré's clean, mud-walled chambers to study the tens of thousands of Arabic texts that Musa and his successors gathered here. Later, on the roof of the mosque, I gazed down at the city, trying to imagine the streets bustling with African and Arab merchants. Here was the medieval world's Hong Kong.

I was eager to see the library at the Ahmed Baba Center, where today approximately 10,000 volumes are housed and catalogued, thanks to grants from UNESCO and from Arab governments and foundations. But, before I could arrange that meeting, I was contacted by the enterprising Abd Al-Qadir Haidara. (I don't know how it was in René Caillié's time, but when visitors arrive in Timbuktu nowadays, everyone from Tuareg traders to Bella beggars shows up to proffer their wares or services in the hopes of "liberating" a few dollars or francs.)

Haidara is a young, strikingly handsome *shariff*, which title means he is a direct descendant of the Prophet. "The Prophet Muhammad himself?" I ask clumsily, as I stared at Haidara's polished ebony skin, his carefully coifed Afro, and long, flowing robes of robin's-egg blue. Then, to compound my faux pax, I continue, "Which tribe are you from?" wondering if his African ancestors were Fulani or Bambara.

"I said that I'm a *shariff*," he responds, pretending not to understand my inquiry. "Let's just say that the Prophet had many wives," he finally concedes, never acknowledging his African roots. He is connected with the other leading families of the city. These families, Haidara told me, have collected, protected, and preserved no fewer than 50,000 volumes in Arabic representing all the multifarious branches of Islamic learning that have been taught in Timbuktu since the days of Mansa Musa, and

Home of a prominent family of Timbuktu

At the height of its glory 500 years ago, the Sankoré Mosque served some 25,000 students, twice Timbuktu's present population.

which, in many cases are still taught there. Would I care to see some of them? I could not resist the invitation, of course.

Haidara led me to his home, a small but airy mud-brick building, the texture of its walls erased by the noon-day sun. We turned left just off the tiny courtyard, facing north, and entered a cramped, dark room. It was full of battered metal steamer trunks and two ancient mahogany armoires. The air was dense with the pungent peppery odor of dry rot, from which I recoiled at first; then I tried to hold my breath for long intervals until I became accustomed to the smell, and to the darkness of the room.

Haidara's story was incredible, but the proof was there before me: In the homes of several of Timbuktu's most prominent families are squirreled some of the fabled city's most precious treasures. For 400 years, these Arabic manuscripts, buried in trunks and boxes, protected from decay by the extraordinarily dry heat of the desert, have been jealously guarded and handed down from genera-tion to generation. Even major scholars of the era have not yet seen this collection.

My eyes adjusted to the gloom, and I slowly came to the realization that I was surrounded by dusty manu-scripts. There seemed to be thousands, a few bound in leather; most were piles of loose papers meticulously tied together, some with gorgeous gold etchings and illustra-tions that would themselves bring thousands of dollars in the world's great auction houses. One was about thirteenth-century law; another, astronomy. Beside it was a 300-year-old history of Islam. If translated, they might completely rewrite the history of black Africa. "What is this one about and when was it written?" I asked Haidara over and over, for much of that scorching afternoon. Standing in his "library," a dusty storage room crowded with old metal trunks piled one on another, I imagined how that shepherd felt holding the Dead Sea Scrolls, per-haps sensing the majesty of his discovery, yet helpless to unlock its secrets. Here, at the "Gateway to the Desert," at the edge of the Sahara's grand sandy superhighway for camels, where two distinct universes have been meeting for a millennium, I held in my own hands perhaps the only remains of the black African world's intellectual achievement. These were the thoughts and knowledge inscribed before the coming of the colonizers, a world that Hume, Kant, Jefferson, and Hegel, at the height of the Enlightenment, had reasoned did not—indeed, could not—exist, a conclusion since ratified by a host of lesser lights.

If only the loaders at Mr. Combie Carroll's Barber Shop could have been there as well.

"Reading in the Street"

The following morning I looked out at the green floodplains extending for miles and miles on either side of the snaking river, wider than the Mississippi, and much, much longer. I cherished the landscape of mud-walled cities rising through the haze like medieval castles on the Rhône, here where the floodplains melt into the Sahara Desert, and the Tuareg ride their camels, followed by the Bella on foot. Through the emptiness of the desert, "roads" made of sand begin, or end, at Timbuktu. It is a threshold between two universes, one brown and nomadic ending at the Mediterranean, the other black and animist, extending south far below the Equator to the Cape of Good Hope. If Djenne is West Africa's Jerusalem, Timbuktu is its Bologna or Paris during the High Middle Ages, a cosmopolitan Islamic bastion against the vast and terrible void of illiteracy and superstition. Despite the cruelties of exploitation, robbery, and rape that have been visited upon these shores, highways such as the Sahara, the Indian Ocean, the Niger, and the Nile bear witness to the irrepressible human impulse to bridge distances, to trade with and encounter others, to grow and learn through the exchanges that only travel enables.

As my travels thus far had made clear to me, so much of the history of Africa's civilizations has been ignored, or destroyed, or devalued as a consequence of European slavery and colonization, and we have scarcely begun to know the achievements of the diverse groups of peoples who have inhabited this continent for millennia. But for all the monuments that have been reduced to rubble and for all the other terrible cruelties visited upon the African people, the denial of their fundamental equality of intellect has been, perhaps, the most long lastingly destructive. It is this denial of the mind of Africa that the legacy of Timbuktu refutes with devastating finality.

146

Dogon mosque: Within the complex system of religions the
Dogon practice, followers of Islam make up 35 percent.

5

SEARCHING FOR THE SWAHILI

The Swahili are essentially a mixed people the result of long crossing between Negroes of the coast and Arabs, with an ad-mixture of slave blood from nearly all the East African tribes. The energy and intelligence derived from their Semitic blood has enabled them to take a leading part in the development of trade and industries.

—ENCYCLOPAEDIA BRITANNICA, 1911

The Swahili is cheerful and happy go lucky as the African: fond of humor, intrigue and power as the Arab. For the proper understanding of the savage African, one must not look on him as a human being, but rather as a superior kind of animal. To judge the African side of the Swahili nature he must be looked at from this standpoint. However, he has another side, the Arab side, a much more complex quality to understand.

—CAPTAIN STIGAND, *The Land of Zinj*, 1913

*Dhow—the foundation of Swahili civilization for
2,000 years*

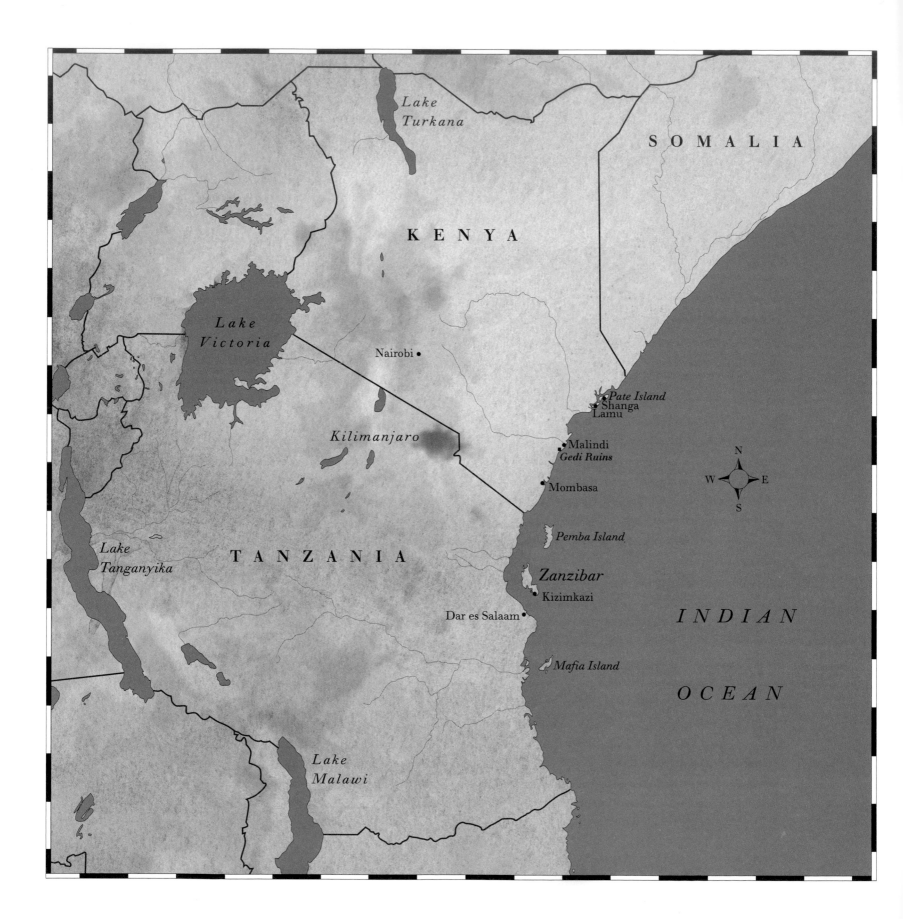

The Swahili language has a special resonance for African Americans. During the Black Panther era of the 1960s, black cultural nationalists such as Amiri Baraka and Maulana Karenga decreed that black Americans could not truly be free until we learned an African language, so as to escape the racism "encoded" in English. The African language they proposed was Swahili. The one African word known to more African Americans than any other must be *kwanza,* the Swahili word to which Karenga turned to name the "African" holiday that he invented as an alternative to Christmas. Even on the original *Star Trek* television series, the sole black person in space was an African named Uhura, derived from the Swahili word for freedom. And as far back as the mid-fifties, when my playmates and I wanted to "speak African," the words that we would utter—picked up from the earliest *Tarzan* movies—were, unbeknownst to us, of Swahili origins: "*Jambo bwana,*" which simply means "Hello, sir." So when the time came for me to choose an African country in which to live for my first visit to the continent in 1970, perhaps for all these reasons I selected a Swahili-speaking country, Tanzania.

If Swahili was a lingua franca throughout a broad band of subequatorial Africa, from Zanzibar west to the Congo, then it also became by the 1960s an ur-language of black identity, the linguistic twine with which to bind ourselves to our lost African past and the key to unlocking the secrets of our hidden or lost "authentic" African identity. The irony of the choice of Swahili—a Bantu language with many Arabic loan words—as the Pan-African lingua franca is that very few of the Africans enslaved and shipped to the New World—our ancestors—would have known Swahili as a first or even second language. Nevertheless, Swahili for most is the sole candidate for a Pan-African language. Even the playwright Wole Soyinka, the first African to receive the Nobel Prize in Literature, has advocated the teaching of Swahili throughout the continent as a means of effecting this goal—and Soyinka is a Yoruba from Nigeria where no one speaks Swahili. Perhaps the choice of Swahili is somewhat less surprising when we realize how extensively cosmopolitan the east coast of Africa has been for the past two thousand years. Europeans, Indians, Chinese, and African traders have been exchanging goods, ideas, religious beliefs, arts and crafts, and genes around the Indian Ocean, on Kenya's and Tanzania's coast borders, for nearly two millennia—a startling fact for those of us raised to think that Africa was "discovered" by Europeans about the same time that Columbus discovered America. The Greeks came here; the mythical Sinbad came here; Marco Polo claimed to have come; the Chinese came here; Vasco da Gama came here. Who could resist the inviting openness of this great sapphire blue ocean, the Indian Ocean, where "earth, sea and sky," as the British explorer Richard Francis Burton wrote of Zanzibar in 1866, "all seemed wrapped in a soft and sensuous repose."[1]

I carried Burton's book with me when I first visited the Swahili coast as a romantic nineteen-year-old, and I had it again as I boarded a dhow—the traditional wooden boat with diagonal lateen sails that has been the foundation of this civilization from its earliest days—to begin my adult travels in search of the Swahili.

The *Periplus of the Erythraean Sea* confirms that people were already living in towns along this coast and trading far across the Indian Ocean when this legendary Greek mariners' guidebook was written in Alexandria, in the first century AD. But it also suggests that even in those days the Swahili coast was a place visited by a few foreign (mostly, if not entirely, Arab) traders, some of whom stayed and married locally:

Men of the greatest stature, who are pirates, inhabit the whole coast and at each place have set up chiefs. The Chief of the Ma'afir is the suzerain, according to an ancient right which subordinates it to Arabia. . . . Arab captains and crews trade and intermarry with the mainlanders of all the places and know their language.[2]

It is on account of this hybrid character that the identity of the Swahili has remained a confusing question for centuries. And it is this hybrid character as well that has allowed so many—including some Swahili people—to challenge this culture's relation to the continent on which it is found.

Among contemporary guidebooks to East Africa, the cultural history of this part of Africa seems unremarkably homogeneous. Directing its mostly European travelers to the stunning white coral beaches of Lamu, an island off the east coast of Kenya, one guidebook describes its coastline as "full of old Arab houses dating back to the day when these towns were important trading centers and part of the chain of Omani Arab ports strung out down the East African coast."[3] With the emphasis on the Omani dominion of the nineteenth century, a people called the Swahili are hardly mentioned, even though their language is identified as the official one of present-day Kenya. The possibility of deep roots of the peoples who once inhabited today's ruins, hidden now by mangroves, dating from the eighth or ninth century and who much later built whitewashed houses made of coral along the most beautiful beaches, is generally ignored, and not for the first time.[4] These ruins and surviving trading towns have long been seen as "jewels" along a "foreign" shore.[5] The hinterland was considered "barbarous" and "African," while the coast was "semi-foreign" or really a province of the Orient.[6] This view typifies the colonialist legacy in traditional scholarship of East Africa, which takes no account of the relation of coastal peoples, or port cities, to inland peoples and their cultures. It is rarely acknowledged that the riches of the Swahili coast depended on the initiatives not only of the Arabs—or even the Swahili themselves—but also on those of the peoples of the hinterland who plied the interior for gold, ivory, and slaves . . . who traded with, and lived in a symbiotic relation with, the coast.

But however much Western histories and travel literature may have contributed to obscuring the African dimension of Swahili identity, an astonishing proportion of the effort, as I discovered on this journey, has been shouldered by the Swahili themselves. Swahili self-understanding is enormously complex and has continuously adapted itself to the winds of change in culture and power that have blown along this coast for two thousand years. The explanations of identity I was to hear would sometimes seem disingenuous to a black man from North America. Nevertheless I continued to ask: Who are the Swahili? Do they belong to Africa at all? Or are they really Arabs who brought their own civilization to Africa? And why, two thousand years on, should it matter?

My journey in search of answers to these questions would take me from Lamu, the famous island resort off the coast of Kenya, south to the port of Mombasa, and finally across the sea to Zanzibar, that legendary island of sultans, slaves, and spices.

Trade gave birth to more than 400 settlements up and down this 2,000 mile reach of East Africa, a shoreline longer even than the distance from Newfoundland to

In Malindi on Kenya's northern coast, Vasco da Gama's pillar stands as a reminder of sixteenth-century Portuguese dominance.

Florida and spanning Kenya, Tanzania, and Somalia. Many of those towns are now abandoned and lie in ruins, but for centuries, they formed a crucial part of the bountiful Indian Ocean trade in which the riches of the African interior were exchanged for the luxury products of the East. By the tenth century, a network stretching from Mozambique to the Mediterranean had been established. A cultural revival in Europe, together with the Golden Age of the Byzantine Empire and the rise of the Fatimid rulers of North Africa, stimulated a further demand for new and exotic materials; when the Portuguese first landed on this coast in the fifteenth century, they were amazed to find not the wilderness they expected, but a string of wealthy mercantile towns like Lamu and Mombasa.

Many of the ancient Swahili towns survive: Malindi, Mombasa, and Zanzibar. Others now lie in ruins. Lamu has kept its original character more than any other of the Swahili city-states.

After a fifteen-hour flight to Nairobi followed by an additional two-hour flight to the airport nearest to Lamu, we finally landed. We were met by Abbas Shekhuna Fadhil, our series fixer who is also a town councilor. He brought us over to Lamu Island by dhow. The small town looked Mediterranean, the whitewashed stone houses with their distinctive arches and cast ironwork vividly outlined by the brightness of the sky. People bustled in the streets—more men than women and more children than adults.

The old town was crowded with vendors, mainly the very young and very old, selling food on the street, while the boys who sit on the edge of the harbor, known as the "beach boys," attempt to sell you anything they can—even themselves. But mostly they sell dhow rides to Shela, Manda, and Pate, the surrounding islands of the

The streets of Lamu

Lamu archipelago. Walking along the gravel road, I couldn't help but notice that the town still had an open gutter system, through which floated human waste, while on the path itself one had to avoid the waste of the donkeys that carried people and goods everywhere on this island with only one car. *Shoeless children and donkey feces don't go together,* I thought.

Lamu is often described by tourist guidebooks as "the best kept secret on the Kenyan coast." In the 1960s and early 1970s, it became a refuge for hippies—Kenya's Kathmandu—drawing many with its unspoiled beauty and easygoing attitude toward strangers. I was worried that all that had made it special in the sixties had turned it into a tourism nightmare.[7] I need not have worried.

Lamu feels ancient and unchanging, like some Greek

Ivory and cloth traders: In the nineteenth century, the street life of East African coastal towns was dominated by trade, as it is today.

island villages still do. The area between the main street and the seafront was built after 1850. Unlike older ones, late-nineteenth-century buildings here have large windows and roofed courtyards, usually on the upper-level; and they often show Zanzibari or Indian influence. One splendid example is Lamu Fort, built in the center of town in 1821 by the Sultan and until recently used as a prison. Now it is completely restored, and boasts a walk-through aquarium and a natural history library among its new amenities.

Lamu is one of the oldest surviving Swahili cities, established by the fourteenth century, though there were small numbers of people from the hinterland here as many as 600 years earlier, lured by the fresh water from the shallow wells that draw on rainwater filtered through the massive sand dunes that lie behind Lamu. Within a hundred years of its founding, Lamu had become a hub of commerce, with small numbers of people from Asia and Arabia settling here. When the Portuguese arrived in 1505, the king was able to pay tribute and avoid having

the town razed. But Lamu would exist for the next 150 years under the thumb of Portugal.

Following a brief period of Omani rule after the Portuguese were ousted, Lamu entered an age of prosperity under the governance of a council of elders. From the end of the twelfth century to the middle of the seventeenth, the town was an emporium to the Indian Ocean. The great mansions I saw were built then, and Swahili poetry and Islamic studies flourished. Trade depended on partnerships between the Swahili and traders who came from the Red Sea area, the Gulf, and India. From the African interior, the Swahili produced commodities coveted the world over: ivory, horn, rare animal skins, gold, and slaves. They also exported more mundane goods like mangrove poles and surplus crops. The foreign traders would arrive in their ocean-faring dhows to exchange their luxury goods—jade and copper jewelry, Chinese porcelain, carpets from Mecca, glassware, and Indian silks and cottons—for the Swahili's raw materials. The shifting of the monsoon winds every six months forced foreign traders to return across the Indian Ocean and leave the Swahili middlemen to collect export goods for the next season and distribute the imported goods to other African traders in the interior.

Around 1700, Lamu became involved in the conflict between the neighboring island city-states of Pate, Faza, and Siyu. These hostilities ended triumphantly for Lamu in 1812, when she defeated Pate and the Mazrui dynasty's forces of Mombasa in the Battle of Shela; but, fearing reprisals, Lamu then called on the Sultan of Oman for intervention and by that fateful calculation lost her independence forever. The Omani would use Lamu for their eventual conquest of the whole coast down to Zanzibar.

It was as part of the Omani empire that Lamu, like Zanzibar, developed a slave-based economy that would last until the turn of the twentieth century, when the

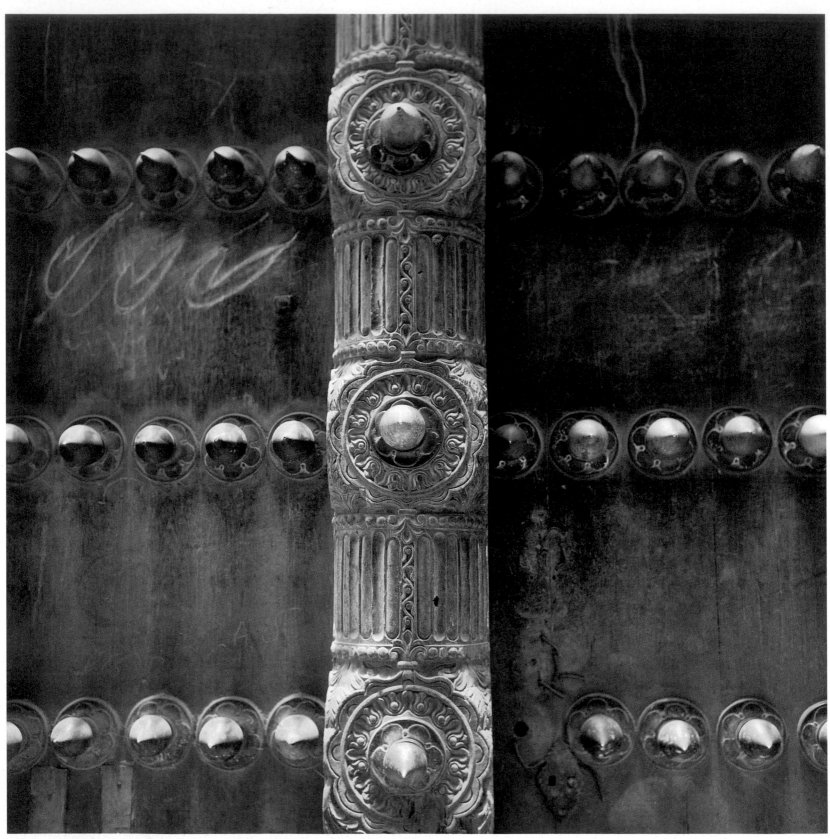

Above: A Swahili proverb warns that appearances can be deceiving: "Nyumba njema si mlango" —a good house isn't judged by its door. Nevertheless, the door was a family's only show of status to the outside community.

Opposite: A small obelisk off the coast of Lamu, designed as a signal to incoming boats.

British forced the Sultan of Zanzibar to sign an antislavery agreement. The immediate result of emancipation was a large pool of cheap labor, and Lamu actually experienced a surge of economic growth exporting ivory, cowries, tortoiseshell, mangrove poles, oilseed, and grains. But Lamu faced a rapid decline after the abolition of slavery within its own boundaries. Much of the town stands as it was then, preserved by its obsolescence.

The following morning, I met up with a Mr. Ahmed Sagaf, an architect and conservationist attached to the Lamu Museum, who took me on a tour of the old town. Sagaf has worked for several years on the restoration of old stone houses in Lamu, much of his labor funded by grants from the Ford Foundation and Scandinavian foundations. He is a member of Lamu's patrician class; his devotion to the town's architectural heritage clearly flows from his pride in issuing from the sort of folk who would have built and dwelt in these grand houses, most of which date from between the sixteenth and eighteenth centuries. Sagaf showed me the massive coral walls and the elaborate carved doorways that marked the houses of the elite, *wa-ungwana,* as they still call themselves, or *wa-amu* (people of Lamu). Many had farms (later plantations) on the mainland, but their wealth came from the monsoon-season trade. The outer walls of rag stone are plain and rather forbidding, in keeping with the Islamic view that it is not noble to make a display of one's wealth.

The courtyard of one of the old houses in Lamu that Sagaf has restored is a vision: Elaborately plastered walls hold alcoves that once would have displayed riches from all over the Indian Ocean: porcelain, metalwork, glassware. But the collections are gone, and every inch is given over to housing the family that lives here now.

Later, over coffee, Sagaf holds forth on the origins of his people. Who were they? He claims that the people who founded Lamu and similar ports were Arabs who came to trade in the area and stayed when they saw that the prospects were good. He offered his own family's history as evidence; he can trace his lineage back twelve generations to Arabia on the computer in his office. "I don't think many Africans can trace their ancestors in the same way." The distinction is vitally important to him: "If you don't know where you come from you are nothing," he told me. Sagaf, I am told, looks like "a Swahili," an observation that is as meaningless as if one had said he looks like an American! But he is culturally and linguistically a Swahili, and wears a white *kofia* (embroidered cap) and *joho* (waistcoat). He is clearly not Arab now, though his sense of identity depends on Arabian roots. In America, he would be taken to be just another African American.

Sagaf, I would discover, is representative of the fascination with genealogy among *wa-ungwana* families of Lamu, and the view that their culture owes little to indigenous African people. I visited more of the old stone houses in Lamu that are inhabited by the descendants of those who originally built them. Usually in these homes, after passing through the *daka* (a deep porch), one approached an intricately carved door, often a family's only opportunity to flaunt its wealth. At most houses men could proceed no further since well-bred Islamic women lived in purdah, isolated from men other than those of their close family. Only a few homes included a room set aside for male business, which was generally conducted outside on stone benches.

The houses were and still are generally built according to strictly hierarchical principles around a central courtyard. Slaves and storage were on the first floor, while the family lived above in long transverse galleries that opened onto the courtyard, not the street. But standing mattered on the upper floors as well. Each member was assigned a place in a gallery according to his position: The head of the family and his wife lived in the innermost chambers, known as *ndani*.

I soon noticed the extraordinary number of toilets: five was not an unheard of number for the grander houses, one for each rank living within. Some were lavishly outfitted with display niches and beautiful plasterwork. The Islamic emphasis on cleanliness and purity figured in the development of these indoor toilets as far back as the thirteenth century, but it was the institution of purdah that created the necessity. It was not so long ago that some Swahili women never really left the houses after their marriages; their only freedom was to travel along the flat roofs to neighboring houses to visit female friends.

The interior of surviving Swahili stone houses, though less lavishly furnished today, retain their original elegance.

The houses of the Swahili middlemen were unique to the coast and were a symbol of permanence, creditworthiness, and cultural affiliation, just as the Swahili stone town, with its walls and mosques, was a zone of familiarity and safety to foreign merchants. As among the bourgeoisie of any other Indian Ocean state, fashionable tea was drunk in quarters decorated with silk, porcelain, beads, and Persian rugs. This symbolism served the Swahili as a way of guarding their trade monopoly with the African interior: Foreign merchants would sooner not deal directly with the Swahili's more culturally remote suppliers among the neighboring nonurban populations, such as the Boni hunters, the Pokomo fishermen and rice farmers, and the Oromo pastoralists. And it was this same symbolism that reinforced a strict hierarchy within Swahili society as well. The coral and rag houses built by the *wa-ungwana* distinguished them from those of the *watumwa* (slaves) who lived on the outskirts of town, and certainly from the dwellings of the

washenzi, who lived outside of the towns and were considered "country bumpkins."[8]

Until recently, Lamu has been more or less isolated from social change in Kenya during this century. Everybody knows who belongs to *wa-ungwana* families and who is the descendant of slaves. Arab ancestry, it seems, is paradoxically similar to the one-drop rule of "descending miscegenation" in America: In Islamic culture and in a patrilineal system, such as that of the patricians (including those Swahili of Omani and Hadhrami descent), a child of mixed race ascends to the status of the more privileged parent. So if the privileged parent is the father and an Arab, his child becomes Arab regardless of who the mother is.[9] Those Swahili who are not patricians, such as the Hadimu and other fishermen of Zanzibar and Pemba, or those of slave ancestry, reckon descent quite differently and have different systems of marriage, divorce, and kinship. But before we encounter any more Sagafs, it will be helpful in understanding the complex evolution of Swahili society to delve a bit into their history from the earliest days.

The best scholarly work being done on the Swahili coast today draws from the sophisticated work done on other port-cities that thrived in the Indian Ocean between 1100 and 1750, when Asia and Africa shared in a complex long-distance trading civilization that predated the Western colonial empires. According to the most recent evidence, the people who are considered to be the proto-Swahili were Sabaki-speakers who hunted, fished, and kept cattle, which they milked and bled. As subsistence farmers, they cultivated coconuts, bananas, wild dates, millet, sorghum, legumes, and rice. They are believed to have been tall and good iron and wood craftsmen.[10]

They emerged from the migrations and interactions of southern Kushitic pastoralists and Bantu-speaking agriculturists from the west and southwest, meeting in the region between Somalia and Kenya. The region is considered the great enigma of East African historiography.[11] By the early ninth century, a form of Swahili was spoken in two clusters of coastal settlements in Lamu and adjacent to the Webbe Shebelle and Juba rivers. From these clusters, a secondary dispersion moved north along the Somali coast as far as Mogadishu, and south as far as Mozambique. Swahili emerged as a separate language during these migrations and later splintered into northern and southern dialects. By the fifteenth century, Swahili speakers were scattered along the coast and nearby islands of eastern Africa, each settlement with its own dialect.

The twelfth-century Arab traveler Al-Idrisi described the Mombasans as skilled hunters.

The Swahili were sailors engaged in trade with other East African peoples as well as with Red Sea mariners. Underneath the stone towns, fishing villages have been unearthed. The social anthropologist John Middleton describes them as a fundamentally maritime people:

[T]he stretches of lagoon, creek, and open sea beyond the reefs are as much a part of their environment as are the coastlands. The sea, rivers and lagoons are not merely stretches of water, but highly productive food resources, divided into territories that are owned by families and protected by spirits just as are stretches of land. The Swahili use the sea as though it were a network of roads.[12]

Periplus of the Erythraean Sea mentions the market town Rhapta, on the coast of Azania, which many scholars believe to be south of Dar es Salaam, although its exact location remains unknown. This was the land, according to Ptolemy's *Geography,* of the black people who made "sewn boats," while Cosmas Indicopleustes, author of *Christian Topography,* called it Zingium, beyond "Barbaria," which roughly coincides with present-day Somalia. The Arabs called it Zanj, "land of the blacks."[13] In the first century AD, the Chinese traveler Tuan Ch'eng-Shih called it Po-pa-li and wrote about it in the *Yu-Yang-tsa-tsu,* a compendium of knowledge that contained the first definite Chinese information about East Africa:

The land of Po-pa-li is in the southwestern ocean. From of old this country has not been subject to any foreign power. In fighting they use elephant's tusks, ribs and wild cattle's horns as spears, and they have corselets and bows and arrows. They have twenty myriads of foot soldiers. The Arabs are continually making raids on them.[14]

The *Periplus* mentions extensive contacts between East Africa and Yemen, and many sources note that there was extensive trading between Arabs and Africans. Pre-Islamic ceramics from the Middle East have been found in both Somalia and Mozambique, mostly of Persian provenance from the Sassanian period. The earliest mosques were built to serve these itinerants. Mark Horton's archaeological work at Shanga shows that the initial phase of mosque building was in the eighth century.

Both Neville Chittick and Peter Garlake, archaeologists, have uncovered early Islamic sites that show evidence of trading both in the interior and in the Indian Ocean, but only Mark Horton since the 1980s has attempted to show that pre-Islamic Africa played a role in the commercial systems of the Indian Ocean trade. Hor-

ton argues that they were an indigenous seafaring society, which settled on the coast around the eighth to the ninth centuries. Moreover, digs at sites underlying the stone towns at Manda, Pate, Lamu, Shanga, and Kilwa have unearthed the remains of early Swahili fishing villages, where earthenware pottery of local manufacture, Sassanian Islamic jars, and white-glazed pottery have been located.[15]

Early Muslim accounts of East Africa indicate that the residents were in the process of choosing to convert to Islam, probably to help with trade and diplomacy. One of the earliest Arab accounts of the Swahili is that of Al-Masudi, who describes a religiously mixed population consisting of Muslims and idolaters. He noted that these "people called the 'Zanj' [blacks] have Kings known as Wafalme [a Swahili word] and holy men use an elegant language by which they preach." He did not regard the Zanj as Arabs or of Arab origin. "The Zanj are the only Abyssinian people to have crossed the branch which flows out of the upper stream of the Nile into the sea of the Zanj. In the same way that the sea of China ends with the land of Japan, the sea of Zanj ends with the land of Sofala and the Waqwaq, which produces gold and many other wonderful things."[16] He also described elephant hunting and the ivory trade, their use of iron, and their use of oxen as beasts of burden and for riding into war.[17]

The Swahili also had important religious and political contacts with the inland gold-bearing regions near Lake Nyasa. Gertrude Caton Thompson, an archaeologist, found there lemon yellow beads and blue-green glass that clearly came all the way from India. There were extensive relations with the Kingdom of Munhumutapa in southern Africa, and with the merchants in Sofala. Al-Idrisi described inland traders, carrying loads on their heads or on their backs to Mombasa and Malindi, where they engaged in trade with the hinterland. Al-Idrisi wrote that in the town of Malindi "Iron was the main source of trade with the peoples of the hinterland" and noticed it as the "source of their greatest profits." Ibn Batuta referred specifically to the "land of the Swahili" in the thirteenth century, and to the town of Kilwa as "the most beautiful and well-constructed town in the world" with roofs built with mangrove poles. The people of Kilwa were described as Zanj, of very black complexion with distinctive facial marks. They were primarily Muslim, but lived side by side with their pagan brethren with whom they engaged in a "holy war."[18]

Indeed, for the Swahili to get at the inland trade, they had to establish a whole range of diplomatic relationships with people who had already been crisscrossing Africa in a series of specific and well-traveled trade routes. It is clear that the people who lived along the area we call the Swahili coast had been a hybrid people for centuries before Arab merchants or European traders arrived.

What this history of the relation of inland peoples to the Indian Ocean coast reveals is that the presence and contributions of black Africans in the development of Swahili civilization is considerable. But you wouldn't learn this from some members of the modern Swahili elite, who contrive to chart a pure Arab lineage at the expense of their African forebears. I encountered the boldest form of this willful denial in Sheikh Said Hassan Badawi, a respected Lamu elder and Muslim scholar.

The sheik's grandson showed Abbas Fadhil, my fixer, and me into a small room lined with shelves of well-worn books. A member of one of Lamu's *shariff,* or Sharifu as the Swahili call them, families—those families that claim direct descent from the Prophet Muhammad—Badawi is shown respect by all around him; those who enter the room bend down to kiss his hand. It was made clear to me what a great honor it is to be granted an audience with the sheik. Slowly, we grew comfortable

with each other, in his library, surrounded by wire-mesh bookshelves, where he sat studying on a thin foam mattress.

Ali Salim (his grandson) remained present to translate, though the sheikh spoke some English. A man in his mid-twenties, Salim was quite dashing: He sported a walking stick and dressed in the long white *kanzu* and *kofia* of old men.

As we grew in ease with each other, the sheikh pulled out genealogies to show us his ancestry. His family descends directly from the Prophet, as do the seemingly dozens of other *shariff* families in town. According to him, the African contribution to Lamu was almost nil; it was the Arabs who built up the region from nothing with their science, religion, and reverence for learning.

Completely unsettled by Badawi's preemptory declarations, I decided to ask Fadhil what he thought. Fadhil considers himself Swahili, but first he is Bajuni. They do not belong to the Swahili elite. They say that they are the indigenous people of the region, but (it comes as no surprise) they, too, somehow claim Arab descent way back in the mists of time. And they claim to have been around longer than the "Arabs." The Bajuni, named for a river on the mainland north of Lamu, make up the majority of Lamu's population.[19]

Fadhil had a slightly different take on the elite's preoccupation with class and Arab lineage, maintaining that they are desperately holding on to a lost heritage in the face of increasing irrelevance. More than 75 percent of Lamu is now Bajuni; they control the town and have little respect for the *wa-ungwana,* whom they think lazy. Not surprisingly, Fadhil had thrashed a *wa-ungwana* candidate in the recent council elections. In his view, things are different now.

Certainly Fadhil's marriage to a Saudi woman is proof of such change. In the past he never would have been

Takwa ruins on the nearly uninhabited island of Manda, Kenya, represents one of the more impressive medieval Swahili settlements.

permitted to marry an Arab woman, since the respectable families think of the Bajuni only as African. When his prospective father-in-law quizzed him on his lineage, Fadhil simply told him that he was Bajuni, and proud to be, but that he did have some Arab blood a long way back, "Persian blood." Fadhil added that he was important in Lamu. The statement "I'm a rich man" seemed to have done the trick.

All Islamic men are allowed four wives at any one time, and divorce in Lamu is easy (it takes a day). Fadhil divorced his first wife before marrying this one, his third.

Marriage is an intriguingly complex and flexible institution in Lamu. It seems perfectly common for couples to divorce after a big row, and then remarry. One can divorce and remarry the same person only two times, though. After the second time, if a couple wanted to get back together again (which they often do), the wife must marry another man first, then divorce, and then they can start all over again. Everybody here seems to be everybody else's brother- or sister-in-law.

On a stroll through the Langoni quarter I quickly picked up on the fact that the women were not wearing veils, nor the men *kanzus*. In general, the Islamic influence is greatly attenuated.[20] In the past, strict segregation would have kept any member of the Arab elite from this area, just as Africans were barred from Mkomani or Lamu's Stone Town. As the Swahili progressively adopted Islam, beginning in the tenth century, they also adopted a social identity that corresponded with the aristocracy of the Islamic world. Unlike upper-class Muslim Swahilis, ordinary Swahilis continued to venerate indigenous spirits, gods, and goddesses; the men still sailed and fished, and the women worked outside. But to the elite, Islam offered a cosmopolitan, universalistic ideology attractive in many of the city-states and countries occupying the Indian Ocean area. Derek Nurse and Thomas Spear write:

> Many Townspeople . . . operated in a wider world than the microcosm of the village, living in towns with other peoples, sailing from town to town along the coast, and trading with the people from across the Indian Ocean. These people lived in macrocosmic worlds inhabited by peoples speaking different languages, having different ancestors, and working in different occupations. In this world the beliefs of the microcosm were too parochial; and what were needed were beliefs that were universal. And so townspeople began to adopt Islam, and in doing so they adopted a set of beliefs and a framework for action that were held in common by others in the town, by people in other towns, and by people from the whole Indian Ocean world.[21]

The Muslim sense of identity, which took many tangible forms, reduced geography to a secondary set of definitions, just as Christianity would do for a brief period in the fourteenth century. The way people ate, dressed, and lived signified to travelers and merchants their personal identities and affiliations. And those significations furnished the basis for credibility—especially in a trading civilization governed by expectations and social ceremony.

By the thirteenth century, the Swahili settlements had grown into a network of commercial towns and city-states along Kenya's and Tanzania's coast, which competed with one another for dominance. By the fifteenth century they were thriving Islamic city-states, each with their own kings and chiefs. The Swahili were engaged in the long-distance trade alongside the great political and commercial nations and towns that dotted the Indian Ocean. At the same time, towns along the East African coast and the surrounding islands became the important centers for the distribution of not only goods, but also of the cultural ideologies and cognitive patterns that constitute the *Dar al-Islam*, "the world of Islam," which would be disrupted when the Portuguese arrived on the coast.

As they became more cosmopolitan, the city-states grew to be more ethnically diverse. The majority of the resident merchants were Swahili-speaking and often of pure "Bantu origin."[22] Others were mixed, the result of unions between local women and visiting or resident merchants, nearly all Muslim, mainly from the Red Sea area, some from Arabia, some from India. There is evidence of Gujerati Hindus and Jains—an Indian Muslim ruler became the ruler of Kilwa in 1502. Direct contact with the Chinese came from two of Cheng "the Eunuch" Ho's seven expeditions in the early fifteenth century. Between 1417 and 1419, his ships got as far as Malindi, and he traveled to Mogadishu between 1431 and 1433, from which he bought ivory, rhino horn, and ambergris for use in aphrodisiacs.[23]

The numbers of Arabs and Persians living on the coast and on the islands at any one time could not have been very large, judging by the absence of comment to that effect among Arab writers at the time. Nevertheless, the upper classes of Swahili society sought to strengthen their position both at home and in the broader Islamic community through marriages to rich Muslims who could claim descent from illustrious families in the Arab world.

In this way the old Swahili legends of the migration of considerable groups of African Muslims to the East African towns in the seventh, eighth, ninth, and tenth centuries are transformed into tales of the migration from Arabia and Persia of ancestors of the Swahili ruling dynasties and the subsequent foundation of many Swahili towns by Persians or Arabs.

Within the Swahili town, Islam would prove politically divisive. Despite its deep tradition of tolerance it gave rise to a set of oppositions that rendered the majority second-class citizens: pious/impious, *umran badawa* (tribal nomadic civilization)/ *umran hadata* (urban settled civilization). Among Swahili Muslim, benevolent *jinn* (or spirits) were associated with urbanity, while the malevolent ones were connected with the bush.[24] The layout of Swahili cities also defined precise social limits and imposed codes of space and rank.

We headed to the town square, where Fadhil and I played *Bao,* the Pan-African board game, which I had learned twenty-seven years earlier when I lived in Tanzania. Brilliant and subtle, it is similar in strategy to the Japanese game of *Go.* Everyone plays, and when they are not playing, they gather to watch, to comment, to offer advice, to referee. But by "everyone," I mean adult males. Dominoes is a distant second in popularity to this ancient game based upon mathematical probability. Fadhil soundly defeated me once, I won once, and our third match was a draw. He then confessed to me that yes, he was a Bajuni, but was far more Arab than African. All Bajuni are, he continued. His grandfather was from Oman and his grandmother from Siyu, a town on Pate Island.

Pate was a place I was eager to see. It is twenty miles offshore in the Lamu archipelago, and so the next day at dawn I found myself on board a dhow headed out to sea. After passing the inner islands and the fishing fleet

165

returning from its previous night's catch, we encountered the more tumultuous Indian Ocean and I got a taste of what the traders had once faced. Supposedly there were towns even older than Lamu on Pate and the islands around it. Their origins are explained in *The Pate Chronicle,* a Swahili account dating to the thirteenth century:

> The beginning of these coast towns, he who first made them was a ruler called Abdul Malik bin Muriani. He heard of this country, and his soul longed to found a new kingdom. So he brought Syrians, and they built the cities of Pate, Malindi, Zanzibar, Mombasa, Lamu and Kilwa.[25]

Pate, a thatched village, came into view around a bend in the mangrove swamps. It would disappoint those expecting a city-state. But the enthusiasm of the local children, who welcomed me with cries of *"Jambo, Jambo,"* quickened my pace as I headed through the village with my host, Mwalimu Dini, a leader here, as well as a farmer and scholar. "Mwalimu" is an honorific that signifies his religious status.

Pate reached its zenith 500 years ago when it was one of the more powerful city-states in the region, a competitor with its younger rival, Lamu. But the town today is somewhat fallen, the result of a long process of decay begun even before the Portuguese arrived in the early sixteenth century. There was an era of resurgence beginning at the end of the seventeenth century; a mixed blessing, since for most of the eighteenth century Pate would be at war with Lamu over trade, only to be defeated in 1812 at the Battle of Shela. Today, next to the nineteenth-century village, lie the overgrown ruins of a large royal palace. Farmers work tobacco fields between the remaining walls of the town. Wattle fences follow the old street pattern.

There is a pillar tomb of one of the sultans, remains of a mosque, and several ruined houses with elaborate plaster niches. The town must have been quite large.

In some ways Pate is quite similar to Lamu, but more isolated. However, the town is marked by the tall stone houses and cramped alleys I had seen on the mainland. And like Lamu, Dini informed me, Pate is a highly segregated town: The upper town is for Africans, while the lower town is older, richer, and more Arab.

We headed on to Shanga, a ruined ancient city on another part of the island. In Shanga, one of the earliest known habitations, I traveled as far back as I would go into the Swahili past. Shanga has given rise to the disputed theory that the origins of Swahili urban culture are to a degree African, and not entirely imported.

I walked through the dense undergrowth looking for ruins with my new guide Mohammed al Badi, who was involved in the excavation of the site with the British archaeologist Mark Horton. They had found a large walled town covering 13 acres and more than 130 stone houses, and a cemetery containing 340 stone tombs. We hacked our way through the thick undergrowth that had sprung up since al Badi was last here, finally reaching a pillar tomb, then a house with the sort of plaster niches I had seen in Lamu. After a while, we came up against the overgrown walls of a mosque.

Al Badi informed me that the archaeologists had excavated through the layers of the ancient city to reach a settlement dating to the eighth century AD, earlier than any other on this coast. The town was laid out in a manner typical of African villages, suggesting that Swahili culture is not entirely indebted to Arabia. Al Badi, a Bajuni, seemed proud to have shown that it was most likely people from East Africa who built these towns more than a thousand years ago—though, with many other sites to

*Pillar tombs near the Friday Mosque in Malindi,
a part of Swahili Afro-Islamic identity*

SEARCHING FOR THE SWAHILI

excavate, he remained cautious about the extent of their influence.

The first traces of Islam—a silver ring with an inscription in Arabic, postholes for three wood mosques—date to between AD 780 and 850, after the initial settlement here between AD 760 and 780. From that earlier, non-Islamic period, Horton found the remnants of a rectangular corral, a group of mud huts, and the same kind of pottery found on the mainland. He believes that only small numbers of people adopted Islam initially, forming an elite then as now.

Shanga seems to have grown into a more advanced society by the late ninth century, complete with its own currency of silver coins. In the next century we see the first coral buildings, and by the eleventh century, signs of increasing trade in the form of coins from the Mediterranean. But Horton believes that the increasing success of the town was not accompanied by rapid population growth, pointing to the fact that the coral mosque built in AD 1000 to accommodate the entire town was only slightly larger than the wooden one it replaced. In fact, he argues, the coral architecture that appeared during this period is not a sign of Arabic immigration, but merely the result of a shift in local style. The town grew until the fourteenth century, when it was abandoned in a hurry; excavation has revealed valuable personal possessions left behind, supporting the popular view that Shanga was destroyed in an attack, though no one knows for sure what happened.

Horton's findings certainly do not exclude considerable Arab participation in the building of Swahili towns. But based on his evidence it seems fairly likely that there were African towns or villages of some sort prior to the Arabs' arrival, and these could have developed later into characteristic Swahili stone towns. Many scholars accurately hold to the principle that the Swahili are necessarily an admixture of Arab and African, a product of their thousand-year encounter on the African coast. Since Kenya's independence a more subtle view emphasizing the African nature of nascent Swahili culture has been gaining credence.

As we left Shanga for Lamu, the captain of my boat—clearly agitated—asked me why I was so obsessed with the distinction between their Arabic and African heritages. I tried to explain that while my own great-great-great grandfather was an Irish man who owned a slave named Jane Gates, I am not considered "Irish" in America. I was therefore intrigued by the convention through which distant Arabic ancestry made a segment of the Lamu population "Persian" rather than African. We discussed America's unfortunate obsession with "race," and my own, as we glided across a sea of the deepest blues—so blue, in fact, that at one point I could scarcely tell where the sea ended and the skyline began.

The Swahili are legendary mariners and traders; in fact, "Swahili" means "people of the coast" in Arabic. Because of this, I eagerly accepted the offer to watch the launching of a dhow. The most famous Swahili sailing vessel is the *mtepe*, a sewn boat made for at least two thousand years until this century, traditionally of teak with coconut matting for the sails. A *mtepe* is a type of dhow.

In Lamu and Zanzibar there are villages famed for their skill in building dhows. Sons learn beside their fathers to construct the craft, which requires three months to build for the small ones, six months (and about $8,000) for the larger. The tools of the boatwright

169

Pillar tombs such as this one in Lamu were the final resting places of sheikhs, chiefs, and elders. Found nowhere else in the Islamic world, they represent a uniquely African adaptation typical of the coast's hybrid culture.

Boats of the legendary mariners setting off full sail

give thanks to the ocean. The men and women exchange words and song, shrill sounds back and forth against a mesmerizing drum riff they call *ngoma*. The chant recounts the colonial invasion and occupation by Westerners. Following the singing, drumming, and sacrifice, according to tradition it is time to throw the captain into the water to prove his seaworthiness. The captain of this particular boat, Captain Athman, is a very large man. The villagers can barely stop laughing as they struggle to toss him into the sea.

That afternoon at a political rally in the town square I was fascinated as a man took the podium to champion his candidate in verse. Al Badi, also a politician, informed me that poetry is at the center of Swahili life, nowhere more than in Lamu, where a candidate stands absolutely no chance of winning if he does not have a decent poet among his supporters. The candidates' poets publicly debate the issues in verse, and generally the best poetry carries the election. Newspapers carry a poetry page, and there are even popular poetry programs on radio, which are a little like public information broadcasts.

Al Badi's brother-in-law, Mohammed Omar, is the

have hardly changed over the centuries: They include a piece of string wound around a wooden spindle with a metal tip. The boatwrights tell me their techniques originated in Arabia. The launch of the boat is the occasion for an important celebration. It often takes most of the day for a large boat to be hauled down the beach on mangrove poles to the water. Banners flutter in the wind, animals are sacrificed and barbecued, and there is much singing and merriment. In the past, it is said that a slave was sacrificed and his blood used to ease the slide of the ship on the mangrove poles.

To watch the launching ritual I headed for the village of Matondoni, a place well known for dhows both small and large. Apparently, Fadhil had passed the word we were filming a movie and so we were treated to a command performance of the ritual, even though the boat had already been launched.

First, the men tie large ropes round the dhow, which sits on the beach. Black-clad women gather, many in veils (*bui buis*), singing and dancing. A goat is sacrificed, to

Nineteenth-century sketch of boat-building on the Swahili coast

spokesman for KANU, the ruling party whose meeting this is. He sings the praises of a local candidate, as well as of Daniel Arap Moi, the controversial president of Kenya, whom many resent for his dictatorial ways. The effect is mostly fulsome, empty praise rather than high art—like the platitudes served up by rock musicians with "causes" who back American politicians.

Lamu poetical tradition begins with Mwenye Shene Ali's *Lamu Chronicle,* an account of inter-island conflicts written at the end of the eighteenth century. It is said that Ali helped win a battle against forces from Mombasa when he summoned rain to douse the enemy's gunpowder. The story is fantastic, but it is a fact that cryptic poetry was used in Lamu's wars to send secret messages.

From the quasi-Mediterranean splendor of Lamu, we caught a dhow—crowded with women cloaked in long black dresses, their faces concealed by veils—and headed to the mainland where we boarded buses to Malindi. The boat seemed dangerously overcrowded, as last-minute passengers packed themselves on board. Our journey would take us south along the coast, via Mombasa, eventually culminating on the island of Zanzibar.

On the mainland, three buses waited to travel in convoy down the coast to Malindi. I had not expected this to be a dangerous journey, but I noticed that soldiers were escorting us. As the buses set off, a fellow passenger explained that Somali bandits had been ambushing cars and buses over the past few years and it wasn't safe to travel without guard. But not to worry, the passenger added, the soldiers are well armed and trained. Since the civil war in Somalia, there are huge numbers of Somalians with guns but not much else.

Today Malindi is a resort visited mostly by Italians, who flock to its many hotels, some of which, it is said, are run by mafiosi who come because Kenya has no extradition treaty with Italy. But 500 years ago, the town was one of the great Swahili city-states, its leaders given to such extravagances as sending a giraffe to China (where it was received with wonder). By the end of the next century, old Malindi was empty, not to be revived until the 1800s and the eventual tourist trade. We stayed in the Blue Marlin, which Ernest Hemingway favored when he visited, before we drove on to Gedi, a spectacular Swahili ruin surrounded by lush foliage.

The town of Gedi, which was walled and covered some 45 acres, flourished between the thirteenth and seventeenth centuries; no one quite knows why it died, though there are many stories. The majority of the 2,500 inhabitants lived on the southern, poorer side of town away from Mecca. The palace and "Stone Town" were in the north. Grand Islamic arches, open courtyards, and a monumental mosque lay in the dappled shade of great baobab trees, hemmed in on all sides by thick tropical vegetation. The major ruins include the sultan's palace, the Great Friday Mosque, and a huge pillar tomb. Both the mosque and the pillar tomb are alien to the Islamic world, suggesting distinctly African forms. On the arch of the northeast doorway of the mosque is a carved broad-bladed spearhead used by East African pastoralists. The pillar tomb associated with chiefs, sheikhs, and community elders is found in many places along the coast, but is no longer made. One of the most striking features about Gedi is its sophisticated plumbing and toilets (probably far superior to those provided for tourists at the entrance kiosk). There is also a form of early "air-conditioning" using an indoor fountain. "These toilets make me proud to be Swahili," the curator told me. "Visitors from Europe are usually a bit embarrassed when they remember that people in medieval London were still emptying their chamber pots out of windows!"

The archaeologist James Kirkman, who excavated Gedi in 1940, was sure that the site could not have been the product of Africans; he wrote, "The historical monuments of East Africa belong, not to the Africans, but to the Arabs and Arabicized Persians, mixed in blood with the African but in culture utterly apart from the Africans who surround them."[26] But the current curator is equally convinced that Gedi was African. Animated in his convictions, he argued, "I am Swahili and I am African. Look at this nose and this hair. Do you think if I went to Arabia they would call me an Arab?" he asked. I confessed that I, too, was baffled by what I had heard thus far.

Later that day, I reached the grand city of Mombasa. As we drove through the city, my taxi driver explained that recently more than thirty people had been killed in riots that seem to have been linked to the forthcoming elections in Kenya. The city's shanties give way to smart, lush suburbs, and we reached the holiday coast of the tourist brochure, but all is not well in paradise.

The luxurious hotel is a Hollywood take on Swahili culture. A doorman, absurdly outfitted in some marketer's idea of a local, escorted me from the cab to the reception. Afterward, I was presented with the display of scantily clad "tribal" girls dancing to an empty lounge.

Kenya's economic problems have turned Mombasa into an irresistible center of affordable sun, scenery, and sex to Europeans, Americans, and Japanese. A two-week tour here is only slightly more expensive than one to the Mediterranean, and the tourists here crowd the beaches and hotels. It is a far cry from the more serene Lamu, where travelers were more innocuous: students shambling through, or the rich on chartered tours.

When the Moroccan traveler Ibn Battuta visited in 1332 he found the people of the town "devout, chaste and virtuous . . . their mosques strongly constructed of wood . . . the greater part of their diet bananas and fish."[27] Another Arab traveler visiting 100 years later found a less ordered society: "[M]onkeys have become the rulers of Mombasa since about 800 Hijriyya (AD 1400). They even come and take the food from the dishes, attack men in their own homes and take away what they can find."[28]

By the late fifteenth century, Mombasa appeared to be the wealthiest of the city-states along the coast. In 1505 a German called Hans Mayr wrote that Mombasans "had built a strong point with many guns at the entrance of the harbor, which is very narrow."

Mombasa is a very large town and lies on an island [about] one and a half . . . leagues round. . . . The houses are of the same type as those of Kilwa; some of them are three storied and all are plastered with lime. The streets are very narrow, so that two people cannot walk abreast in them, which makes the streets even narrower. . . . The town has more than 600 houses which are thatched with palm leaves. . . . In between the stone dwelling houses there are wooden houses with porches and stables for cattle.[29]

In 1505, the Portuguese came in force with fourteen men-of-war to avenge Vasco da Gama's rebuff seven years before. After a violent battle, they proceeded to plunder the town for two weeks, a preview of Portuguese raids for the next hundred years. In 1593, they staked a powerful claim to the coast in the form of Fort Jesus, though its walls and cannon would prove no guarantee of security; by 1875, it had passed back and forth nine times between the Portuguese and the Arabs.

Malindi today depends on tourists drawn to its spectacular coral reef. Five hundred years ago it was one of the great Swahili city-states.

The East African coast was not subject to any foreign political control before the arrival of the Portuguese, who stumbled across small clan-based sultanates of patrician clans and independent city-states. The Portuguese linked the Swahili coast to Lisbon and Brazil and to the west coast of Africa, clumsily interfering in traditional patterns of trading. Not only did they raise taxes to intolerable levels, but they were notoriously cruel toward the Muslim inhabitants of the coast. A bull of Pope Nicholas V granted to the King of Portugal for a monopoly of trade with African peoples stated that they must "fight all the Saracens, Pagans, and other enemies of Christ, wherever they may be."[30] As a result, the fortunes of the stone towns rose and fell. Each coastal city has its own rich history, which tells of its origins and relationships with the Portuguese and the strangers who followed them. However, the glory of most of the stone towns turned out to be ephemeral, their political life crumbling as their trade faltered. In the eleventh century, Mogadishu, in Somalia, was an extremely wealthy town, noted by travelers for its size and wealth. By the fifteenth century, Mogadishu's Webbe Shebelle region was overrun with the nomadic Somalis and the Oromo peoples, and their trade routes into the interior were cut off and the whole town declined in economic importance. Mogadishu lost its monopoly over the gold trade to the southern town of Kilwa.

By the 1650s Oman, assisted by Gujerati merchants, had begun its imperial expansion and, determined to control the Indian Ocean trade, pushed the Portuguese out of Muscat and sacked Pate and Zanzibar. The Omani Ya'rubi dynasty attacked Portuguese settlements across the Indian Ocean, sacking Mombasa in 1661, and raiding Mozambique in 1670. In December 1698, they captured Mombasa, officially ending Portuguese rule on the

Fort Jesus, scene of a violent confrontation between the Portuguese, the Mombasans, and the Omanis.

Swahili coast. Then, from 1700 to 1749, Oman was distracted by a civil war that would ultimately bring the al-Busaidi dynasty to power. Briefly, during the war, Mombasa achieved de facto independence under the Swahili Mazrui rulers. But by the mid-eighteenth century, the al-Busaidi, thwarted in India by the British, established themselves in Zanzibar, and by 1837 they were able to assert control over Mombasa with Zanzibar their principal seat of power on the coast. The Omani dominion would last for almost two and a half centuries. Although freed from Portuguese Christian nobility, the Swahili were hardly regarded as brethren by their overlords and fellow Muslims. Initially, the Omani attempted to distance themselves from the Swahili, tending to regard them as unorthodox and socially impure. It is yet another twist in this peculiar history of the construction of Swahili identity that I was to learn as I traveled down this coast.

* * *

Stone arch in Mombasa—built by missionaries, it housed a bell rung to warn the town's inhabitants of approaching slave traders.

If any Swahili custom embodies the complex confluence of nature with foreign and colonial influences, it is the practice of the spirit cult. I next visited one of those societies.

Swahili culture has long been marked by the existence of spirit-possession cults. Islam accommodates local spirits easily, contrary to what many people think; even though the more conservative do look askance and the truly orthodox shun them as heresy, the spirits are given Arabic-based names and all is well. Sometimes the incantations and charms are drawn from the Koran in the case of Arab spirits and one observes the sacred word of Islam at play in the world of cosmic African understanding.

In a village just outside Mombasa, I visited with Thureya Mohammed, a traditional doctor ("*Mganga*") who had arranged for us to film a healing ceremony. As a *Mganga*, she is able to rid people of evil spirits since she herself is under the influence of good ones. Mohammed tells us that she is supported by a coterie of believers whom she has cured; she has considerable influence over their lives. With a saucy laugh, she added that her husband isn't allowed into the bedroom on Thursday nights—Thursday is her night with the spirits.

At the back of her house, Mohammed, who looks uncannily like Aretha Franklin, has a room with shrines to her three personal spirits. Oromo (Galla) is African, Pemban is Swahili, and there is also an Arab one—the three components of Swahili society. Her joke about the Arab spirit's bossing around the other two reminded me of Fadhil's dim view of Lamu's elite. Outside, she has another shrine that houses a powerful spirit. This is the disposal place of the exorcised spirits, transferred onto ritual objects.

Mohammed introduced me to her helper, Juma—a "spirit cult practitioner" and professional in the art of exorcism. The ceremony begins in the healing room,

where the patient, an old man who apart from his spirit possession also had malaria, was lying down. Mohammed and Juma began chanting and coaxing the spirit to reveal itself. Outside the room, a group of men, women, and children offered chant in response. Covered in a white sheet, the old man rocked and moaned. Mohammed suddenly crouched down on all fours and in a very high voice screeched like a dog, letting the spirit know that she meant business, she later explained to me.

Juma led the session outside, talking to the spirit, asking what it wants. Once the spirit is identified, everyone proceeds to the backyard to another sacred shrine. Those in attendance are brightly clad in reds and blues, playing instruments and chanting songs in Arabic as they swayed back and forth to the drumbeat. They encircled the old man, who sat entranced by the spirit or the continuous movement around him. The sun seemed to pound. A rooster is sacrificed. They mix its blood with honey in a mug. The old man drank the mixture and ate bread soaked lightly in blood. The idea was that the spirit would travel through the blood into a jar where it can be held and kept from reentering the body. Later, toward the end of the ceremony, Juma annointed the body of the man, back and front. They led him out, so he could be taken to the hospital to be treated for malaria! The patient appeared to move much better than he had before undergoing the ritual, and seemed quite relieved.

Swahili cults may involve themselves in possession by a whole variety of different spirits. *Kiarabu* (Arab) spirits are very powerful, but also dangerous. They reflect the Arab cultural hegemony of the nineteenth century. Their ceremonies, which use Islamic ritual forms, must always precede those of other types of spirits, which use more

African forms of music and dance. The spirits recognized as most "Swahili" are the *kipemba* from Pemba. Their cults focus on the medicine bag and employ many of the same charms used by traditional healers/diviners (*waganga*) among the non-Muslim neighbors of the Swahili. They also use the distinctive regalia of the Shirazi rulers said to have dominated the coast before the Omani Arabs. But there are as many types of spirits as there are cultures that have influenced the Swahili; each is appeased with its own rituals and utensils. There are Congolese spirits (from the slaves); Masai (neighbors); Comoran (immigrants to the area); Portuguese (occupiers); and Nubian (mercenary soldiers). One of the more notable cults, the Habeshia, was introduced to Zanzibar from Ethiopia by a concubine in the sultan's harem. Participants in its rituals included the Omani royal family—even today the cult is popular with the urban elite. Whatever denials or repressions in which some of the Swahili may indulge themselves, the world of the spirits at least attests to the extraordinary heterogeneity of their culture.

It was time to head for my ultimate destination, the island of Zanzibar. Perhaps only the name "Timbuktu" is as exotic and mysterious in its resonance. I first visited Zanzibar in 1970, sailing all night from Dar es Salaam by dhow. This time I sailed on a dilapidated Greek cargo ship. It was here in this irresistibly charming sea resort that I would confront the long shadow that hangs over this complicated civilization. Slavery is the Swahili coast's figure in the carpet, the underlying pattern or foundation upon which issues of racial identity have been constructed.

* * *

A wrecked slave dhow

The port was awash in disembarking passengers and unloaded cargo, a flood only more chaotic because of late travelers pushing past the aggressive salesmen to make their boats. I retreated down a narrow alley between menacing stone buildings, past children playing with homemade toys in dark doorways to reach my hotel. The lobby, done up in the favored Swahili style of heavy wood and cane furniture, offered a cool, dark respite from the frenzy outside. Later, from my room, I surveyed the town, wondering if consciousness of the slave past was an explicit part of Zanzibar's national traditions.

The following morning I met a journalist named Ummi Mahsouda Alley Hammid, a direct descendant of the infamous black Zanzibari slave trader Hamed bin Mohammed El Marzebi, known as Tippu Tip. In 1865, Tippu Tip had become one of the most powerful African slave traders, controlling an empire throughout Central and East Africa. First, Ummi took me to the ruined nineteenth-century palace of Sultan Barghash. The stone pillars now compete with palm trees to support the sky: The only roofs are the domes of the Hamman bathhouse where the sultan kept his harem. It should not surprise us that so many Swahili here can claim Arab roots—the sultan alone is said to have had ninety-nine concubines.

From the seventeenth century, the coast around Zanzibar was increasingly under the influence of the sultans of Oman. By the nineteenth century they had shifted their capital to the port, which had long since outstripped the ancient towns of Lamu, Kilwa, Pate, and Mombasa.

Many of the narrow streets are lined with grand houses built of coral stone by wealthy Arabs and Indian merchants in the nineteenth century, similar to the ones seen in Lamu and elsewhere: massive plain outer walls with large, ornately carved front doors and rooms that are arranged along galleries overlooking an inner courtyard. Sultan Barghash's palace is a large, square building with wrought-iron verandahs. It became known as the House of Wonders because it was the first building in sub-Saharan Africa to have electric lighting and an electric elevator. (Zanzibar Town was in fact the first in sub-Saharan Africa to have electricity and electric street lighting.)

Half the sultan's palace is now a museum found on the Mizingani road, next to the ocean. It is a large, castellated building built in the 1890s. After the 1964 revolution it languished for a while before being given over to presenting the history of the sultans of Zanzibar, whose belongings visitors can still admire. Their Omani forebears came to the area in the middle of the seventeenth century to fight at the side of Queen Mwana Mwema against the Portuguese at Zanzibar and Pemba. By 1668 they controlled the coast down to Mozambique. Thirty years later they sent the new ruler, Queen Fatuma, into exile and placed her son Hassan on the throne as their puppet.

In 1840, Sultan Seyyid Said bin Sultan transferred his court from Muscat to Zanzibar, which was now a thriving center for trade. The population had swelled with immigrants from India and Arabia, and the island was so

Seyid Said bin Sultan, the Omani sultan who transferred his court to Zanzibar as the island's wealth swelled

wealthy that the Omani ruling class was more focused on establishing plantations on Zanzibar than on opportunities in Oman. Principally they grew dates and cloves, a crop that would continue to expand until the Second World War, by which time Zanzibar and Pemba would account for almost four-fifths of the world's production.

The Portuguese had devastated the Indian Ocean trade; Zanzibar, under the Sultan of Oman, turned to slaves in order to replace it. In the 1700s, the port began providing labor for local plantations, European colonies in Africa, and a very few even ended up on American plantations.

This is not to understate, as some have, a fairly constant East African trade in human chattel since the earliest times. As we have seen, pharaonic Egypt bought slaves

Built in the 1890s, the sultan's palace is now a museum.

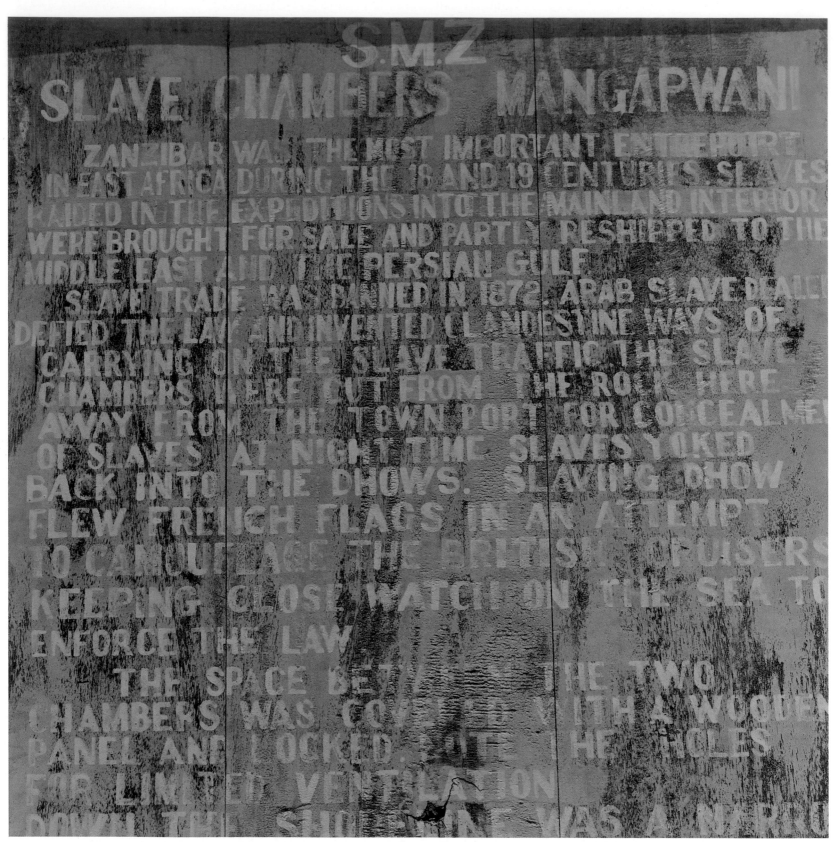

S.M.Z

SLAVE CHAMBERS MANGAPWANI

ZANZIBAR WAS THE MOST IMPORTANT ENTREPÔT
IN EAST AFRICA DURING THE 18 AND 19 CENTURIES. SLAVES
RAIDED IN THE EXPEDITIONS INTO THE MAINLAND INTERIOR
WERE BROUGHT FOR SALE AND PARTLY RESHIPPED TO THE
MIDDLE EAST AND THE PERSIAN GULF.

SLAVE TRADE WAS BANNED IN 1872. ARAB SLAVE DEALERS
DEFIED THE LAW AND INVENTED CLANDESTINE WAYS OF
CARRYING ON THE SLAVE TRAFFIC. THE SLAVE
CHAMBERS WERE CUT FROM THE ROCK HERE
AWAY FROM THE TOWN PORT FOR CONCEALMENT
OF SLAVES AT NIGHT TIME SLAVES YOKED
BACK INTO THE DHOWS. SLAVING DHOW
FLEW FRENCH FLAGS IN AN ATTEMPT
TO CAMOUFLAGE THE BRITISH CRUISERS
KEEPING CLOSE WATCH ON THE SEA TO
ENFORCE THE LAW.

THE SPACE BETWEEN THE TWO
CHAMBERS WAS COVERED WITH A WOODEN
PANEL AND LOCKED. BUT THE HOLES
FOR LIMITED VENTILATION
DOWN THE SHORELINE WAS A NARROW

The slave chambers of Mangapwani consisted of a cave cut out of the island's coral.

from the land of Punt, as did Nubia and Arabia, and African slaves were certainly known in ancient Persia, Parthia, and India. The Chinese, too, acquired slaves in the twelfth century from all shores of the Indian Ocean.

Pointing to the fact that Arab writers hardly acknowledge it, Basil Davidson and other like-minded historians have contended that an East African slave trade must have played only a small role in the economy of the area before the nineteenth century.[31] And it is telling, they say, that there are no significant African minority populations in any of those countries that traded for so many centuries with the Swahili coast. It is only guilt, their argument runs, that leads Europe's apologists to shift responsibility for creating the slave trade to an earlier era, since in the nineteenth century most of the slaves were shipped to European colonies.

Other recent writers have gone so far as to argue that slavery as practiced on the East African coast before the eighteenth century was somehow relatively benign. This view holds that the people of the interior exchanged some of their own people as a kind of pledge of loyalty, and perhaps with the expectation that those slaves would eventually become incorporated into wealthy coastal society. It is certainly true that domestic and agricultural slaves in earlier Swahili society did not always suffer the same lot as those who would work on commercial plantations. Still, the number of Africans enslaved is considerable. Scholarly estimates of the total number of slaves shipped across the Sahara Desert between AD 650 and AD 1600 vary from 3.5 million to 4.8 million. Estimates of the total number of slaves shipped from East Africa through the Red Sea and across the Indian Ocean since the latter half of the first millenium AD and AD 1600 vary from 2.4 million to 4.8 million. The problem of arriving at an accurate estimate of the total stems from two factors: first that slavery in East Africa has had such a long

history, and from the fact that very few if any records were kept, unlike the transatlantic slave trade. "However elusive the precise figures," the historian Edward Alper notes, "it is certain that during the century from 1770 to 1870, the slave trade in eastern Africa grew to previously unimagined heights, with disastrous consequences for many of the peoples of the region."[32]

Still, there is no justification to minimize the extent of the early slave trade. The numbers may not have been on the same scale as the transatlantic trade, but all the same, it clearly involved more than a handful of people. There is even a fairly convincing argument to be made that the slave trade was sizable enough to factor into the motivation of the Swahili in converting to Islam: Here was a way of ensuring their own freedom, since Islam forbids the enslavement of Muslims. The same reasoning may also explain why Islam never spread farther inland than the coastal settlements; Mark Horton suggests that it would have been against the commercial interests of the Swahili to seek to convert the people from among whom they were drawing a lucrative number of slaves—although Ali Mazrui questions this interpretation, pointing to west Africa's encounter with Islam.

All arguments about origins pale when confronted with the flood of slaves that poured into Zanzibar in the nineteenth century. After the worldwide supply was reduced by the British embargo in West Africa, Omani and Swahili traffickers expanded their efforts in the east, reaching all the way to Lake Nyasa (Malawi) and Lake Tanganyika in their attempt to find new territory. The number of slaves passing through Zanzibar each year was estimated at about 15,000, though in 1839 one British witness thought the number to be more on the order of 45,000. Arabia, Egypt, and the various countries around the Persian Gulf absorbed about half of these; the rest were secreted to the Portuguese at Mozambique, and

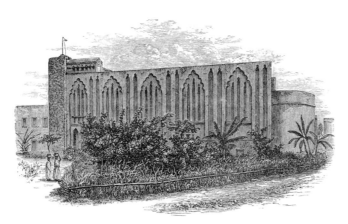

Zanzibar's Anglican cathedral was built on the site of the former slave market seven years after the abolition.

then on to the New World. Zanzibar was thriving: Not only was it awash in slaves and cloves, it also became an exporter of ivory to the United States, where it was used to make piano keys and billiard balls.

Zanzibar's Anglican cathedral marks the ground once polluted by the slave market. It was not until 1873 that the British, who had outlawed slavery in their empire sixty-six years earlier, were able to force the sultan to the negotiating table by initiating a blockade of all the slave-trading

The British among the Swahili during the Omani dominion: The colonialist presence would endure until the 1960s.

ports on the mainland. With the slave trade ended in Zanzibar, the terrible market was shut down, and its site passed to the Universities Mission in Central Africa.

In 1889, the sultanate was dismembered by the European colonial powers; the Germans established their colony of Tanganyika and the British declared a protectorate over the islands of Zanzibar and Pemba and the ten-mile-deep coastal strip of Kenya, which legally remained an appendage of Zanzibar. The island became sharply segregated along racial lines; the Old Creek provided a definite marker between Stone Town where Arabs, Asians, and the British lived, and Ngambo, the area reserved for "natives." The Swahili were not given a role and were subsequently ignored in wider East African political, economic, and educational developments. A stereotyping of them as "slave-trading" Arabs, or collaborators, was prevalent among the demoralized peoples of the interior. During the last decades of the nineteenth century, the British ruled through a titular sultan. Indeed the red flag of Zanzibar flew over British colonial buildings until the al-Busaidi dynasty was ended by the revolution of 1964. Once allies of the British, the Swahili fell out of favor. With the exception of Zanzibar, it was peoples of the mainland and of the Kenyan interior who took over after independence. In parts of the coast, however, although Swahili is the culture of the majority of people—their conversations, cuisine, dress code, songs and music, traditions of the mosque, Ramadan and circumcision rites, and funeral and marriage rites—it has often been considered peripheral in any national debate.[33]

I wanted to talk to people in Zanzibar about the Shirazi. People who say they are Shirazi claim to be descended from Persians. So I set off by "bush taxi" for the village of Kizimkazi in the south of the island.

Persian baths built by the sultan in 1850

I stood on the beach, a popular spot for watching dolphins, with Abu and Mohammed Kombo. Gesturing out to sea, they asserted, "Our forefathers came from Persia; we are 'Shirazi,' from Shiraz in modern Iran." They took me to a nearby stone mosque, where they said the Shirazi first made landfall before establishing Kizimkazi. Inside, they proudly pointed to an Arabic inscription dating the mosque to the twelfth century. Neither of them appear particularly "Persian," but Mohammed is incensed that his children are taught by their teachers to consider themselves African.

There *was* a Persian influence in Zanzibar at one time. The most famous Zanzibari artist of the late twentieth century is Ali Darwish, who though culturally and linguistically Swahili apparently knew enough of his Iranian genealogy to have received Iranian citizenship in 1970. And there were people before the revolution days who were almost definitely of Iranian origin, but, paradoxically, these were not the same who called themselves Shirazi. Indeed, though there were a small number of noble families on other parts of the coast who claimed Persian ancestry the identification seems necessarily based on speculation, particularly since there was never significant Persian immigration to the area. What's more intriguing, however, is whether Zanzibaris who claim to have originated in Persia are descended from the East African slaves who rose against the Abbasid imperial caliphate (AD 868–883) in the famous Zanj uprising. This rebellion started in Iraq and spread to Iran where it briefly established a black dynasty before it was crushed by imperial forces. The political leaders of the rebellion were East African, but the main religious leader of the revolt was a Persian Khanjite, Ali bin Muhhamed. It is not known whether the Zanzibaris are the descendants of those returning heroes of the Zanj dynasty.[34]

But the Persian connection is still far less than many

Last of the old "kings" of Zanzibar. Believed to be of Persian and African descent, the Mwenyi Mkuu ruled Zanzibar before the Omani sultan and retained some power during the latter's reign.

Zanzibari Shirazi assert, and it was the sort of identification I was growing accustomed to; the desire for Shirazi heritage was a variation on the theme that status depends on assertions of culture. Here, as in some of the other cities on the Swahili coast, the choice of Arab lineage was not so much a *rejection of Africa* as an expedient move to increase one's chances.[35]

The forces behind the need for the Shirazi identity are not so complex. By the turn of the century, Zanzibar's prosperity was waning and the heavy-handed Omani puppets were as unpopular as their British masters. Swahili families were understandably seeking some way to distance themselves from the Omani Arabs; their solution was to claim descent from Persians. It was a bold stroke that managed to assert residence in Zanzibar long before the arrival of the Arabs even as it refused to admit any African heritage. The Shirazi banner was eventually hoisted by all classes, a nationalist standard to brandish against the sultan.

I drove back to Zanzibar's Stone Town, somewhat befuddled by what was beginning to seem a willingness on the part of the people I had met to claim any lineage, as long as it wasn't black African. But it was not until I decided to visit the grand Anglican cathedral that I began to comprehend this phenomenon. It was here at the site of the former slave market that I gained an insight into the darker side of Zanzibar's history, the intolerable truth that compelled the island's peoples to construct an alternative narrative of origins.

I was escorted about the cathedral by Canon Thomas Godda, who told me that it had been completed in 1880, seven years after the abolition of the slave market. He attempted to answer my difficulty with the preference for Arab ancestry by taking me beneath the Santa Monica mission next to the cathedral. There I stood in the chambers that had served as sweltering dungeons for thousands of slaves in the last century. Upstairs again, in the relative cool of the nave, he pointed to the font. "If the baby of an enslaved woman was crying as they took her to market, the traders would take it from her arms and bash its brains out on a stone on this spot, where its blood would run down into the creek. The font was put here so that its holy water would cleanse the sins of this place." The high altar is a memorial as well, an attempt to redeem the spot where the men were lashed to test their tolerance for pain and the women were bent over to reveal their sexual potential.

Many of the slaves were exported, while others were put to work by their Omani masters on their thriving spice plantations. In the 1870s, it was estimated that up to two-thirds of the Zanzibari population were slaves. The fact is that the vast majority of the people who call themselves "Shirazi" are descendants not primarily of Persians, but more directly of slaves from the African mainland. Why the fabricated identity? Slaves, of course, have always been at the bottom of Swahili society, and nobody wanted to be associated with them. On the other hand, nobody wanted to be classified as Arab, which came, through the Omani, to be synonymous with colonial collaboration and cruel slave drivers. "Shirazi" was a way of creating a new identity; of rejecting the two objectionable realities of slaver and slave; and, finally, of cleansing the century-old heritage of slavery.

Today the past is not forgotten, only ignored. Godda explained that in schools filled with the descendants of slaves and slave owners alike it is policy not to teach Zanzibar's history. Having witnessed harmony on the island between people of different backgrounds, I was quite surprised. Slavery had ended in the last century; was there really that much anxiety? If Canon Godda's claims were true (I realized he was a Christian in a Muslim society and had a specific viewpoint), one needed to question the theory of benign cultural fusion on the Swahili coast.

It seems that the Swahili were made to feel culturally inferior by the Arabs and racially inferior by the Portuguese and the British. The cultural prejudices of Arab rule had a huge impact on the Swahili sense of self. The "colonial mentality" created an imperative to become culturally Arab. "Arabness" became a mark of status, and eventually the norm for Swahili society. In the nineteenth century the ascent of Arab cultural superiority, linked as it was with the slave trade, intensified a sense of ethnic hierarchy and social stratification. In the Arab view of social distinction, skin color was only one element; lineage and cultural assimilation ranging from linguistic mastery to pietistic scholarship were paramount.[36] European visitors made skin color a more important issue. "Africanness"

was suddenly an even greater liability, and Arab ancestry became the only path to redemption. Africans suffered under British legal semantics. To be categorized as "native" in British East Africa ensured political and economic liability. "Natives" were given smaller rations of cornmeal, while anyone who could claim to be Arab or Shirazi was eligible for rations of the more highly prized rice. Lots of people discovered a new identity for themselves. People who were before British rule designated as solely "African" by the system were now divided in order of superiority into "semitic," "hamitic," and "negroid."[37]

Listening to the canon, I thought of how consistent this tendency in Zanzibar to "forget" the past has been, at least since the construction of the Cathedral. The baptismal font constructed over the place where crying babies were killed is a metaphor for this tendency. It would take an ocean of holy water to cleanse the sins of slavery from this stunningly beautiful island, but the culture of studied denial of that slaving past means no true reconciliation will occur.

When I visited the grand house of Tippu Tip, the legendary slave dealer who was a black African, his great-granddaughter Ummi told me that during its construction, forty slaves are said to have been slaughtered and buried in the foundation "to make the walls strong." It had never occurred to me that a descendant of slaves could ever stand face-to-face with a black descendant of a black slave trader, especially in East Africa. When I suggested it was at least theoretically possible that an ancestor of hers might have enslaved an ancestor of mine, she responded that, while she regretted the horrors of slavery, she could not have imagined how Tippu Tip could have done otherwise. "You know," she said slowly, "back then, you could be only two things: a slaver or a slave. He made the better choice." I had never thought of my own family's participation in slavery as a matter of choice, but I had to concede that faced with the same possibilities, they no doubt would have elected the path of Tippu Tip.

The next day—after three weeks on the Swahili coast—I set sail by dhow for Dar es Salaam. As the Swahili mariners let out for sail, I thought about what I had found here. This 2,000-year-old culture, born of the Indian Ocean, has undeniably created a unique people and culture, a fusion of influences that has never conformed with outsiders' definitions of Africans. But for all the wonders of this culture one cannot help but be troubled by the brutal history from which it issues or the manner in which that history has been repressed.

Swahili history is remarkably complex, a complexity that has undoubtedly contributed to much of the controversy surrounding their identity. Racially, they've considered themselves, and have been designated as, African, Arab, or both, a self-conception that has changed depending on different historical periods. Again, when convoluted semantics in British colonial law threatened to dispossess "natives," a category that included the Swahili, of their land through burdensome taxation, many renamed themselves "Arab" or "Shirazi." This can

Above: The legendary slave trader Tippu Tip, who was a black African
Opposite: Slave cavern of Mangapwani, Zanzibar

appear at times, from a North American perspective, to be evasive. But the Swahili might counter this by arguing that such a form of classifying people is an imposition rooted in the racial politics of North America, having little or nothing to do with the historical realities and continuous interaction blacks have had with the Middle East.

Who are the Swahili in history and why do the ruins of a once-thriving civilization, hidden beneath the mangrove bushes, still have the power to enchant? I thought about how once there had been a thriving East African economy trading equally with Asia and the Middle East, and how that trading world became subsumed by a Western empire based on inequality and force. I thought about the peculiar colonial racial interpretations that were at play in East Africa, and how early scholars wrote about East Africans, and how some Swahili began to write about themselves. James de Vere Allen wrote that "there can be few historic peoples whose identity is as elusive as that of the Swahilis . . . For all that Swahili identity is elusive, it is only relatively recently that western historians have questioned their historical importance and that some have even queried their existence." He also asked how "[t]he African element in cultural patrimony [could be so] modified by Islam and later distorted until many Swahilis themselves lost sight of it, while some non-Swahili denied it altogether."[38]

Historians did not write about Cambay in Gujerat as being built or constructed by outsiders, even though that city may have been simultaneously Islamic, Indian, and Portuguese and its people may have felt more allegiance to Mecca than to Bombay! The Swahili are a Bantu-speaking people, an African people with an Afro-Islamic culture. They are distinctive in their relationship to an Afro-Asiatic world and distinctive on the East African coast in their history of urbanity in classical Africa. My attempt to delve into Swahili history had to take into account the questions of racial, cultural, and ethnic identity, for in no other place in Africa have the questions being asked been so misleading, nor the answers so vague and contentious, nor the tourists so misinformed. These differing accounts of that attempt to cast light on who the Swahili are, and their achievements—as sophisticated writers, traders, and fishermen, as poetic politicians—demand a careful study of their history in relation to Africa and the Middle East as well as a rethinking of the way in which we persist in thinking about race and ethnic grouping in Africa.

For instance, the Swahili have always defined their collective identity in cultural terms rather than racial terms, and neither Eurocentric nor Afrocentric interpretations have been able to pigeonhole them into neat definitions. Their identity is inclusive and hybrid, which is also true of more African ethnicities than is commonly imagined. And that is not merely the legacy of the Swahili, but for most of a cosmopolitan Africa today.

On the other hand, in spite of the apparent tensions within Swahili history and in Swahili historiography, perhaps it is the very way that the Swahili have reimagined and forgotten their origins time and time again with such conviction that forces us to look at the way we self-righteously imagine our own. When I was growing up in the fifties, we used to chant, "If you're black, get back; if you're brown, get down; if you're white, you are all right." I never dreamed that I would encounter a variation of those attitudes nine thousand miles away from black America. As I watched Zanzibar's coast disappear on the horizon, I remembered this verse:

> Then I'll go sailing far,
> Off to Zanzibar
> Though my dream places seem
> Better than they really are.

Slave chambers of Zanzibar: Today the past is not forgotten,
only ignored.

6

THE TREE
OF FORGETFULNESS

But, am I African? Had some of my ancestors sold their relatives to white men? What would my feelings be when I looked into the black face of an African, feeling that maybe his great-great-great grandfather had sold my great-great-great grandfather into slavery? Was there something in Africa that my feelings could latch onto to make all of this dark past clear and meaningful? Would the Africans regard me as a lost brother who had returned? . . .

"Didn't your mother or grandmother ever tell you what part of Africa you came from, sar?"

I didn't answer. I stared vaguely about me. I had, in my childhood, asked my parents about it, but they had no information, or else they hadn't wanted to speak about it. I remembered that many Africans had sold their people into slavery; it had been said that they had no idea of the kind of slavery into which they had been selling their people, but they had sold them . . . I suddenly didn't know what to say to the men confronting me.

"Haven't you tried to find out where in Africa you came from, sar?"

"Well," I said softly, "you know, you fellows who sold us and the white men who bought us didn't keep any records."

Silence stood between us. We avoided each other's eyes.

—RICHARD WRIGHT, *Black Power*

To get power, sell your mother. Once you have power,
there are many ways of getting her back.

—ASANTE PROVERB

You who are breath and giver of my being
How shall I dare refuse you forgiveness
Even if the offense were real

—WOLE SOYINKA, *Death and the King's Horsemen*

193

View of Elmina's bustling port, as seen from
the former slave castle of the same name

NIGER

BURKINA FASO

NIGERIA

GHANA

Niger River

TOGO

BENIN

Benue River

Lake Volta

Niger River

• Abomey

ASANTE

S l a v e

Kumasi •

C o a s t

Gold Coast

Accra •

Ouidah •

Cape Coast

Bight of Benin

Elmina • •

N

W ✦ E

S

GULF OF GUINEA

Bight of Biafra

At my elementary school in West Virginia during the late 1950s, "Black History" was virtually nonexistent. It took form only on those few days devoted to discussing the slave trade in Africa, which our teachers represented mainly in terms of its beneficent effect of rescuing our ancestors from the savagery and barbarism endemic to the Dark Continent. I'm not certain if the lessons taught on these "slavery days," as I called them, were devised with any thought to how they would make us feel. But the more I heard about the supposed vacuity of the African past and the role of the southern plantation as a veritable finishing school that saved our own people from themselves, the more embarrassed I felt. I learned to hate slavery days, and would have done anything to make them go away.

There was little consolation in the admission that the agents of our forebears' deliverors had acted with wicked intent. The Europeans, our teachers had made plain to us, had arrived on the west coast of Africa and, willy-nilly, begun to capture its inhabitants with all the sublime indifference of fishermen casting their nets for tuna. If there were an evil force in this wretched, if ultimately redeeming, drama it was surely they—the Dutch, the Spanish, the Portuguese, the English, and the French—who had embarked upon the trade in human beings to furnish the principal source of labor for the economic machine that they called the New World. By the same token, if there were innocent victims of war and commerce it was surely the Africans themselves, whose efforts to resist proved hopeless in the face of the overwhelming technological superiority of the Europeans. Such a neat division between Africans as victims and Europeans as agents was perhaps necessary somehow in the portrayal of the slave trade as a divine plan whereby Africans were brought to the Americas to receive the blessings of work, morals, and manners. Only a divine plan, revealed by a perfect moral symmetry, could possibly mitigate what must otherwise be understood as the collective guilt of the Europeans for the primal rupture in African history caused by the slave trade. The idea that the Africans themselves might be anything but uniformly innocent in this redemptive sin was not broached by my teachers, if indeed it had ever occurred to them.

My friends and I little understood the unmistakable humiliation we felt on slavery days. Perhaps we were embarrassed to be the descendants of slaves, and worse, of the savage Africans depicted in our textbooks whose saving grace had been enslavement in the New World. Later, in college, I would learn that my classmates were not the first to feel this way. Writing at the turn of the century, the great political leader Booker T. Washington urged his fellow American Negroes to forget about the past, to turn their backs on slavery, to fabricate a new identity, "a new Negro for a new century." Even historians—black historians—were loath to touch the slave legacy. While many wrote books about abolition, the Civil War, or Reconstruction, it was not until 1972—more than a hundred years after the Emancipation Proclamation—that John W. Blassingame became the first black historian to write a book about slavery from the point of view of the slave. No, for generations slavery was not embraced as the awful definitive experience of our people, one entitling us to claims of inherited victimhood; rather, it was the monster chained in the basement of the American consciousness—a creature we would all do well to avoid. It was during my undergraduate years at Yale that the subject I had longed to avoid as a schoolboy became one of the principal intellectual concerns of my adulthood. Doubtless, the fact that Blassingame, a Yale professor, had published *The Slave Community* during these same years afforded me some inspiration. Since then I have written extensively about the literature cre-

François-Auguste Biard's 1883 painting Slaves on the West Coast of Africa *captures something of the insouciance of European participation in the slave trade.*

The Secret Relationship Between Blacks and Jews. The aim was to divert attention from the dramatic extent of black enslavement in the pre-Islamic Arab world, and in the Muslim world since the eighth century.

But the least well known—and for African Americans the most painful—truth concerning the extraordinarily complex phenomenon that was the African slave trade is the role of black Africans themselves in its origins, its operation, and its perpetuation.[1] It was an uneasiness and anger about this truth that fueled Richard Wright's barely concealed contempt for his Ghanaian kinsmen in *Black Power* and that led many African Americans to view their New World culture as *sui generis,* connected only tenuously to its African antecedents, if at all. Western images of African barbarism and savagery, of course, did not endear us to our native land. But for many of my countrymen, the African role in the slave trade of other Africans is both a horrific surprise and the ultimate betrayal, something akin to fratricide and sororicide. Imagine the impact of a revelation that Sephardic Jews

ated by slaves. It therefore bears some explanation why I found myself dreading the trip I was to make to film and write about the slave trade in Ghana and Benin.

The darkest secret about African slavery, as I had discovered years after the slavery days of my youth, was not the horror that the Europeans visited upon their captives, as unimaginably barbaric and inhumane as this was. The despicable European role in the enslavement of Africans is amply documented and widely known. Also familiar (though markedly less well documented) is the extent of black slavery in the Arab world, a phenomenon of surprisingly large proportions predating Europe's involvement by well over a millennium. It developed, as we have seen, through the trade of the kingdoms of Nubia, Meroë, Axum, Mali, and Zanzibar, among many others. It was surely an anxiety about precisely this part of the history of the African slave trade that compelled Minister Louis Farrakhan's Nation of Islam—through its "research department"—to fabricate a major role in the slave trade for Jewish merchants and bankers according to its book,

A company of captives—men, women, and children—being driven to the coast

had served as the middlemen in the capture and incarceration of Ashkenazi Jews during the Holocaust, and you can perhaps begin to understand Richard Wright's disgust. Therefore, even though I had known the unpleasant truth all my adult life, it was with the most visceral apprehension that I went to investigate it firsthand during my trip to Ghana and Benin, two of the former capitals of the West African slave trade.

My journey took me first to Ghana's bustling port of Elmina, the first European slave-trading post in all of sub-Saharan Africa, built originally to protect the gold trade; but, following its capture by the Dutch in 1637, it came to serve the Dutch slave trade with Brazil and the Caribbean. From there, I headed inland to Kumasi, the center of the great Kingdom of Asante, before traveling east on the trails of the infamous kings of Dahomey (Benin). Finally, I made my way back down the coast to Ouidah (also in Benin), the most dreaded slave port of them all, from which the last slave ship departed hardly more than a century ago.

As we have seen in detail, African slavery dates back virtually as far as civilization itself. African slaves crossed the Mediterranean, the Red Sea, the Indian Ocean, and the Sahara desert beginning in ancient Egyptian times and continuing through the classical Greco-Roman period and beyond. But the single most dramatic transformation in the trade occurred with the discovery of the Americas and the almost simultaneous discovery of the Atlantic coast of Africa by European explorers and traders beginning at the end of the fifteenth century. The search for gold and an eagerness to circumvent the Muslim domination of this trade across the Sahara; the quest

for a new route by sea to the Indies; and the perennial dream of finding the legendary Prester John of Ethiopia and his wealth all led the Portuguese down the coast of West Africa and eventually around the Cape of Good Hope, up the Swahili coast, and then east to India. Along the way, what the Portuguese discovered, and were able to transform into unprecedented profit, was commerce in black human beings.

Studies undertaken by a group of historians under the direction of David Eltis at the W.E.B. Du Bois Institute at Harvard have revealed that between 1519 and the nineteenth century approximately 12 million people were captured from Africa and shipped to the New World. Of these, 27 percent came from the Gold Coast (the colonial name given by the British to the coastal area of present-day Ghana) and the Bight of Benin, and Dahomey, now the Republic of Benin.

Why and how were people sold on this coast? What was happening when, according to the Ga people's traditions, the "earth was spoiled by slave raiding"?[2] In simple terms, money was the driving force behind slavery's logic, but the structure of that logic was in fact quite complex.

By 1417, the Portuguese were the first Europeans to inch their way around North Africa, in the hope of obtaining direct access to the fabled wealth in gold that their local trade contacts had led them to believe existed. But obtaining access to these routes was going to be harder than the Europeans had imagined, for they soon learned that the goldfields of any significance were situated inland somewhere, and that the gold flowed, unabated and beyond their reach, northward via established Muslim land routes—which seemed to be completely monopolized by the inland kingdoms. Fate, though, appeared to be on their side for, between the mouths of the Tano and Volta rivers, the Portuguese stumbled on small states that appeared abundantly endowed in gold, and ruled by quite regal men who were ready to trade gold dust for European goods.

At the time the Portuguese arrived the Guinea coast was a complex amalgam of ethnicities, numerous coastal kingdoms, and large interior empires.[3] Eager to navigate the myriad interests, one Diego d'Azambuja, the Portuguese captain who oversaw the building of Elmina Castle, arranged to meet one King Caramansa of Edina. Before an awesome display of ceremony and artifacts (wooden stools, drums, ivory trumpets), d'Azambuja offered to trade. But the Africans had their own trade in metals and materials, and the only other trade items, horses, quickly succumbed to the equatorial sun. Eventually, the Portuguese identified a commodity that the coastal traders would value sufficiently in return for their gold: servants. The sixteenth and seventeenth centuries coincided with the Akan people's push into the rain forest of central Ghana, placing a premium on labor, and hence precipitating a big demand for slaves. The Portuguese began to buy slaves from the Kingdom of Dahomey, shipping them up the coast to the Akan state of Asante. As John Reader writes:

> Perversely, [they] discovered there was an African commodity that the Akan would readily accept in exchange for their gold; furthermore, it was a commodity that was abundantly available to the Portuguese a relatively short distance (up to 800 km) along the coast: slaves.[4]

In 1471, the Guinea trade ("Guinea" from the Moroccan "Aguinaw" or "Gnawa," meaning "black") had begun in earnest with the blessing of King John of Portugal. After the discovery of gold on the Guinea coast, Portuguese maritime expansion was swift and spectacular—they accumulated by some estimates one-tenth of the

Coastal African traders rarely sold their own into bondage but drew upon their prisoners from the hinterland.

world's known gold supply.[5] The Portuguese and the other Europeans who followed took ample advantage of the Akan economies' commitment to gold-dust currency.

But by the seventeenth century, the Akan states stopped exchanging gold for slaves and began instead to sell slaves in exchange for gold, the resource underpinning their economies. This reversal occurred for a few reasons: First, in 1662, the Dutch won the *asiento* from Spain to supply slaves to the Spanish New World possessions; so from the mid-seventeenth century, Europeans flocked to the slave coast to participate in a trade driven by the economic imperatives of the New World's plantations. Hence, there was an explosion of demand for slave labor. In addition, the Africans grew anxious to reassert control over trade in the precious metal so central to their economies. The Akan kingdom of Akwamu, the predecessor of the Asante (not even as rich in gold as Denkyira, Assin, Wassaw, and other Akan states), was eager to control trade routes to Accra, which was one of the busiest gold markets on the West African coast by the seventeenth century.[6] In 1707, it placed a ban on gold exportation; adopted cowrie currency from the Aja/Fon peoples further east; and dealt, instead of in gold, in cowries, slaves, and cloth for European trade goods, European gold, and European cloth.[7]

The switch from selling gold to selling slaves was also precipitated by the powerful Akan wars of consolidation and expansion in the seventeenth century. Akwamu defeated Accra and the coastal states to the east between 1677 and 1709. It in turn was defeated by Akyem and its allies in 1730. Asante defeated Denkyira in 1701 and Akyem in the 1740s. The political model of enslaving one's vanquished foes, identified by the scholar Philip Curtin, began with the wars of conquest and consolidation, which spewed slaves into the Atlantic slave trade continuously until the abatement of this political turmoil. But few states, not even Asante, had the military means to control a large internal slave class. The slave trade proved instrumental in absorbing male captives and eliminating the need to kill them, adding a new economic dimension to warfare.[8] Especially after 1750, the profitability of the trade encouraged the rise of African entrepreneurs who specialized in the slave trade.

As gold-supplying centers like the coastal ports Assini and Axim ceased to sell gold, they gained some notoriety as suppliers of slaves.[9] Some Akan groups neglected gold prospecting altogether and decided that in the new climate of endemic insecurity, raiding was better than being raided. Slaving also required less work while being more lucrative. For a male slave in 1704, the English were offering merchandise worth nearly three ounces of gold. General William de la Plama wrote in 1704, "[S]o that the Negroes seeing this, now pay more attention to the slave trade than the gold trade, as they do better by it."[10] And Director General William Butler of Elmina complained that the gold trade had decreased in volume by 50 percent due "to the very heavy payments, which the Negroes receive for their slaves."[11]

Kwame Anthony Appiah describes the three principal sources of the slaves:

Some were captives, taken in war. A second group were kidnapped by slave-raiders. And a third were people from the same societies that sold them: criminals, dependents, people acquired from their families in exchange for loans—so-called debt pawns. (As societies that lived off the slave trade arose, the distinction between those kidnapped and those taken in warfare is not always easy to make.)[12]

The effects of the demand for slaves, first by Africans for use as gold-mining and agricultural labor, including forest clearance, and then in unprecedented numbers by Europeans, were astonishingly devastating. As Appiah puts it:

Between the mid-fifteenth and the late nineteenth centuries, perhaps as many as 13 million people left Africa and were submitted to the appalling conditions of the Atlantic slave trade, with 10 to 20 percent of them dying in the infamous Middle Passage. Millions more were traded across the Sahara or the Red Sea, or from the East Coast and the South Atlantic. The historian Patrick Manning has suggested that as many as 21 million people were captured in West Africa between 1700 and 1850, to produce the 9 million or so slaves who left the region in the Atlantic slave trade in that period; millions died, and as many as 7 million never left, remaining as slaves in Africa.[13]

This latter figure—of seven million remaining on the continent of Africa, slaves enslaved by Africans for use in Africa—is as remarkable to me as the number of Africans shipped to the New World. Slavery had become an essential component of the fabric of the African political economy, especially among the peoples of Asante and Dahomey.

By the first two decades of the eighteenth century, the Gold Coast was increasingly identified with the slave trade, while the gold trade had decreased in volume by something like 50 percent. Six years later another report indicated that the gold trade had dwindled to nothing. This transformation was accelerated by the increased demand for slaves from the New World plantations, and higher prices. To the West Africans gold had always been more than just a medium of exchange, and they were reluctant to part with it. Also, the king of Dahomey had banned the export of gold from his kingdom, and many traders on the Gold Coast accepted only gold for slaves.

Ghana has occupied a special place in the African American intellectual's imagination, and in Pan-African cultural politics, at least since the publication of Richard Wright's withering polemic, *Black Power,* in 1954. Not only had Ghana become a republic in 1957, but its first president, Kwame Nkrumah, proclaimed it the "Black Star" of Africa's independence movement, inviting American Negroes to think of this land as their true home and to repatriate there. Scores of them did emigrate, most notably Maya Angelou and W.E.B. Du Bois. Du Bois would die here on the eve of the great march on Washington, D.C., in August 1963, a citizen and loyal patriot.

Although I had been to Ghana before—the first time in 1971, ending a transcontinental hitchhiking trek that had begun in Dar es Salaam with a pilgrimage to Du Bois's grave—I had never been to the slave castles that dot this part of the coast. It was with my head full of slavery's facts and figures and my heart loaded with the deepest dread that I landed in Accra, bearing a sepia-toned photograph of Jane Gates, my family's earliest known ancestor, a woman brought to America as a slave whose own ancestors we believe hailed from this very coast.

Elmina is about a two-hour drive from Accra. It seemed to take forever to escape Accra's city limits, but the countryside was gorgeously lush and green. The road was paved the entire way, a luxury that I appreciated after nine months of travel in Africa. Huge waves pound the coast; the undertow here makes swimming dangerous. But one can easily discern the lure of this region for the Portuguese; indeed, Elmina even today recalls a Portuguese fishing village. Its inviting white sands could very well be on the Mediterranean.

FORTS AND SLAVES

From the fifteenth century onward, Europeans built trading forts along this coast, blessed with natural harbors, coves, and several promontories. These structures were intended to facilitate the trade in gold and to house the hundreds of officials and merchants who had transformed the coastal villages into thriving centers of commerce. But as the slave trade took off, the forts' storerooms came to serve as slave dungeons as well. Today about sixty fortified trade posts survive along 300 miles of coast. The largest of these are three enormous castles: Elmina, originally the headquarters of the Portuguese and then later of the Dutch; Cape Coast, built by the Swedes and taken over by the British; and Christiansbourg Castle, the Danish stronghold in Accra that became the site of Du Bois's original grave in Ghana. (His body is now buried in a mausoleum.) Several hundred rusty guns and cannon on bastions point toward the sea as though still ready to fight rival Europeans.

The oldest European structure along the coast, Elmina Castle was built by the Portuguese in 1482 as a bulwark against Spanish competition. The name means "the port" in Arabic, though in Portuguese it means "the mine," as in "Elmina de ouro," "the gold mine." For more than a hundred years, the Portuguese traded their cloths, metals, and hardware for gold, ivory, and eventually slaves until their monopoly was challenged. In 1598, the Dutch, having only recently overcome their Spanish rivals, captured the Portuguese forts at Butri, Moure, Kormantse, and Kommenda. They stormed Elmina Castle unsuccessfully in 1625 but took it finally in 1637. And with the successful capture of Axim in 1642 the Portuguese claim to the Guinea trade was effectively ended.

The Dutch were now the main suppliers of goods from Asia and Africa and came to enjoy a trading advantage even in Lisbon. They undercut their enemy's prices by so much that one of the chiefs at Asebo sent two ambassadors to Holland to see if the Dutch wished to build a fort at Moure. Fort Coenraadsburg on St. Iago Hill became the headquarters of a Dutch West Indies company whose principal business was to supply labor for the New World plantations. Meanwhile, at Elmina, the Dutch turned the Portuguese Catholic church into a slave market where luckless men, women, and children were brought before being transported to the New World. Eventually, the Dutch sold Elmina to the British, who had been present on the coast since 1660. The British Royal African Company wouldn't take over most of the Dutch forts until the 1770s, but by early in the eighteenth century, the British had become the kings of the slave trade.

I began my journey at Elmina, located in Cape Coast, seeking to discover the effects of the slave trade on the history of West Africa. Elmina is a hugely popular destination for American tourists. Indeed, like many other forts along the coast, it has become a place of pilgrimage, carrying for many African Americans the sort of emotional charge that Auschwitz bears for Jewish people. It is on these tours that many African Americans learn that their ancestors were sold by other Africans; I joined a group of black Americans to observe this process for myself.

I had been to a slave castle once before, at Gorée Island, just off the coast of Dakar, Senegal. I had chosen to visit alone. At one point during my tour, I had walked into the room designated for "the crippled and infirm." And, despite my tendency toward ironic detachment in places hallowed by history, to my enormous surprise, I found myself crying uncontrollably. I hate this sort of public display; it makes me suspicious of motivation. And I have always been wary of slavery's power to inspire the sort of hyperbole that lends itself to kitsch and to sentimentality. But on that day I could not help wondering how any human being could have withstood the physical and psychological ravages of capture, enslavement, and the Middle Passage. I do not believe that I myself could have. Yet, someone in my lineage had, some brave soul who had summoned more courage to survive than I could imagine. I cried, I believe, out of admiration for that courage.

Moving deeper into the castle at Elmina, the group and I left the governor's well-appointed rooms and

Built by the Swedes with slave labor in 1652, Cape Coast Castle in Ghana was used by its successive occupants to defend against the incursions of rival European powers, not Africans. Its hundreds of now-rusty cannon point toward the sea. The British captured it in 1665 and retained it as their headquarters until 1876, when they moved their capital from the Cape Coast to Accra.

descended to the dungeons directly below. The governor, we were told, lived immediately above the cramped quarters from which issued the cries and groans of the slaves, so many of whom died before they were forced on their horrific journey across the Atlantic. From his balcony, he was able to select any of the slave women for his pleasure. It was this revelation that moved several members of our group—as it happens, mostly women—to tears.

I interviewed some fellow visitors as they emerged from the dungeons into the sunlit courtyard, where they posed for photographs by the Gate of Tears, the infamous portal through which slaves boarded the ships bound for the New World. Why had they come here? What did they expect to find, on this return to our putative homeland? What did this place make them feel? Sheer horror and the deepest rage at European brutality was the shared answer. They had come both to indict the European oppressors and to experience that awful point of departure where Africans became African Americans.

The tour guide concluded his lecture with the admission that the captives bought by the European slavers on this coast were sold by African traders. The stillness in that castle was palpable. For most African Americans, the slave trade is still understood in terms of a literally black and white opposition, the one I had been taught as a boy. While anger at the Europeans flowed freely from those in our group, few were prepared to confront the curious ease with which black Africans could sell other black Africans to the white man. "Surely they couldn't know how terrible it would be," one woman mumbled almost to herself. "They could not possibly have," another added. As we walked out of the castle grounds, our tour guide confessed to me his relief at this group's response. Many African American visitors, he acknowledged, become quite resentful toward their hosts at this part of the story. Some Ghanaian guides have even begun to

change their accounts, omitting the role of the African slave traders. To my surprise, even I was not immune to these emotions: Despite rejecting outright any claim that guilt is heritable—a repulsive and irrational notion—I felt a profound discomfort in Elmina, a discomfort that would recur on this trip everywhere I met a descendant of the black Africans who had sold their fellows—perhaps an ancestor of mine—into slavery. I had experienced this complex emotion before, unexpectedly and without examining it fully, when I met the great-granddaughter of the infamous slaver Tippu Tip in Zanzibar.

As I walked away from the castle grounds toward the fish market, a little boy hailed me, asking for a donation:

"You have to know that we are one Africa, which simply means we are the same people. It is only because of the European's slave trade that you have lost your motherland to another country called the United States of America. And this is the time we must learn from each other to understand ourselves as brothers and sisters. *Sankofa*—literally, looking backwards, on returning to the past to learn from it—is not a taboo. May those of our ancestors who died on the way to America and who died in the cause of slavery rest in peace."

I was flabbergasted by the child's words. And how could I, as a teacher, not be smitten by his knowledge of history? I handed him ten dollars. Looking amazed, he thanked me profusely, then ran away. *This kid is a genius,* I thought; *maybe he'll become a scholar.* The next morning, two other schoolboys approached me and delivered, verbatim, the same speech—which turned out to be a standard school lesson all Ghanaian children must commit to memory. Here at Elmina, the more clever among them trade on it for profit, wandering the grounds of the castle, searching for sentimentalists like me.

Elmina Castle, the coast's oldest European structure. From his balcony, the governor, who lived above the hellish slave dungeons, could select any slave woman for his pleasure.

Slave trader. The introduction of firearms figured prominently in the rise of the powerful slave-trading kingdoms.

the best cloths, the most prestigious luxury goods, and, crucially, firearms.[14]

Guns had been introduced to Africa in the sixteenth century in the western Sudan when the Moroccans used them in their war against the Songhay Empire at the Battle of Tondibi. But as a result of the European presence on the coast during the slave trade, a new traffic in firearms developed.[15] William Bosman, a Dutchman and a fort manager, remarked wryly that the Europeans were providing the Africans with a "knife to cut our own throats." Presumably, he also meant theirs, too, for the area was wracked with warfare throughout the eighteenth century, and guns made all the difference between victory and defeat in the ensuing wars of expansion.[16] This gradual dispersion of weapons by the eighteenth and nineteenth centuries coincided with the rise and consolidation of the inland states like Asante and Dahomey, whose military prowess was based partially on the firearm. Guns also became part of their regalia and were integrated into various ceremonies.

The effect of the slave trade was not only to build up the wealth of kings in the short term, but to create conditions of instability in African politics in the long term. The conditions were laid in place not only for the exportation but also the domestic use of slaves. The slave population in the whole of Africa in the nineteenth century was roughly equal to the New World's slave population from the seventeenth to the early nineteenth centuries. And the nineteenth-century growth of the slave trade not only expanded the scale of African slavery, but also instigated a new set of social transformations. The heritage of slavery is still evident in Africa today—in its strict class distinctions, in its stunted population size, uneven sex ratios, and in its labor systems that still rely on migration, on compulsion, and on low pay.[17] Despite knowing full well that Africa's poverty and retarded economic devel-

Today, Elmina stands flat against the sea, its economy sustained by tourism and fishing. But from 1487 to 1489, an estimated average of 8,000 ounces of gold flowed far from this town to the royal treasury in Lisbon. By 1496, the output was about 22,500 ounces. And within a few years, a small fishing village on the west coast of Africa had been transformed into a principal supplier of bullion for the world market, exporting more than half a ton annually.

For Africans, the profits of the trade were deceptive, short-term, and ultimately pernicious. The trade brought an immediate expansion in the African money supply but not a long-term improvement in African economic welfare, as there was little or no creation of wealth for the general population. Only elites benefited by obtaining

Wealthy West African rulers and merchants were the only Africans to prosper from the slave trade.

opment were all but guaranteed, initially at least, by colonialism, Richard Wright wondered (irrationally) whether the Africans' commodification of their fellow black human beings for sale to the white strangers, and the absence of expiation for this sin, had resulted in a kind of curse, or, if you like, divine punishment for the crime of fratricide. But one hardly need resort to supernatural explanations; that the depletion of tens of millions of people would devastate the Continent is clear by any rational analysis.

The day after I visited Elmina Castle, I met with Dr. Akosua Perbi, who teaches in the history department of the University of Ghana at Legon, just outside of Accra. She has written extensively on indigenous slavery and the African involvement in the slave trade in this part of West

Africa and frequently gives lectures to visiting African Americans. Dr. Perbi wanted to put the slave trade into historical context, and to talk about what Ghanaians today think about that history.

Dr. Perbi noted that slavery had existed in Africa (indeed, throughout the world) long before the Portuguese arrived; the reason that the Portuguese were able to obtain slaves so easily was that the states along the coast already utilized slave labor extensively—it was embedded in the culture. Soon, coastal chiefs began to broker to the Europeans slaves they had purchased from the interior, most of whom were prisoners of the Akan and Fante kingdoms. Gradually, kingdoms like Asante grew more powerful and drew people to live near the coast.

But the European understanding of slavery was quite different from the African. In Africa, slaves could hope to be released from servitude and join a family clan. Even while enslaved they retained some rights, and it was not necessarily expected that their children would be slaves as well. And, of course, in Africa slavery could not give rise to a racism based on skin color. Dr. Perbi contrasted this mode of slavery with the inhumane European system in which the captives were brutalized and stripped of their rights, as their offspring would be, in perpetuity.

Dr. Perbi maintained that the distinctions between the two systems could not have been lost on the people living along the coast, much less the individuals actually involved in the trade. They lived close enough to the castles to observe the cruel conditions of the holding cells—and to see how many were buried before even reaching the ships.

In Ghana it is a breach of decorum to be too interested in slavery. After all, many Ghanaians are the descendants of slaves incorporated into family clans and might take offense if asked a lot of probing questions. But, truth be told, slavery for most Ghanaians is not something in which they feel implicated; it is mostly a concern of Americans.

Dr. Perbi, while entirely sympathetic with my concerns, cautioned me to remember that to Africans slavery was not about "race," but about power and money. Those Africans who were rich and powerful enough to get involved in the trade did so—in their view, at least—on an equal basis with the Europeans. Forts such as Elmina were built on land leased to European powers by powerful African rulers. And in these parts the power belonged to the Asante. To know the origins of the slave trade, she advised me quietly, one must know the Asante. And as far as they were concerned, she added, an Asante herself, they were not selling their brothers or sisters into slavery, they were selling strangers, foreigners, enemies, and captives. The concept of "the African" was invented by European colonials. "Ask yourself: An African to whom? But did they know what horror they were selling these people into? They must have," she added.

Who were the Asante, and what part did they play in the slave trade? In search of answers, I set off for a journey inland by bus to Kumasi, the capital of the Asante kingdom. Beginning in the seventeenth century, Kumasi was a vibrant cosmopolitan center of about 20,000 inhabitants and the seat of power in this part of West Africa for two hundred years.

In the seventeenth century, unlike the Fante and Ga coastal kingdoms, the Asante were virtually unknown to the Europeans. Jean Barbot in *A Description of the Coasts of North and South Guinea* (1720) wrote:

Nothing can be said of Ashanti which is utterly unknown, for want of correspondence; but that it is very rich in gold, some parcels whereof are brought

down to the Gold Coast, in peaceable times, by the Akans, who trade thither, when the roads are open.[18]

The first European account gives a picture of the kingdom at the height of its splendor. It was a confederacy of states based on military power, over which the Asante-hene (King of Asante) reigned supreme from Kumasi. In the pseudoscientific racist imagination of Europe in the eighteenth and nineteenth centuries, the Asante warriors joined the "war-like Zulus," Dahomeans, and Masai in commanding admiration for their martial valor, courage, and nobility.[19]

In *Mission from Cape Coast Castle to Ashantee* (1819), T. E. Bowdich described the Asante infantry wearing war caps with eagle feathers, attending Moors in large cloaks of white satin who "slowly raised their eyes from the ground as we passed with a most malignant scowl," and the torches that preceded the king displaying the splendor of his "regalia with a chastened luster, and which chanced to make the human trophies (skulls) held by the soldiers more imposing." The king stopped by Bowdich and his companions "to enquire our names a second time to wish the visitors good night; his address was mild and deliberate," Bowdich writes. The king was followed by his aunts, sisters, and others of his family, with rows of fine gold chains around their necks. Bowdich estimated the number of Asante warriors in the procession at 3,000.[20]

Writing about another encounter with the king and his chiefs, Bowdich is virtually transfixed by the opulence of the Asante court.

The sun was reflected, with a glare scarcely more supportable than the heat, from the massy gold ornaments, which glistened in every direction . . . [and] massy gold necklaces. Some [The Caboceers] wore necklaces reaching to the navel entirely of aggry beads; a band of gold beads encircled the knee, from which several strings depended; small circles of gold like guineas, rings, and casts of animals, were strung around their ankles; . . . manilas, and rude lumps of gold, hung from their left wrists, which were so heavily laden as to be supported on the head of one of their handsomest boys. Gold and silver pipes and canes dazzled the eye in every direction. Wolves' and rams' heads as if live, cast in gold, were suspended from their gold handled swords, which were held around them in great numbers; . . . immediately behind their chairs (which were of black wood, almost covered by inlays of ivory and gold embossment) stood their handsomest youths, with corslets of leopard's skin covered with gold cockle shells, and stuck full of small knives, sheathed in gold and silver, and the handles of the blue agate; cartouch [sic] boxes of elephant's hide hung below, ornamented in the same manner; a large gold handled sword was fixed behind the left shoulder, and silk scarves and horses' tails (generally white) streamed from the arms and waist cloth: their long Danish mukets [sic] had broad rims of gold at small distances, and the stocks were ornamented with shells. Finely grown girls stood behind the chairs of some, with silver basins. . . . The Kings four linguists were encircled by a splendor inferior to none, and their peculiar insignia, gold canes, were elevated in all directions, tied in bundles like fasces. The keeper of the treasury, added to his own magnificence by the ostentatious display of his service; the blow pan, boxes, scales and weights, were of solid gold.[21]

The Europeans had not encountered such a lavish use of gold anywhere else in West Africa. One almost feels sorry for the early Portuguese traders, who had been driven from their coastal forts before discovering the region's riches.

AKAN KINGDOMS AND THE RISE OF ASANTE

The Asante are the last major Akan kingdom, and they remained hidden to the outside world for ages. One view holds that they migrated from the north and other parts of West Africa. Another suggests that the Akan were a people who always lived in the forest areas and absorbed many influences from the cultures of those that participated in the trade network of the Macina area of Mali, and, particularly that of Djenne, between AD 1200 and AD 1600.

According to oral tradition, the first Akan state to emerge was Bono, founded sometime in the fourteenth century. Its capital was Bono Manso, in the region of present Tekyiman. Founded by the Aduana (or Amono) clan, Bono was situated at the end of the trade route stretching to Djenne and the Niger region. Its growth is said to have been accelerated by the discovery of the Banda goldfields during the reign of Kumfi Ameyaw I, during which time gold dust was established as the sole currency and standard weights by which to measure it—still used by the Asante—were fixed. The Europeans noted that the Akan were the most important and knowledgeable inland traders, who brought gold and ivory to the coast and manufactured beautiful cloth.

After Bono, there was a long succession of Akan kingdoms and clans. Thus, most Asante today say their founding ancestors came from the Adanse and Amanse districts of modern Asante, although the people of Kumasi (from the district of Kumasi) say they came out of a hole at Asantemanso in Asumenya, a few miles south of Kumasi—that is, they were autochthonous. After 1650, Akyem, Denkyira, and Akwamu emerged as the most important states in the hinterland. Akyem became the region's main supplier of pure gold during this period. The Akwamu state secured control over the inland trade routes of the Ga kingdoms when they defeated the Ga in 1680–1681. They were able to reap revenue in rents from European settlements at Accra and outlying beaches. By the end of the seventeenth century, the kingdom of Denkyira came to dominate the region by controlling its richest veins of gold, as well as the coastal trade. It held the Asante as a tributary state, but the arrogance and the arbitrary demands of the Denkyira king [Denkyirahene]—so the Asante say—developed into one of the immediate causes of the Asante-Denkyira wars (1698–1701).

In the years preceding those wars, the Asante settled in the Adanse area, traveling southward to form larger towns, but paying tribute all the while to the more powerful Denkyira state. Tradition has it that the king of Kwaman, Nana Obiri Yeboa, dreamt of unifying Asante clans and freeing them from the yoke of the Denkyira. A shrewd politician, he persuaded the other Asante rulers to form a confederation, centered at Kumasi, but he was killed in battle in the 1660s before his vision was realized. It was left to the legendary king Nana Osei Tutu (1697–1717), a clan leader from the Kumasi state, to make the dream of Asante unity a reality. One of Tutu's wives, it is said, was raped by the Denkyirahene, which may have strengthened his resolve. But whatever his inspiration, he rather miraculously managed to defeat the great empire of Denkyira, reducing the Asante's former masters to vassals between 1699 and 1701.

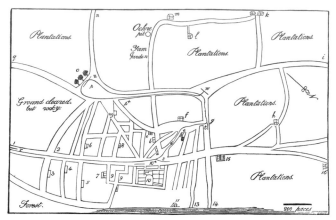

A plan of Kumasi, seat of the unified Asante kingdom, as drawn by the nineteenth-century traveler T. E. Bowdich, who highlighted his more notable experiences. Point t *is where he "halted to witness human sacrifice."*

It was during Osei Tutu's glorious reign that the sacrosanct Golden Stool, symbol of Asante unity and nationhood, first appeared. In 1701, the priest and chief of Angona, Nana Okomfo Anokye, had informed the king that God had commissioned him to summon from heaven an object that would contain the spirit of the nation. Apparently, as the story relates:

On the appointed day, the chiefs met, each waiting to be the paramount chief elect. The atmosphere looked calm. Okomfo Anokye appeared amidst drumming and dancing. After some magical dances, he paused a little, jumped here and there and began to call something from the sky. Drumming started again and the priest conjured. The sky became tense and a deafening noise was heard. Then a stool studded with gold descended on to the lap of Nana Osei Tutu. It therefore meant that he had been chosen by the ancestors and the gods as the unquestionable king of all the kings of the Asante Nation.

This was the origin of the famous "Friday's Golden Stool," which still survives today with its unifying power unimpaired. It was decreed at one time that the Stool should never touch the earth, nor be sat upon, even by the Asantehene. A palm tree still grows in a grove near the museum at Awukagoa that bears the marks of Anokye's sandals.

I have long admired Asante civilization. There is an entrancing sophistication and beauty to its material culture—from the elaborately carved gold objects to the colorful kente cloth—as well as an ancient literary tradition rich in proverbs. But perhaps above all I admire the self-confidence of this complex society, its assuredness in its own worth and traditions. Long before the Europeans arrived on the coast, the kingdom relied on a well-organized bureaucracy and benefited from an intricate trading network. And when the Europeans did come, Asante was able to force them into a formal commercial relationship of its own design. Much of Asante's power, it must be acknowledged, came to be based on its arsenals of firearms. With these guns, the Asante were able not only to subjugate their neighbors, but also to remain independent of Great Britain until 1896. But this wealth of weapons could not have been built were it not for the wealth derived from black slaves, which the Asante possessed and traded for guns just as eagerly as the Europeans accepted them. Ironically, then, Asante could insure its independence only by virtue of the armaments it secured by engaging in the slave trade. This is, for me at least, the great paradox of Asante's civilization, and the cause of a certain ambivalence toward its historical glory.

Gold and traditional kente cloth still make their appearance at Asante festivals.

Perhaps the late Asantehene (the Asante king, or Otumfuo) could have shed some light on this paradoxical history. His Majesty Otumfuo Opuko Ware II, an English-educated barrister who had held power for twenty-six years, died on February 25, 1999. When I visited he was in London receiving medical treatment. It was his great-grandmother who fought off the British at the turn of the century, an accomplishment commemorated at the Palace Museum, where her effigy keeps guard, rifle in lap.

Not unexpectedly, the presentation of the king was

traditionally one of the most materially elaborate rituals of this culture. In royal procession, he was adorned with swords, umbrellas, gold pipes, sandals, and cloths, and preceded by a huge retinue, including his precisely regimented official drummers, ivory-horn blowers, the umbrella and fan bearers (to protect him from the sun and flies, respectively), as well as hunchbacked clowns who were reported to have exquisitely sweet, high-pitched singing voices. F. A. Ranseyer and J. Kuhne of the Basel Missionary Society (which was captured at Annum in 1869 by the Asante army and held until 1874) described the Asantehene in this way:

> After a number of such personages had passed, the great monarch himself approached. He was heralded by some eighty individuals, each wearing a cap of monkey's skin, adorned by a golden plate, and each holding his seat in his hand. Then came the dwarfs and buffoons in red flannel shirts, with the officials of the harem; there were also sixty boys, every one of whom wore a charm sewn up in leopard's skin, with written scraps from the Koran, which were highly valued; this train was followed by five tastefully carved royal chairs, hung round with gold and silver bells, and richly ornamented with jewels . . . under an enormous silk sunshade, appeared the actual throne chair, encased with gold . . . still larger umbrellas and fans now approached . . . Led by an attendant under a magnificent sunshade of black velvet, edged with gold, and kept in constant motion, the royal potentate appeared. Boys with sabers, fans and elephant tails danced around him like imps of darkness, screaming with all the power of their lungs, "he is coming, he is coming. His majesty the lord of all the earth approaches!" Golden sandals adorned his feet; a richly ornamented turban was on his head; his dress was of yellow silk-damask; his hands and feet glittered with gold bracelets and bangles. Half a dozen pages held him by the arms, back and legs, like a little child, crying continually, "Look before thee, O lion! Take care, the ground is not even here."[22]

Today the Asantehene is revered as a traditional ruler, even though Ghana has been a republic since 1957. Asantehene Ageyman Prempeh I returned to Kumasi in 1924 as

The reception given for the British in 1817 shows nineteenth-century court pageantry in all its dazzling color.

An Asante caboceer, *or chief, suited for battle*

a private citizen, after the British had sent him into exile. He was recognized in 1926 after his return as Kumasi-hene, or chief of Kumasi. His successor, Prempeh II, presided over the official restoration of the Asante confederacy in 1935. He was followed by Otomfuo Opuko Ware II. He was also the uncle of my dear friend and Harvard colleague Kwame Anthony Appiah. I had met him once and dined with him in Westchester County in 1985, during a state visit to America. On the same occasion, I met his son, the Oheneba, whom I saw again at Appiah's father's funeral in Kumasi. (Joe Appiah was the brother of the Asantehene's wife, Victoria.) The Asantehene's palace stands on velvet lawns patrolled by squads of peacocks. It is the successor to two previous buildings: the misleadingly named Old Palace (now a museum), which served as the Asantehene residence and legal court from 1926 to 1956, and the original palace razed by the British.

People now can choose whether to present their cases to courts of law or to the traditional council that meets in the Old Palace to decide constitutional and private disputes. Every Monday and Thursday between noon and 2 P.M., the council renders verdicts on such matters as conflicts over land and the number of wives a man is permitted to take. The Asantehene himself is available to visitors every sixth Sunday at noon; it is said that he is quite partial to guests who come bearing a bottle of schnapps!

During my visit, I was granted an interview with the Asantehene's son Oheneba Aduesi Poku, but first I had the opportunity to see the Queen Mother of Asante. The Queen Mother plays a crucial role. She is regarded as the mother of the nation, though she is not actually the Asantehene's mother, but rather the nearest female relative he deems qualified for the position. She is one of his most trusted advisors and serves on the council that will determine succession upon his death.

Because Asante society is matrilineal, the only son of the present Asantehene cannot be his successor—though he is a formidable man in his own right, with a PhD in international relations from Tufts University and extensive diplomatic experience. He is limited to a position in court as a senior chief, a job best understood as "Prime Minister of the Palace." As we sat down to talk, I thought how frustrating it must be to be so well equipped to rule, yet disqualified on account of tradition. I was deeply impressed with his knowledge of the kingdom's history, but we had never discussed slavery before.

He was proud that Asante had been able to hold the European powers at arm's length for centuries: It was only in 1902 that the British, after a hundred years of colonial machinations, were able to subjugate the kingdom and make it a part of their empire. That state of affairs would endure only fifty-five years, until the Asante Union asserted its independence and joined the new country of Ghana. But he was ambivalent about the trade of slaves for guns that was the dynamic behind Asante's strength. He asked (not really wanting an answer, it

Scenes within the walls of the Asántehene's palace. The upper panel shows how skulls of the vanquished were used ornamentally in this warrior kingdom.

been defeated and enslaved. Negatives being impossible to prove, his logic was unassailable; I wondered if such an excuse had been given at the time.

The Asantehene's son was frank when I ventured my question as to the guilt his people might feel nowadays. Little, he replied: It was just business. His forebears had sold slaves to Europeans in order to receive specific luxury goods they could not obtain elsewhere. As for the slaves they had used to work the fields and mines, that had simply been a part of the culture then, however outmoded and repugnant it seems to us now. I reminded him of an Asante proverb I had come across: "To get power, sell your mother; once you have power there are many ways of getting her back." He smiled; well, the Asante are still renowned as the real businessmen of Ghana.

The Asantehene's son obviously took great pride in his people's accomplishments, however funded. He pointed out that had the British not conquered Asante and set in motion the sequence of events that led to its absorption into Ghana, the territory would still be known as the Asante Empire. Even so, the kingdom maintains a significant role in Ghana, operating in parallel to the national government led by President Jerry Rawlings in a relationship marked by civility and interdependence. So many other traditional African kingdoms have withered that for the Asante to have survived is notable; that they have thrived, remarkable.

As I left Kumasi, I thought about the predicament that the Oheneba had described—trade for guns, expand, or be enslaved yourself. It brought to mind Tippu Tip's granddaughter's dilemma, presented to me on the island of Zanzibar: "There were only two states of being— either you were a slave trader, or a slave. Which would you prefer? What would you have done?" I also thought about Dr. Perbi's insistence that however pervasive the

seemed) whether the Asante could have understood the brutality of the trade they were furthering? He clearly wanted to believe that the answer was no, that had the Asante understood the difference between the traditional indigenous form of slavery and its crueler American cousin they never would have permitted the trade. He allowed, however, that his forebears were trapped in a terrible situation: If they did not trade slaves for guns, their neighbors would have, and they themselves would have trade, the Asante knew exactly what horrors they were selling their captives into, just as the people along the coast had. They had known, and it had not mattered. Survival was survival.

Heading toward Accra, where I would spend the night before continuing to the Republic of Benin, where I would confront the legacy of the kings of Dahomey, I tried to think through my confused feelings about the slave trade and the complicity of Africans. While in the Asantehene's court, I found myself longing for someone to apologize, as preposterously ritualized as such gestures have become in our culture. As it happens, several people did oblige this unspoken wish. But the effect somehow fell short, not because of any lack of sincerity, but, I believe, because of my own deep ambivalence about the fate of Africans brought to the New World, and that of their descendants, compared with the fate of those left behind and the generations that succeeded them. Nothing—absolutely nothing—can justify the sale of other human beings into bondage. And there can be no doubt that the socioeconomic misery afflicting so many African Americans today has its roots in two and a half centuries of enslavement, followed by another century of *de jure* segregation. Nevertheless, I wonder how many African Americans would change places with the Africans descended from those we left behind on the Continent? That is the paradox we face, whether we want to admit it or not. When I asked the members of the tour group at Elmina Castle whether, given that option and power to travel back in time, and knowing what they now knew, if they would elect to prevent their ancestors' capture and sale to the Europeans, only one said yes, curiously enough. The others, however reluctantly, all said that even knowing the full extent of the agony that awaited

they would have allowed their ancestors to board the ships.

Whatever the unforeseen and unintended ultimate benefits of slavery for the descendants of the first Africans to become American, the question of the moral status of the Africans who facilitated the passage was for me still unresolved. It came down to a question of what they knew of the cruelties of New World slavery. As I continued my journey, somehow the answer to that question mattered to me above all others.

We drove all day and late into the night to Cotonou, in the Republic of Benin, crossing the country of Togo in less than an hour; we finally checked into our hotel at midnight. The next day we headed inland to Abomey, to the royal palaces of Dahomey's kings.

Dahomey was not only Asante's rival, but also, as we have seen, the supplier of its first European-bought slaves. In fact, slavery was so fundamental to Dahomey's enormous wealth and power, which lasted longer here than anywhere else in West Africa, that even Asante's role in this nightmare is dwarfed by comparison. But I wanted to learn how it became so great. Dahomey was also the home of Vodou, the Yoruba and Fon-based religion that the slaves would transport to the New World. It remains today, in its various complex forms, the most widely practiced African religion in the Caribbean and throughout North and South America. It is yet another irony of slavery's legacy that such an important element of Pan-African culture should have its origins in the kingdom that became the most brutal player in the African slave trade.

The area east of Asante was the site of a number of empires and kingdoms. These included Allada, Dahomey, Porto Novo, Kétou, Benin, Ife, Oyo, and the city-states of Lagos, Bonny, Brass, Nembe, and New and Old Calabar. Of these, the three mightiest were Oyo, Dahomey, and Benin, situated on that section of West Africa between the Volta and Lagos rivers known to the Europeans as the Slave Coast. In the sixteenth century, the initial supplier of slaves was the kingdom of Allada. This role shifted to the kingdom of Ouidah in the seventeenth century and to the inland kingdom of Dahomey in the eighteenth. The origins of Dahomey's famously terrifying kingdom lie in the old medieval coastal kingdom of Allada.

The people of Allada were Aja peoples who had originally come from a place called Tado (in present-day Republic of Benin) along with the Ewe peoples. Ten different myths explain their origins, most beginning with the coupling of a leopard and a human being whose offspring fathered the Agasuvi royal lineage. Out of Allada sprang forth towns and kingdoms that became so crucial to the slave trade, such as Grand Popo, Ouidah, Jakin, and Porto Novo. Recognizing Allada as their father kingdom, subsequent states attempted to legitimize their ruling elites through association with the Agasuvi at Allada.

The ruling family of Dahomey was no exception. Richard Francis Burton, the English adventurer, observed in 1864:

> The Dahomians look upon Allada as the cradle of their race . . . The tradition touching Allada, which is not found in books, but is known to every boy in the kingdom, is this . . . About AD 1620, an old and wealthy king of Allada proper died, and left his property to his three sons. These agreed that the eldest should reign in his father's stead, which he did, in peace and prosperity . . . "De," the youngest, or some say the second, rounded the upper Nohwe [Lake Nokue] and founded Hwebonu

[Hogbonu "brother"]. The cadet Dako [in some other accounts, called Dakodonu] . . . went north [and founded Dahomey].[23]

In fact, the succession was somewhat more disputatious, compelling one of the brothers, Do-Aklin, to lead his followers sixty miles from the coast in about 1620, where he founded the town of Abomey. His successors would usurp power from the local Igede chiefs who were already inhabitants of the area; his two immediate successors, King Wegbaja (1650–1685) and Akaba II (1685–1708) conquered the neighboring districts to the south and southeast of Abomey. Out of the mingling of the Aja and the local inhabitants the Dahomean people evolved. The ruler who inherited this nucleus of a kingdom was Agaja Trudo (1708–1752), a contemporary of the Asante kings Osei Tutu and Opuko Ware. He built a large, well-organized army as well as a military academy and instituted intelligence-gathering. Thus empowered, he also embarked on several wars of expansion.

Indeed, a few historians think that Agaja Trudo was actually trying to stop "by stages the slave trade in the Aja country [in order] to substitute it for a general trade in

Entry into Abomey, seat of Dahomean kings

216

agricultural produce."[24] One view is that he conquered the surrounding coastal states first to ensure their own safety and second to prevent the rapaciousness of the coast from spreading further. By 1700, then, the kingdom of Dahomey covered the southern part of the present-day Republic of Benin. Between 1724 and 1727, King Agaja Trudo conquered all of the smaller and older states surrounding Abomey, and in 1724 and 1727 added the kingdoms of Allada and Whydah, or Ouidah, to his empire, the coastal states most embroiled in the slave trade. Other scholars disagree with this magnanimous interpretation, arguing that Dahomey was situated in very infertile soil with no significant mineral reserves. Its economy *was* the slave trade, and the trade structured the state. Dahomey's profession *was* war. When the slave trade was replaced with the palm oil trade, Dahomey's eastern wars were aimed at capturing lands rich in palm oil.[25]

Despite the debates on how Dahomey's involvement in the slave trade began, it was clear that Europeans were far more involved in the internal politics on the Slave Coast than on the Gold Coast. As the slave trade generated even vaster riches than the trade in gold, Europeans could ill afford *not* to meddle, and pursued a reckless policy of intervention with the complicity of circles of debauched nobles on the Slave Coast. Between 1670 and 1708, all three kings of Ouidah (one of the coastal ports) were European nominees. King Aisan, the last of these, was installed by the English director before the townspeople even knew that their previous ruler was dead—a complete contravention of the traditional system of succession. The Dutch, English, and French dominated the court of Ouidah, the French trading there from 1670. Until 1671, an estimated annual average of only about 3,000 captives were exported from Aja ports. But by 1700, the trade was completely out of control.

The damaging effects of the slave trade were seen in the paralysis of courtly politics: Until 1670, King Tefizon of Allada opposed the unrestricted European trade in slaves. He had warned both the Dutch and the French that he wanted neither their ships nor their merchandise at his ports. At the same time, however, he faced opposition from sections of his court, and rebellion smoldered in his provinces. Jakin, a major port, had already broken away, hoping to monopolize trade with the Europeans. No sooner had it been brought back into the fold than Ouidah asserted its independence. The English arrived in Ouidah in 1681; the Dutch in 1682; and the Brandenburgers in 1684. There were numerous Portuguese and Brazilians living there. In 1704, the mélange of resident Europeans unilaterally declared Ouidah a free port and in 1708 enthroned King Huffon, then only a thirteen-year-old boy. The growing commerce in slaves rested in the hands of a few hereditary groups that themselves continually split into competing lawless factions. This chaos seemed to be spreading to Abomey.

One could interpret the Dahomean king Agaja Trudo's invasion of Allada in 1724 and Ouidah in 1727 as designed to correct the breakdown of authority on the coast, or conversely as his play to take advantage of this very degeneration. Either way, his first move was to abolish the ruling dynasties of the two kingdoms, placing their governments in the hands of two of his most senior ministers.

Agaja Trudo not only brought the nobles of Allada and Ouidah into line, but also wreaked havoc on the European slave trade, burning and looting factories and besieging foreign military forts. Dahomean soldiers blocked the routes by which captives were taken from the interior to the coast. One Portuguese report read, "He stops the passage of slaves and robs the negroes who go into the interior to buy them . . . Daomé closes the roads by which the Negroes come down," and the English traveler Captain William Snelgrave complained that "the trade at Whidaw is almost ruined; the far-inland people having now no markets to carry their slaves to, as formerly . . . few negroes are now brought down to be sold to the Europeans."[26]

The disgruntled slavers, the British in particular, sought new ports, and found Badagry in present-day Nigeria as an alternative slave mart. In 1725, King Agaja Trudo sent an ambassador to England inviting Europeans involved in virtually any trade except slavery. One Mr. Bullfinch Lamb, an agent for an English African company, who found himself a hostage of Trudo, wrote, "If any tailor, carpenter, smith, or any sort of white men that is free, be willing to come here, he will find very good encouragement, and be much caressed, and get money if he can be contented with this life for a time, his majesty paying every body extravagantly that works for him."[27] Agaja Trudo had already begun to use captives otherwise diverted from the slave trade on royal farms, in the hope of increasing agricultural production.

So it is uncertain when Dahomey's gruesome reputation as a participant in the slave trade began; its politics fluctuated somewhat depending on the faction in power. But the real terror is thought to have begun under King Tegbesu; by the 1740s, Dahomean commercial organization, expansionist tendencies, and a brutally efficient military made Dahomey change its policy on slavery. Within Dahomey, the king asserted monopoly rights over the disposal of war captives. Soldiers were obliged to surrender their prisoners to the king at the end of each campaign, receiving a payment for each in return. In principle, Dahomey sold only foreigners as slaves, whether captives or slaves purchased from other countries: King Wegbaja had made it a capital offense to sell citizens. Snelgrave noted in 1727 that "the king of Dahomey never sold the

European prisoners before Dahomey's omnipotent king

slaves employed on his farms unless they are guilty of very great crimes."[28] But this moral stance created such an acute shortage of slaves in the 1770s that kings Kpengla and Agonglo removed the oppressive restrictions and gave merchants full freedom to trade. Dahomey at times operated as a middleman, redistributing slaves from other territories. And when the royal monopoly over the sale of slaves was not in effect, brokering through various private merchants was allowed.[29]

Tebgesu IV (1740–1774), Kpengla V (1774–1789), and Agonglo (1789–1797) continued the wave of expansion and annexed the Mahi region to the north and the Upper Weme, the Mono, and the Porto Novo areas to the southeast and southwest. But Dahomey was still a small country kept in check by the huge empire of Oyo, in present-day Nigeria. Oyo attacked the rising kingdom four times between 1726 and 1730, chasing Dahomey from her southwestern trade routes and Porto Novo before Dahomey agreed to pay tribute in 1730. When Oyo started to disintegrate, however, racked by civil war, King Adandoza (1797–1818) decided to halt payment. His successor, Gezo (1818–1858), inflicted defeat on an invading force in 1821 and broke free of Oyo completely. He pushed northward and conquered more of the Mahi country and in 1841 and 1851 attacked the western provinces of Oyo, especially Ketu and Abeokuta, before dying of smallpox during a siege of Ketu. Kings Glele (1848–1889) and Behanzin (1889–1894) continued to attack the western districts, ultimately capturing Ketu but not Abeokuta. Attacks on the southeastern districts brought Behanzin into conflict with the French, who defeated him in 1894, signaling the end of the kingdom.

In Abomey, this history of violent warfare is enshrined on the walls of the royal palaces. As soon as I entered the grounds, I thought of how enormous and imposing the seat of this savanna kingdom must have appeared in the nineteenth century, especially to its prisoners of war. Equally awesome, and terrifying, would have been the art adorning the walls of the building. The exteriors are covered with reliefs of gods and animals and—more dramatically—horrible scenes of warfare, warriors decapitating their captives, and holding their severed heads and limbs like trophies of war. Inside is a wall covered with carved royal icons of different animals: a blue chameleon, a copper lion, a hyena eating a goat. On another wall are giant appliquéd tapestries. One shows Gezo beating an enemy over the head with the victim's own detached leg. Incongruously doll-like figures of Dahomean warriors behead equally doll-like Mahis. Elsewhere what seems like a toy horse parades with the head of a Yoruba chief. "The whole place looks like a nightmarish puppet show."[30]

Such was the glorification of martial brutality in this dominion whose king is said to have sat on a throne decorated with the skulls of his victims. I asked Dr. Joseph Adande, an art historian who accompanied me through the palace, if Dahomey really deserved its outsized reputation for brutality in war and for the orgy of human sac-

King Gezo, who led the Dahomeans in a successful revolt against Oyo rule

rifice believed to have been so central to court life. Was this image of bloodthirstiness propagated by Europeans bent on garnering support for the continuation of the slave trade through an argument that enslavement was a better fate than the one the captives of this kingdom would have otherwise met?

Adande explained that one must understand the his-

King Gezo's sprawling palace is one of two Dahomean royal dwellings that survive today.

An orgy of human sacrifice: Was the kingdom's reputation for bloodthirstiness fully deserved?

tory of Abomey to put that question in proper perspective, arguing that their level of war and violence was typical of any expansionist kingdom. But how many similar kingdoms, I wondered, celebrated their victories in such an openly ghastly way?

The palaces of Dahomey covered vast expanses of land. Each regent was obliged to build his own and to construct what Robert Cornevin called an "architectural genealogy."[31] Today only Gezo's and Glele's palaces sur-

vive. Both have been restored as museums surrounded by a labyrinth of dwellings and altars. Agaja Trudo built the first palace as well as a large moat that was the source of the new city's name—"agbome," meaning inside (me) the moat (agbo)[32]—Abomey.

Throughout the eighteenth and nineteenth centuries, Abomey was famous for its military force. European writers and travelers were fascinated by lurid tales of women warriors whom they called Amazonians after mythical women first mentioned in Homer's *Iliad*. The *gbeto,* as the Dahomeans called them, were a military unit and a corps of bodyguards around the king. They protected him and fought in battles against the Oyo and, eventually, the French. "They were tall well-proportioned women dressed in dull brown petticoats, and indigo-dyed tunics, with black sashes, profusely ornamented with magic relics . . . Their guns were heavy, wide-bore muskets, and their ammunition was carried in black leather pouches," wrote J. Alfred Skertchly, a British entomologist who spent eight months in Dahomey between 1871 and 1872. They were first used as troops under King Agaja Trudo in 1727 to fight King Huffon of Ouidah. Snelgrave wrote that Agaja Trudo

Reliefs in Gezo's palace glorify the Dahomean custom of brutality toward their enemies

A romantic depiction of Dahomey's women warriors, or gbeto,
who made up the core of the king's personal guard and terror-
ized his enemies with their reputation for ferocity in battle

1764. In peacetime, the *gbeto* made pottery, engaged in
long-distance trading, and handled the king's finances. In
return, the king took care of them. They were said to eat
raw meat, shave their heads, and file their teeth into
sharp points.[34]

Today, the descendants of the *gbeto* are a living part of
Dahomey's culture as dancers at court. I attended one of
their ceremonial performances before King of Abomey,
descendant of Dahomey's kings, King Dedjelagni, who
wore a leopard-nose mask as a sign of royal lineage and in
honor of his nation's founding myth. Perhaps eight or
nine years old, the girls entered from behind the throne
and danced joltingly while singing battle songs and
swinging play weapons, toy axes and knives, in the air.
When I told the king, at the ceremony's conclusion, that
I was a descendant of slaves from this coast, everyone
assembled, including the *gbeto*, started to clap. The king
responded that it was wonderful to see that a descendant
of slaves had become successful.

ordered a great number of women to be armed like
soldiers, and appointed officers to each company,
with colors, drums, and umbrellas [symbols of
rank], according to the Negro fashion. Then order-
ing the Army to march, the women soldiers were
placed in the Rear to prevent discovery. When they
came in sight of the Whidaw army, the latter were
much surprized to see such numbers of Danhomé
soldiers, as they supposed them all to be, marching
against them . . .[33]

At the sight of the dreaded Dahomean host, most of
Ouidah's army fled, probably well acquainted with their
tactics of torture and ferocity in battles. Asante traditions
tell of women in the opposing forces when the kingdom
was routed in their one and only clash with Dahomey in

Today the descendants of the gbeto *are still central to court rit-*
ual, using play weapons to reenact their ancestors' bloody
exploits.

Dahomey's reigning king congratulates the author on his success as a descendant of slaves.

here invented to escape the terror of Dahomey. The floating village of Ganvie on the way to Cotonou was constructed in 1732 when the Tofinu people decided to take advantage of a Dahomean religious taboo forbidding warriors from entering or crossing water. An entire community moved into the center of a large lake, using rocks and sand to build small islands upon which their bamboo houses were set on stilts. I wove in and out of Ganvie's watery "streets," passing women trading from their pirogues. Today, the village's residents, numbering approximately 17,000, make their living selling fish farmed beneath their stilt houses to the nearby markets.

These well-choreographed dancers, with their pretend weapons, offer a harmless pantomime of the ferocity of their namesakes. It is hard to imagine the terror that once reigned here among a people living with the constant threat of losing their lives, either to slavery or more absolutely in ritual murder. Before going to Ouidah, I went to see one of the more ingenious ways the people

My final destination was Ouidah, the center of Dahomey's slave trade under the nineteenth-century dominion of the Brazilian Francisco de Souza, the infamous Viceroy of Ouidah. Ouidah's decayed and despondent atmosphere evokes its troubled past: This was the port through which so many of the two million or so slaves were shipped from the Bight of Benin to the New World. Ouidah is a quiet, sleepy town, with its mixture of small colonial-style whitewashed houses.

Given the horror here, it is little wonder that Ouidah also became a religious center, the Vatican of Vodou. Martine de Souza, one of Francisco's many descendants—he had forty wives and ninety-nine sons—was my guide for Ouidah and Cotonou. De Souza is college-educated and arranges tours of the city. She is married to one of Benin's most accomplished artists. She took me to the *fetish* market (in Cotonou), as it has been called since the days of the Portuguese, who considered Vodou's liturgical and medicinal objects to be such. Here hundreds of tables are spread across several rows, filled with the jaws, heads, legs, and even whole carcasses of a wide variety of animals. Dog heads, de Souza explains, are used to bring

The floating village of Ganvie, built on a lake to defend against the Fon, forbidden by their religion from entering water

harm to one's enemies; the chameleon is a treatment for heart ailments; snails are for good luck; the duck's head is useful if someone is bringing a court case against you: When they rise to accuse you, words will fail them. Virtually every type of animal and plant is available in dried, smoked, or pickled form. The stench was overpowering. Vodou is ubiquitous in Ouidah as well. Walking from the market to the main square, we passed shrines decorated with portraits of the religion's gods and goddesses, altars carefully constructed next to homes, and houses flying the white flag of the priesthood.

We visited the Temple of the Pythons, Vodou's most sacred house, located in the center of town just a few hundred yards from the Roman Catholic Cathedral of Notre Dame. Many attend morning mass on Sunday and then participate in the rites at the Temple of the Pythons later in the day. De Souza herself is a dual worshiper. I had assumed the name of the temple to be figurative until I noticed its floor starting to slither. It was full of snakes, handled easily by the priests after we had presented them—and the gods—an oblation of gin.

Ouidah is the Vatican of Vodou, and the Temple of the Pythons is the faith's most sacred cathedral.

Late in the nineteenth century when Brazilian slaves returned to this place in successive waves as free men and women, determined to set up their lives again in Africa, many in Ouidah were shocked to see them, having believed that those who were captured as slaves could never return to these shores again. From about the 1840s, priests of Afro-Atlantic religions now based in the Americas regularly returned to Benin and Nigeria for spiritual inspiration and training.[35] To New World blacks, this quiet town can be as evocative as other cities, such as Harlem, Lagos, Salvador da Bahia, or Havana. The memory of this place where so many disembarked is still nurtured in many New World communities from Creole New Orleans to Cuba, Brazil, and especially Haiti. Wherever the much-maligned and misunderstood religions of Vodou, Cuban Santería, and Brazilian Candomblé are found, Ouidah is also present, serving much as Ethiopia did for the ancient Greeks, as a sacred place from which several gods and goddesses originate.

This port was also the home of the Chacha Francisco Felix de Souza. When Gezo came to power following a coup d'état in 1818, he instituted the new position called Chacha, to which he appointed this Brazilian trader. The Chacha replaced the king's agents and oversaw the shipment and marketing of slaves at Ouidah, thus combining functions earlier divided between European and African traders. Along with his monopoly over the slave trade, de Souza had administrative authority over the European traders residing at Ouidah.

Martine de Souza took me to her family compound, a maze of walls within walls, the series of homes built by Francisco de Souza, whose property was once as vast as his powers. De Souza's home is as one might expect: quite grand. His bedroom, appropriately enough, is his shrine: He is buried next to his four-poster bed. His portrait hangs above his tomb, conveying an image of a Brazilian *mestizo* with steely green eyes. Slavery was just a business for de Souza. When I discussed his role in the slave trade with Martine's uncle, Marcellin de Souza, he argued that his ancestor, the viceroy, had saved thousands of slaves from certain death by shipping them to the New World—because otherwise they would have been sacrificed. "He bought their lives," Marcellin said. "He also brought cassava and palm trees to this area. He was a good man who is rightly venerated annually by his descendants." After her uncle had left, Martine confided to me that he gets quite angry when Francisco de Souza is criticized. She, however, feels differently and refuses to participate in her family's annual ceremony. She is ashamed of her heritage. I wondered who has a more difficult burden: we who know that we are descended from slaves but destined never to know a homeland, or those who know that their ancestors willingly, eagerly wallowed in this evil. The words of Tippu Tip's great-granddaughter once again came to mind as I stared into Martine's warm brown face: "You were either a slaver or a slave."

After talking with Marcellin, we went to the slave market to walk the two and a half miles of the Route des Esclaves, the road down which the shackled slaves made their way to the ships waiting on the coast. De Souza built the slave market so that he could watch from his window as slaves were sold, then marched to sea.

The route is now a UNESCO World Heritage Site, marked by subtle sculptures along the way, the work of contemporary Benin artists. We stopped at its various stations. A large statue of a mermaid signifies that the sea was the sole destination beyond this point. Just behind this sculpture stood a recently planted tree. Martine explained that there was once a tree here called the "Tree of Forgetfulness." Incredibly, the kings of Dahomey forced the slaves to walk around this tree—the men nine times, the women seven—so that they would forget the horrors of slavery. The kings sought to protect themselves against the wrath of the slaves' spirits returning to curse them. They wanted to force their spirits to forget.

Just after the Tree of Forgetfulness is an area known as "Zomai," an open square where two statues of bound slaves stand. Zomai is the place where light cannot go: here the slaves were kept, waiting in dungeonlike conditions, for weeks and weeks, waiting for the slave ships to arrive. Nearby is the common grave where those who died were dumped.

The next stop is the "Tree of Hope," where once again the Dahomean kings forced the slaves to circle to signify that, despite appearances, they would still not abandon all expectations of freedom in this world, or the next. Martine confessed that she refuses to walk this route in the dark for fear of confronting angry spirits burdened with the weight of a dreadful past. I told her that I do not think that I could have survived this torture.

At the end of the route, we finally arrived at the "Gate of No Return," a huge sculpture at the edge of the beach. Egun statues symbolize that the spirits of slaves, the dead, are welcome home through this gate. Martine suddenly said that she would rather be the descendant of a slave than of a slave trader. I wondered how many descendants of slaves would agree with her?

At the edge of the water I was overwhelmed by the beauty of the coast. It seems a paradise. The thin, swaying palms line up toward the sea; lush green grasses are

The Gate of No Return, one of the stations on the Route des Esclaves, the road down which shackled captives were forced on their way to board the slave ships headed for the New World

Slave dungeon of Cape Coast Castle. Did the African slavers know what horrors awaited those whom they sold into bondage?

set apart by the brick redness of the earth. The contrast between this startling loveliness and the sinister transactions and rituals performed here must have struck even de Souza's men, who somewhere in their hearts must have known that not all business is simply business. Here it occurred to me—the answer to the question that had haunted me throughout this journey—had the African slavers known what horrors attended slavery in the New World compared with slavery as practiced at home? The Tree of Forgetfulness was my answer. They had known, and devised a ritual of continual expiation to assuage their guilt, which they resisted nonetheless. The glory of Asante and Dahomey was constructed on a foundation of human suffering, the awareness of which demanded perpetual repression.

Slavery, we know, has left a hole in the hearts of African Americans. But it has also had the most devastating effects on the African societies left behind. Does this legacy haunt Africa today? For even while guilt itself is not heritable, could it be that the consequences of that guilt somehow persist? How can a society expiate such sins of the fathers? These are the thoughts, this is the despair, that I suppress when thinking about the history of the slave trade, and the centrality of black African involvement in it.

In so many ways, "Africa," as a place, and "Africans," as a people, were born as a direct outcome of European commercial interests, initially in exploiting the continent's vast supply of black bodies and then much later, at the turn of this century, in the colonization of entire "countries." The torrent of cultural, economic, and political forces resulting from the slave trade was, in its way, as grand and as traumatic as that released by the Renaissance, as Du Bois once observed, and as fraught with implications for the subsequent shaping of the modern world. Unlike guilt, privilege is heritable, and so, too, is the lack of it: It is from the lingering consequences of a systematic, legalized deprivation that such a large part of the African American people will be struggling to emerge a century hence.[36] But who can say when black Africa, its people brutalized for centuries by the slave trade and its resources then plundered by an additional century of colonialism, who can say when Africa will escape the effects of its past? Sometimes I envy Wole Soyinka and Kwame Anthony Appiah for the easy familiarity each has with his people's history and cultural heritage, the unbroken access to the names and birthdates of his ancestors and to their gods. And despite all that we envy in our African kinsmen, all that we long to recover from our broken and lost African past, the conundrum of our longing is that remarkably few African Americans, when given the opportunity over the last two centuries, have embraced the idea of repatriation. For us, Africa has tended to be an idealized imagined community. Our "Africanness," while a palpable presence, has been forged in a "New World."

7

SOUTH AFRICA
AND ZIMBABWE:
LEGENDS OF LOST CITIES

It can be taken as a fact that the wood which we obtained actually is cedar-wood and from this that it cannot come from anywhere else but from Libanon [sic]. Furthermore, only the Phonecians [sic] could have brought it here; firstly, Salomo [Solomon] used a lot of cedar-wood for the building of the temple and of his palaces: Including here the visit of the Queen of Seba [Sheba] and, considering Zimbabwe or Zimbaöe or Simbaöe written in Arabic, (of Hebrew I understood nothing), one gets the results that the great woman who built the rondeau at [Great Zimbabwe] could have been none other than the Queen of Seba.

—CARL MAUCH, 1871

Zimbabye [sic] is an old Phoenecian residence and everything points to Sofula [sic] being the place from which Hiram fetched his gold[.] [T]he words "peacocks" in the [B]ible may be read as parrots and amongst the stone ornaments from Zimbabye are green parrots the common kind of that district[.] [F]or the rest you have gold and ivory also the fact that Zimbabye is built of hewn stone without mortar.

—CECIL RHODES, 1891

The curving walls of Great Zimbabwe

ZAMBIA

Beit Bridge

ZIMBABWE

• Harare

Great Zimbabwe Nat. Monument ■

Bulawayo •

Matopos Hills

Shashe River

BOTSWANA

Limpopo River

Mapungubwe •

Kruger

Thulamela •

National

Park

Limpopo River

Pietersburg •

(BOPHUTHATSWANA)
Sun City •

Pretoria •

Soweto • • Johannesburg

SOUTH AFRICA

N
W ✦ E
S

I went to college in the late sixties and early seventies. Mine was a generation that had come to believe the goal of a liberal education was to create "a tributary to society, not a sanctuary from it," as the president of Yale, A. Bartlett Giamatti, once put it. For us, there was an implicit connection between the life of the mind and life in the world, whether in the ghettos of America or in the townships of South Africa.

No one epitomized our commitment to the world beyond academe more than Nelson Mandela. Among the familiar icons of opposition to war, racism, and other evils, only the "Free Mandela!" poster was truly ubiquitous. We could all agree, if we could agree on little else, that apartheid, and Mandela's imprisonment on Robben Island, were the very epitome of evil and injustice. And we believed that we were fighting for his release just as surely as we were fighting against the war in Vietnam and racial segregation here in America. I saved the "Free Mandela!" poster that graced the walls of my own college dorm, and when our first daughter was born, I was proud to hang it on the walls of her nursery.

On the morning of his release, my wife and I woke our daughters early, just so they could watch Mandela walk out of prison. When he finally emerged, we were overwhelmed and teary-eyed at the sight of his straight back, his unbowed head—his nobility! There walked the Negro, as my father might have said; there walked the whole of the African people, as regal as any king.

When my wife and I returned our daughters to their bedroom, I gazed upon my Mandela poster, now twenty years old. That poster was wrong, I thought: Mandela is not only free today—Mandela has *always* been free.

Interest in South Africa among African Americans has a long and noble history, at least since the turn of the cen-

Mandela in triumph—for our generation his imprisonment was the epitome of evil

tury in the form of a black American missionary presence. Du Bois condemned apartheid as "a medieval slave-ridden oligarchy"; in 1950 he predicted with great foresight that before the year 2000, the black majority of South Africa "would take over this wretched and reactionary section of the world and make it into a new democratic state."[1] Not surprisingly, his statement was banned in South Africa. For his part, Martin Luther King, Jr., often proclaimed that "the American Negro cannot be free until his brothers and sisters in South Africa are free."

It was the similarity—or the perception of similarity—between apartheid in South Africa and racial segregation in the United States that generated a pronounced measure of sympathy among African Americans for their African brethren throughout the twentieth century. No other African conflict and certainly none between any two black ethnic groups—whether between Yoruba and Ibo, or Hutu and Tutsi, or Luo and Kikiyu—has ever generated the same level of understanding, passion, and commitment. It may simply be that conflict among black peoples, unexampled in the American experience, has seemed to us irrelevant—at least, judging by the embarrassing failure of our political leadership to mount successful campaigns against atrocities such as those perpetuated by Idi Amin in Uganda, Mobutu Sese Seko in the Congo (formerly Zaire), General Sani Abacha in Nigeria, or any of several equally evil and petty dictators throughout the African continent since 1960. But the oppression of blacks by whites such as that in South Africa was a phenomenon we felt we understood implicitly, even congenitally. If slavery had a counterpart in the contemporary world, for us it was apartheid. The Republic of South Africa was Georgia and Arkansas, Alabama and Mississippi, two centuries of slavery, all rolled into one. Mandela was their Martin Luther King, Jr., Johannesburg, their Birmingham. Indeed, we believed the entire continent could not be free of its colonial past until South Africa was free. And so the day that Mandela was released represented to all of us an emancipation from half a millennium of European racism brutally visited upon our forebears and, until that moment, still tyrannizing our black brothers and sisters on the Continent.

I came to South Africa partly to investigate one of the most insidious aspects of apartheid: the systematic denial of a black African contribution to the creation of virtually any form of civilization. Until recently, it has been officially promulgated that the land now called South Africa was totally uninhabited before the arrival of the first white settler, Jan van Riebeeck, in 1652. Likewise all institutions of governmental and cultural authority advanced the "scientific claims" that the great art and surviving architecture of the Shona people of South Africa and Zimbabwe were actually the creation of Phoenicians, Arabs, or other nonblack peoples. Such misrepresentations have prevailed since the founding of this country. In order to justify and perpetuate their imperialism and oppression of black Africans, the white settlers developed a mythology, a counterfeit history that was intended to deny the Africans the very capacity to create culture, to embrace reason, even to enjoy beauty. If we can imagine the aspersion cast upon African artistic and intellectual agency by Hume, Kant, Jefferson, and Hegel and a host of lesser lights, fully blown into an all-encompassing, suffocating ideology of repression—reflected in textbooks, historical novels, journalism, museums, and even in archaeological and historical scholarship—then we can begin to understand the depth and extent of the bizarre intellectual forms that apartheid assumed during the past one hundred years. Rarely has the complicity between scholarship and racist politics been more direct, or repressive, than under the colonialist governments of Rhodesia and South Africa.

It was as much to explore the effects of this ideology as to discover the great but systematically obscured achievement of the original inhabitants of South Africa and Zimbabwe, that I came to southern Africa. My journey would take me from Johannesburg, and the infamous township of Soweto, to the Palace of the Lost City at Sun City Resort, then 500 miles north and east through the heart of apartheid country on the trail of the lost cities of Mapungubwe and Thulamela, then across the Limpopo River to Great Zimbabwe, Zimbabwe, in search of the magnificent stone city that inspired the popular novel and film *King Solomon's Mines.*

"What's the word, Johannesburg, said, what's the word?" That Gil Scott-Heron song, popular when I was an undergraduate, was our fight song in the campaign to free South Africa. Like many of my generation I vowed never to come here, never to visit Johannesburg, until Nelson Mandela and this land were free. This trip was my point of entry as I visited the new, the free, South Africa.

Johannesburg is known as the "City of Gold" because of its role in South Africa's extensive gold trade. In fact, long after Europe had succeeded in ending the African slave trade and long after slavery was abolished in the United States, a kind of neo-slavery—systematized exploitation of black labor—was allowed to continue in South Africa, precisely because of its gold supply and other mineral wealth (especially diamonds). Exorbitant profits were realized as black workers were paid slave wages to perform some of the most hazardous, backbreaking work in the world. Under pressure from white capitalists, Western governments—especially those of the United States and Britain—continued to recognize the apartheid government, citing "security interests."

The West was shockingly slow both to acknowledge the inevitability of the collapse of white rule in southern Africa and to foresee the rise of a majority government, as Du Bois had done half a century ago. As late as 1987, Britain's conservative prime minister Margaret Thatcher famously noted that "anyone who believes that the African National Congress will ever rule South Africa is living in cloud-cuckoo-land."[2] Three years later, Nelson Mandela emerged from prison, and political apartheid came to an end soon thereafter. But while the political strictures of apartheid may have been dismantled, the effects of the old order on the consciousness of South Africa's people—including their understanding of their nation's history—will take much longer to undo.

I began my journey in South Africa escorted by Sophiso Ndolovo, a graduate student in the new postapartheid precolonial history course at Witwatersrand University. I asked Ndolovo to show me Soweto, the sprawling black township outside Johannesburg where in 1976 more than one hundred black schoolchildren were shot dead by security forces in an uprising against apartheid.

The biggest surprise about Soweto is its size: Its estimated population is three million. It is not so much a suburb or a borough as a city unto itself. The second biggest surprise is its socioeconomic variety, its residents from all classes: from the poorest who live in shanties with no electricity or running water, to middle-class professionals, to members of the black upper class. In this sense it reminds me of Harlem in the 1920s. When I remarked upon this variety, Ndolovo gently reminded me that all black people were forced to live here, however rich they were. It became clear to me that while *de jure* segregation may be a thing of the past, anything remotely resembling an integrated society will take generations to achieve.

I asked Ndolovo how he, as a historian, weighs the impact that apartheid had on the way that history was taught in South Africa. He replied that the official version held that there were no black people living here when Dutch settler Jan van Riebeeck arrived on the Cape of Good Hope to establish a colony for the Dutch East India Company in 1652. In fact, precolonial history, his specialty, was not even offered at his university before the African National Congress (ANC) took power. He explained how the Afrikaaner settlers and their descendants used history as an instrument of power: "So in a way what you do in that instance, you decide to push to

Seventeenth-century drawing of European ships arriving at Table Bay on the Cape of Good Hope

the back the history of the people who have been here. You start your time line, if I may say, your chronology, when as a colonist you arrived."

"Before 1652, then," I interrupted, "there was nothing here?"

"Nothing. This was an empty land," Ndolovo continued. "And then they came with the myth of the empty land, they came with various theories that most of the African people that you find here migrated from sub-Saharan Africa and probably they reached these shores the same time as the white people in 1652."

"And so from that point," I suggested, "history unfolds as the survival of the fittest?"

"Then it's survival of the fittest."

For most South Africans—black, white, and colored—the past is another country. When I ask them where I might find their ancient history, most, irrespective of color, point me to a place called "The Palace of the Lost City," located two hours or so from Johannesburg. For well over two millennia, Africa had been a *tabula rasa* onto which Europeans projected both their darkest fears and their noblest aspirations. As the archaeologist Martin Hall put it, "Africa was anticipated in Europe long before

it was experienced."[3] One important motif of their projection has been the legend of the lost city. "He had found in the interior a ruined city which he believed to be the Ophir of the Bible. This story of an ancient civilization long since lapsed into the darkest barbarism, took a great hold of my imagination." This is a passage from the nineteenth-century best-seller *King Solomon's Mines*.[4] It was published in 1885 when Europe was on the point of carving up Africa and typifies twin desires: one to ascribe a glorious past to Africa, and the other to dissociate Africans from it. H. Rider Haggard's adventure story became the ultimate colonial fantasy about lost cities hidden deep in the Dark Continent. When Europeans did come upon real ruined cities they refused to believe that Africans had built them.

The infamous Sun City is located in the Northern province in a region established by the former apartheid government as the black independent homeland called Bophuthatswana. At its heart is the Palace of the Lost City: a twentieth-century embodiment of every European fantasy of cities buried deep in the heart of Africa bursting with fantastic wealth and graced with sophisticated culture, a realization of the Queen of Sheba's Ophir or the palace of Prester John. With this hotel and casino constructed between 1990 and 1993, surrounded by the largest man-made forest ever created (consisting of imported trees), the billionaire developer Sol Kerzner incredibly has constructed for $260 million what no European had been able to find. It is a favorite resort of Michael Jackson's, who was staying here when I visited.

Centuries before tall ships were ever dreamed about and long before the dawn of a western civilization, nomadic people from northern Africa set out to seek a new world. Eventually they found a land of peace and plenty in a secluded valley, shaped by an ancient volcanic crater. The gold these people mined brought them great riches and they built a mighty palace for their benevolent king, whose hospitality became renowned throughout Africa. But one terrible day an earthquake destroyed their homes, aqueducts, fields and mine shafts, sparing only the palace on its foundations of rock, and the people fled. Vegetation slowly concealed the ruins and all that remained was a memory, the legend of a Lost City . . . until in 1991 it was "rediscovered" at Sun City and restored to its former splendor by the following year. A new era of hospitality had begun in an exciting and amazing leisure resort.

So reads Sun City's "official history."

I met the highly regarded and charming American architect responsible for the "restoration" of this entirely fictitious African city, Jerry Alison. Its history is a product of his fertile imagination, and he freely admits that his main inspirations were the Tarzan comic books he read as a child, films like *The African Queen,* and Indiana Jones. He told me that in most of the other places he had worked, such as Malaysia, he was able to reflect the local heritage in the buildings he designed, but that this area of Africa didn't have much of a heritage. He therefore invited his design team to construct stories for the place's made-up history. He explained the Monkey Springs Plaza, for instance, as a story conceived by the man who also designed the casino: "Henry Congraasano came up with a tale about the monkeys that saved the village during a drought by going to the treetops to gather juice for the village people. This is created in their [the monkeys] honor." The entire complex of the Lost City was built according to "the legend," which consists of twenty-eight such stories, each relating to a different site at the resort. One can wander through the jungles and rain forests, or

head for the Royal Baths in the Valley of the Waves with its imported sand beach and an enormous pool that boasts a wave machine to make surfing possible. Beyond is the Bridge of Time, which shakes every hour on the hour because of an artificial seismic tremor. Alison's programmed earthquake is meant to "re-create" the catastrophe said to have destroyed the "Ancient Ones" who brought their civilization to southern Africa from "the north," a realm undoubtedly close to, if not descended from, ancient Egypt.

As Alison and I were ending our tour, I asked various tourists how they gauged the historical accuracy of this artificial city; nearly all, irrespective of color, thought it true to the past. One, an Indian physician, gave a typical response: "You are now seeing the Africa that Africa used to look like in those days. This is truly African," he concluded, "or Africa as it was supposed to be." Alison told me that he considers such blurring of fact and fantasy in the minds of visitors his greatest achievement. For him, the Palace of the Lost City is as innocent as Disneyland. I asked the archaeologist Martin Hall, whom I met when we drove to Pretoria, South Africa's administrative capital, whether he agreed.

For Hall, the very popularity of the Lost City, its attractiveness and its freehanded fabrication of the past, only makes it more difficult to promote the rediscovery of the true history of black civilizations in South Africa and Zimbabwe, a history more than a thousand years old. It is difficult for a painstaking, inevitably incomplete representation of the indigenous medieval Shona kingdom (of which Great Zimbabwe is thought to have been the capital) to compete with the fully formed, made-to-order legend of the Lost City. "Shona history is simply not show business," he lamented. "The world has one role for Africa—as a destiny for other people's expeditions, and as the home of dark forces. Rider Haggard,

Wilbur Smith [the author], and Sol Kerzner have all seen this point, and all have become wealthy." Today the challenge is merely to make the actual past as palatable as fantasy, but only a few years ago, the lot of scholars was far more difficult. The politics of academic work were enormously complex under apartheid. Those whose research depended on the support of a public university or museum were under tremendous pressure to make their scholarship conform to the official claims of official ideology and either to denigrate or deny the existence and contributions of black ethnic groups before 1652. Some became blatant apologists for apartheid; others, desperate to protect the truth as well as their jobs, sought to circumvent the political strictures by publishing descriptive rather than interpretive reports of their findings.

I began my journey into South Africa's actual past the next morning. My initial destination was Mapungubwe, located 500 miles north of Pretoria near the border with Zimbabwe. Nearly 1,000 years old, it is a forgotten city: Though it was discovered seventy years ago, almost no one in South Africa has heard of it. The work of making known what had been so assiduously concealed is only just beginning.

The drive from Pretoria to the Limpopo River and Mapungubwe is long and straight. South Africa was the eleventh African country I had visited in my nine months of travels, and the contrast of its infrastructure to those of previous African countries I had visited was startling. All the roads on which I traveled were in excellent shape; the gas stations and restaurants along the way recalled those back home in America. The stunning modernity of its railroads and communication system were likewise unrivaled, except perhaps by those of Egypt. Were it not for the presence of poor black shanty settlements dotting the landscape, I just as easily could have been traveling in North America or Europe.

Since apartheid's end, academic reform has become an urgent goal of the ANC. A project called "Curriculum 2005" aims to transform completely the teaching of history, drawing upon archaeology and oral traditions to recover what had been officially repressed, or denied.

Mapungubwe is perched on a plateau 985 feet long and 164 feet high, surrounded by sandstone cliffs, near the confluence of the Shashe and the Limpopo Rivers where the countries of South Africa, Zimbabwe, and Botswana meet. Like Debra Damo in Ethiopia, it can be reached only by rope. Remarkably, its Iron Age inhabitants managed to transport to the very top 2,000 tons of soil for farming. This is only one of the many extraordinary attainments of a civilization that thrived here in the eleventh century. Building wealth through cattle herding, they produced astonishingly intricate gold artifacts, including a finely wrought gold plate rhinoceros that's one of the most beautiful representations of an animal ever found on the African continent. Also found at this site were thousands of beads manufactured as far away as India and China, proving Mapungubwe traded through the East African–Indian Ocean network that we encountered on the Swahili Coast, exchanging ivory, animal skins, copper, gold and other exotic goods to East Coast merchants. The civilization that founded Mapungubwe was part of a series of Shona states that would establish hundreds of stone settlements in southern Africa, culminating in Great Zimbabwe.

THE EARLY SHONA STATES

The indigenous hunter-gatherer communities of southern Africa are known as the San. About 2,000 years ago, shepherd nomads moved southward through the western parts of the subcontinent. They are often called the Khoi, but because they were physically similar to the San and spoke a related language the two groups are collectively known as the "Khoisan" (although all these names are of dubious validity). Then, somewhere between AD 1 and AD 300 farming communities began to move south. These people were genetically distinct from the Khoisan, and spoke very different languages (of the Bantu family). Archaeologists label this the Early Iron Age, because these people used iron and grew crops and kept cattle. There was direct historical continuity from the Early Iron Age through the Late Iron Age and into the historical period; Early Iron Age farmers, who moved into southern Africa some two thousand years ago, are the direct ancestors of the majority of modern South Africans.[5]

Mapungubwe, and after it Great Zimbabwe and its successor states in southern Africa, were part of this history, and represent the emergence of complex forms of social organization: trading economies, social stratification and kingship, monumental architecture, etcetera. This is much the same historical process that occurred everywhere else in the world from the Chinese feudal states that developed from peasant villages, to the appearance of cities of the Indus valleys, to the rise of European states.

Martin Hall explains how the scholarly re-creation of this historical process was distorted by the racist ideology of apartheid. "Because archaeologists have no written records, they have to reconstruct southern African history from material remains. Mostly they have collections of thousands of potsherds. They sort these into groups of similar appearance and mostly contemporaneous manufactures, and call these groups 'cultures.' By custom, these 'cultures' are named after important archaeological sites. Hence the 'Leopard's Kopje culture,' the 'Gokomere Culture.' This archaeological idea of 'culture' is common

the world over. But in South Africa, it has fitted rather too easily with the reductionism of apartheid ideology, for instance in the government's identification of the Bantu as static tribes without history. What could be more consistent with this ideology than a version of history that characterized people by the style of their kitchen utensils, tied all other aspects of their identity to this single marker, and then mapped out their distribution according to where their distinctive kitchenware could be found?"[6]

In the ninth century, a proto-Shona-speaking civilization arose all over the middle Limpopo valley and then moved onto the Zimbabwean plateau, which might be termed the cradle of the Shona civilization. This region, home to groups now named after their pots, such as Leopard Kopje, Gumanye or Gokomere, Harare, Musvengi, and Zhiwa, built stone towns and cities that are to be seen as contemporaneous and continuous with one another. The chief distinguishing characteristic of their

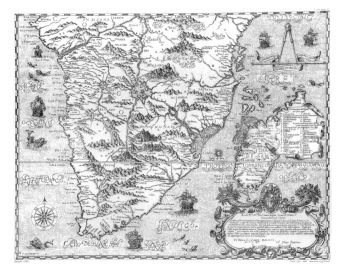

In the golden age of the Shona, from the fifteenth to the eighteenth century, the Mutapa Empire stretched across present-day Zimbabwe, Botswana, Mozambique, and South Africa.

civilization was the construction of stone platforms on which huts and other buildings were erected.[7] They also mined gold, traded in copper, salt, cloth, and ivory, and owned vast herds of cattle. The civilizations that were based at Mapungubwe—Great Zimbabwe (from the thirteenth to the end of the fifteenth century), Torwa (from the fifteenth to the sixteenth century), and the Mutapa kingdom (fifteenth to eighteenth century) ruled by the Munhumutapa—shared a tradition of elaborate stone-wall building and were also significant religious and political urban centers. The *zimbabwes* are the most visible remains of the early Shona states and kingdoms, and their construction occurred during a time of political stability and economic vitality, the Golden Age of the Shona-speaking people. There are about 500 *zimbabwes* scattered throughout Zimbabwe, Botswana, Mozambique, and Transvaal. To the northeast, the most celebrated is, of course, Great Zimbabwe, sixteen miles south of Fort Victoria.

As Mapungubwe, one of the first settlements in this civilization, became drier—it has been plagued by drought during much of this century—other stone settlements emerged, as the Shona migrated in search of better grazing land for their cattle. They moved north, to today's Zimbabwe, where more than 300 such settlements have been found. As the economy developed here from the sale of the cattle, surplus wealth accrued and this region began to be integrated into the larger trading network of the Indian Ocean coastal cities. Arab traders spoke of the "Land of Sofala" with its purported "meadows of gold." While the claims were typically hyperbolic, gold and ivory were indeed traded to the coast, while beads and cloth were traded deeper into the interior. Legends of the gold of Sofala—a city on the coast—spread to Europe, fueling the search to explore the heart of Africa.

The Shona people's sacred plateau of Mapungubwe: Archaeological discoveries here contradicted Afrikaaner ideology and were suppressed for decades.

Thus were channels opened between the Limpopo River basin and the outside world.

Mapungubwe was deserted in the twelfth century and resettled by a group known as the Baleya under a leader named Mapungubwe or Mhungubwe (the jackal), after whom the place eventually took its name. The Baleya built the stone walls that are visible today. The reasons for the original community's desertion are unclear. It could be that they migrated north to live at the newly created Great Zimbabwe in the Limpopo valley, or perhaps ecological reasons forced their relocation.[8] There is quite a consistent pattern of peoples relocating from different *zimbabwes* after a few hundred years or so.

On my visit I was accompanied by Johan Filmater, the regional director for the National Park Service, who supervises these excavations. Together, we ascended the plateau, using a rope to scale the narrow cleft of rock, into which footholds were carved 1,000 years ago.

Mapungubwe was "discovered" sixty-seven years ago by a white farmer, E.S.Q. Van Graan, who persuaded a young African to take him and his party to what he knew to be a sacred site. According to Leo Fouché, an archaeologist, Mapungubwe was regarded as so holy that most Africans "would not so much as point to it and . . . would keep their backs carefully turned to it. To climb it meant certain death. It was sacred to the Great Ones among their ancestors."[9]

Piles of boulders were nestled at the summit, to be rolled down upon unwelcome visitors. Here Van Graan's party found the typical remains of daily life: broken pieces of pottery, bone fragments, spindles for weaving, pieces of iron and copper. But they also found a tantalizing wealth of gold objects: a scepter covered with gold plates expertly hammered to within a five-thousandth of an inch in thickness, free from holes. A magnificent rhinoceros fashioned from gold plate tacked down with gold pins onto a core of material that had long since disintegrated. There were graves bearing skeletons adorned with gold and glass beads, and wooden headdresses that had been covered with gold sheathing, as well as a superbly crafted golden bowl. Altogether, they found 25 ounces of gold. While Van Graan's party initially had decided to keep their discovery secret, Van Graan's son changed his mind and contacted Fouché at Pretoria, where the younger Van Graan had studied ethnology.[10] The university soon embarked upon the main excavation. In 1934, graves containing fragments of twenty-three skeletons, one adorned with 70 ounces of gold, another with 12,000 gold beads, were found. No wonder myths of a city of gold located in Africa's interior circulated centuries ago.

Mapungubwe quickly became the most excavated site in South Africa, but the results of these efforts went virtually unpublished since the existence of the oldest urban

Godi bracelets and beads found in graves at Mapungubwe

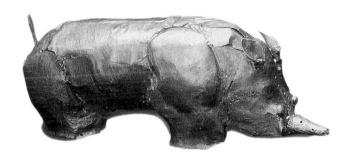

The gold rhinoceros of Mapungubwe. One of the most magnificent representations of an animal to be discovered on the African continent was hidden from public view but can now be found on several websites.

settlement discovered in southern Africa flatly disproved the Afrikaaner myth of origins. Even today, some of the more remarkable archaeological finds from Mapungubwe are kept under lock and key in the archaeology department at the University of Pretoria, where Professor Andre Meyer would later give me a rare tour. I asked Johan Filmater if he had seen the artifacts. He had not, he admitted, a bit embarrassed, because access was restricted. He said that he would like to see a museum constructed near the site, to make these artifacts accessible to the public. No such plans are in the works; however, several websites exist now, replete with photographs and texts.

Then Filmater offered to show me where the less valuable artifacts, those not deemed worthy of being shipped to Pretoria, are kept.

We climbed down the rope from the plateau, and he walked me to what could charitably be called a shack, covered only partially by a deteriorating corrugated roof. Stacks of crumbling cardboard boxes exposed to the weather and to animals house the lesser treasures of Mapungubwe's civilization. It is as if these rare artifacts were left so scandalously unprotected in order to facilitate their decay and disintegration, thereby relieving apartheid South Africa of the embarrassment of Mapungubwe's achievement. But whether deliberate or not, the shoddy treatment of these precious remains by a university as sophisticated as Pretoria, in a country as wealthy as South Africa, is, to put it bluntly, one of the most inexcusable examples of academic irresponsibility that I have ever encountered. Had these artifacts confirmed the early presence here of Phoenicians, Egyptians, or the Greeks, Mapungubwe would be the site of a great museum and tourist attraction. The ANC government, faced with formidable economic challenges, has understandably only begun to direct its attention to matters such as these.

Mapungubwe exerted great influence over a wide area,

and is thought to have been the center of major political and economic developments in this region. It enjoyed a temperate climate and was populated with thousands of farmers who also raised cattle. By as early as 1175 at least, it was the capital of a state with several subcenters or districts. It was a highly structured society, with a clearly delineated class system, as the excavation of its graves has revealed. The king and the elites were buried in splendor on the plateau, while the rest of the population were interred at the bottom of the hill in simple graves, their remains unadorned.

After Mapungubwe, we drove to another stone settlement, this one only recently discovered: Thulamela (which means "place of giving birth"), located in the Kruger National Park. Established by the ancestors of the Shangaan, Tsonga, and Venda peoples, this settlement thrived between AD 1350 and AD 1650 and was in regular contact with traders from the great Swahili states along the coast. Today the stone-walled hilltop site is covered with ancient, sprawling baobab trees.

Thulamela is clearly a part of the larger trading and metalworking empire associated with Great Zimbabwe and related to similar settlements found in Zimbabwe, South Africa, Botswana, and Mozambique.

The contrast between the government's handling of Thulamela and Mapungubwe could not be greater: First excavated in 1996, this site has been reconstructed from the original stones found by archaeologists from the University of Pretoria, in the atmosphere of openness created by the ANC government. People living near the site have been actively engaged in the excavation, sharing oral history with the scholars. Thulamela proves that black South Africans had evolved sophisticated mining skills long before Europeans arrived. Their metalworkers succeeded in converting iron ore into carbon steel for use in tools and weapons.

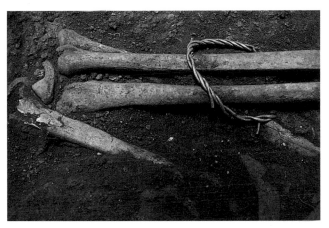

At left, the skeleton of a woman buried in the traditional "losha" position, discovered at Thulamela. Above, detail of forearm adorned with a gold bracelet

A female skeleton buried here in the "losha" position—the posture in which Venda women traditionally greeted men by bowing slightly with their palms pressed together under the left temple—was found wearing a gold bracelet and a necklace consisting of gold beads. The grave of a male found nearby contained ostrich shells, gold, and iron. Thulamela is a tourist site; postcards identify the gold-bedecked skeletons as those of a king and queen.

From Thulamela, I drove across the "great grey-green greasy Limpopo" River, as Kipling called it, across the Beit Bridge into Zimbabwe. South Africa's northern provinces have the feel of Appalachia, where I grew up. The night before we crossed the Limpopo, I stayed in a popular Afrikaaner holiday camp in the heart of what was once the Afrikaaner frontier. When the film crew and I walked into the camp's restaurant, virtually everyone stopped eating and stared at us. I felt as if I had just walked into a trucker's stop on the Pennsylvania Turn-

pike in the Allegheny Mountains three or four decades ago. I was so uncomfortable that I found it difficult to eat. Then, realizing that it was karaoke night and since this place reminded me of home, I sang John Denver's "Country Roads," to surprisingly generous applause from the crowd. The appreciative Afrikaaners asked for more, but I elected to quit while I was ahead.

Zimbabwe has been independent for almost twenty years, fourteen longer than South Africa. Formerly known as Rhodesia, the country was named after Cecil Rhodes, the famed entrepreneur and imperialist. I spent much of my adolescence longing to win a Rhodes scholarship to study at Oxford University. But if Rhodes—who notoriously liked to quip, "I prefer land to niggers"—could have known how many individuals of African descent his endowment would send to England, he might have thought twice about his generosity. When Rhodes first arrived in the town of Bulawayo, he managed to deceive the Ndebele king, Lobengula, into signing away his land, and thus opened the region to gold prospectors, many of whom became grave robbers. The exploitation of this area's tremendous natural resources went hand-in-hand with the destruction, or erasure, of centuries's civilization.

We drove through the Matopos Hills, a stunning outcrop of enormous boulders piled high in the midst of the savannah. Matopos is a deeply spiritual region, home to several rain-making cults. Even Cecil Rhodes was not immune to its spiritual power: He chose to be buried here, haunted, as he confessed, by the majesty he encountered. He also wanted to show his mastery over the African people whose land and wealth he had taken.

For the Ndebele, Matopos Hills was not merely one sacred place among others. The equivalent of Heaven for Christians, Matopos was where the very souls of the departed dwelled for all eternity. I made my way to the summit called World's View accompanied by Calvert Nkomo, a guide for the Parks Service.

Following his death from a heart attack in 1902, thou-

Matopos today

sands of Ndebele gathered to bear witness on the day of Rhodes's burial. When the whites attempted to fire a twenty-one-gun salute, the Ndebele protested, fearing that the noise would disturb the spirits of their ancestors. They pleaded and were granted permission to offer Rhodes a traditional farewell instead. Calvert Nkomo reenacted their enticingly melodic chant. When I asked him what it meant, he interpreted: "It means, 'We're burying a white man. Forgive us.'"

On board a bus from Bulawayo to Great Zimbabwe, my ultimate destination, I asked a schoolboy in an adjacent seat if he knew anything about Great Zimbabwe, the most famous of all the stone *zimbabwes* (or *madzimbabwe* as the Shona call them). He told me that it was the center of a great civilization, built by the Shona people, and that they lived in dome-shaped huts. It turns out that many schoolchildren in Zimbabwe are brought to Great Zimbabwe on field trips every year. In this country, the awareness and appreciation of the black precolonial past is much more evolved than what one encounters in the more recently democratic South Africa. In fact, the ruins of Great Zimbabwe constitute a national source of pride

Rhodes's sacrilegious burial in hallowed Matopos

244

Precariously balanced boulders of Matopos

President Robert Mugabe in 1981, witnessing the repatriation of national treasures

that is the legacy of all citizens, regardless of ethnicity. These ruins are the symbolic center of the independent republic, a tribute to African agency and black precolonial civilization.

It is no coincidence that the nation has renamed itself after Great Zimbabwe, that the medieval stone settlement appears on the national coinage. But it was not always so. When white explorers such as Carl Mauch first stumbled across this incredible city in 1871, they were unwilling to believe that Africans could have built anything so grand. Even a century later, in the 1970s under white rule, guidebooks were censored by the government. As in South Africa, archaeologists were compelled to deny that this city was built by Africans, even though evidence gathered proved beyond doubt that this was the capital of a vast and thriving African state that had lasted more than 300 years.

Before Robert Mugabe's Zimbabwe African National Union Patriotic Front (ZANU-PF) took power in 1980 from the embattled white-minority government in what was then Rhodesia, Zimbabwe's past had long been central to the propaganda efforts to preserve the racist regime.[11] In 1979, only a year prior to the end of white rule, Prime Minister Ian Smith remarked, "I think few people realize at the beginning of this century there was no civilization, so to speak, here amongst the black people."[12] Such musings had been the basis of a seventy-year dictatorship under which Africans—Shona and Ndebele—lived separately as legal citizens.

As we have seen, the stone ruins, or *zimbabwes,* scattered across the Limpopo valley and plateau, extend as far as Botswana, Mozambique, and the eastern Transvaal. They were always the awkward physical refutation of Bantu inferiority and the apparent civilizational nullity of the ignominious "kaffir."[13] To the Shona, the largest ethnic group in Zimbabwe whose ancestors were the builders of the ruins, these structures were emblematic of a past "greatness" embodying notions of ingenuity, will, resistance, and strength.[14] During the 1896 rebellion in Mashonaland and the civil war of the sixties and seventies, names of the spirit mediums who lived in the early Shona states reappeared as symbols of nationalist inspiration.[15] Realizing their power, the Smith regime apparently tried to co-opt these symbols through interesting antiguerrilla tactics. In 1973, for instance, leaflets written in Shona were distributed by plane to villagers. One was from the Great Medium of Mhondoro Mutota and read as follows:

I know that my children Nehanda, Chidyamawuya and Chiwodza Memera have been captured by the terrorists. And I see that Chiwawa [presumed to have been a medium supporting the guerrillas] has committed a great crime. The ancestral spirits do not want bloodshed in this country. I shall work with the Government. I shall not die helping the terrorists, no. I know them. When the terrorists come to this area they must be destroyed by the people working with the soldiers.[16]

Zimbabwes scattered through the Limpopo valley posed a silent rebuttal to the Rhodesian government's claim that the black southern (Zimbabwean and South Africans) Africans had no culture of their own to speak of.

But more pervasive than such insidiously clever attempts to use African culture against Africans were the systematic efforts to deny the indigenous character of that culture altogether. To explain away Zimbabwean ruins and the surviving art of the Shona, European historians and anthropologists constructed myths of a one-way cultural diffusion whereby Africans were the beneficiaries of the Semitic Phoenicians or Sabeans. In fact, colonialist historiography maintained British and South African settlers were only the latest of a series of colonists—beginning with the Semites, who were succeeded by the Portuguese—of whom the Shona have always been the servants. And according to the tenets of pseudoscientific racism, left to their own devices, the Africans could never have evolved beyond a Stone Age culture. It is tempting to believe such fabrications were without influence except within Rhodesia's borders, but I for one first heard of Great Zimbabwe in 1974, reading the Oxford scholar John Baker's magnum opus *Race* for a class at Cambridge: Baker argues that much of the greater part of the building took place only after contact had been made with foreign traders (Arab, Indian, Persian, and Indonesian) on the coast.[17]

Great Zimbabwe is the largest of the extensive group of stone ruins situated on the high granite country of the Zimbabwean plateau. We only have a few primary written sources on Great Zimbabwe, although we know from archaeological evidence that this community seemed to inherit the primacy of Mapungubwe and was situated at the western edge of a large hill on the southern fringes of the Great Crescent. It has been estimated that about 150 ruins built in the Great Zimbabwe style, or in the later Khami style in this area, and perhaps as many as another fifty have been destroyed since the 1890s by reckless excavators.[18]

The wealth and influence in this region seem to have grown both with the increasing size of their herds of cattle and because they were able to extend their control over trade routes and force traders, especially to the southwest and southeast, to pay them tribute.

The builders of Great Zimbabwe copied features of the stone walling at Mapungubwe, but greatly improved the inherited techniques, creating their own massive walled city with hardly any straight faces, right-angled junctions, or rectangular spaces. Granite rocks were collected from the slopes of the low, bare granite hills around the city. Slabs were quarried from the parent rock by firing, and then rapidly quenched with cold water before being broken up into blocks and sheets and trimmed by hammers and iron chisels to make the components of the high, broad walls. Natural rocks were also incorporated into the building.

The blocks were fitted together in the bottom layer of the walls. In subsequent layers, their faces were very carefully matched for thickness. They were fitted together so closely there was no need for mud between the blocks. Entrances through the thick walls were rounded, set off by low buttresses and stone pillars. Decorative turrets were built along the tops of the outer walls. Not an ounce of mortar was used throughout the whole stone construction. Dry-stone walling was of course common in medieval Europe for boundary walls on farms; but unlike those in Europe, the stones of Great Zimbabwe were standardized in shape, size, and weight to permit a smooth and regular finish to the wall face. There is also no bonding of the stones at wall intersections. The builders must have possessed considerable technological sophistication.

* * *

There are two groups of ruins, one on the hill and one in the valley below, which by AD 1250 was well populated, perhaps with as many as 18,000 people.[19] It appears that royalty dwelled within the great walls, and farmers and workers lived outside. The walls of the main enclosure were built in a series of irregular curves to match the rounded edges of the *daga* (clay) huts; some of the walls partitioned and adjoined thatched *daga* huts to form a single integrated unit. These huts were sometimes more than 30 feet across with thick external walls built entirely of *daga* and finished with colors ranging from pale ochre tones to rich dark reds. Their surfaces were painted and decorated with moldings of abstract patterns creating the effect of sculpture rather than architecture. These "huts" were sometimes massive structures equivalent in some cases to two- or three-story buildings.[20] The ordinary townspeople lived in cramped conditions, while on the hill there were probably nearly fifty separate households living behind the stone walls. David Beach conjures up a picture of what urban living may have been like at Great Zimbabwe:

Inside the wall that enclosed the main site, the huts were so close together that their eaves must have

Panorama of Great Zimbabwe, Africa's largest stone structure south of the pyramids

been touching. Judging from the more modern settlements of the Shona, Zimbabwe must have had an appearance and atmosphere far different from that of today. A great deal of the valley, now green, must have been trampled bare by the passage of feet. From cockcrow to the evening, the noise must have been tremendous. In certain weather conditions the smoke of hundreds if not thousands of cooking fires would have created conditions approaching that of smog. And, since so far there is no evidence for more elaborate arrangements, the people can't have gone very far to defecate, with the result that disease may have been as much a factor at Zimbabwe as in some of its European counterparts. Zimbabwe has often been viewed through an aura of romance, but perhaps a cloud of smoke and flies would be more appropriate from a standpoint of archaeological accuracy. The contrast between the ruler and the ruled must have been quite striking.[21]

The western enclosure was, perhaps, also the home of spirit mediums. The structures here are hauntingly beautiful, having double entrances—for the use of spirits as well as men. If the relationship between the ruler and the spirit mediums was as important as it was in nineteenth-century Shona society, then the former controlled the political, military, and legal spheres as well as the distribution of the land, while the national spirit medium (the vehicle for communicating with the ancestors) conducted many of the ceremonies necessary for rain, fertility, and harvests; ratified and selected rulers; and would have had separate dwellings.[22]

While such arguments are inevitably speculative, most historians agree that Great Zimbabwe's decline around 1500 had largely to do with ecological degradation: over-population and the corresponding depletion in arable

Farmers and workers dwelt in the valley surrounding the great walls within which lived the Shona royalty.

land, clean water, and other sustaining resources. Under these pressures, members of the stone-building culture migrated to the north and to the southeast to found the Mutapa Karanga states and the Torwa kingdom, respectively. The construction of stone *zimbabwes* would cease in the seventeenth century in the south, slightly earlier in the north. The Portuguese explorer Antonio Fernandes actually saw one in the process of being built in the north in 1511.[23] But his is the last mention of the construction of a *zimbabwe* and thereafter, Portuguese explanations of the "ruins" are linked with the Biblical story of the Queen of Sheba.

Great Zimabawe's origins were a metaphor—the central metaphor—for the intelligence of black Africans and their right to govern their own land and nurture their own traditions. What is most ironic is that Europeans located many of their most far-fetched fantasies in the depths of sub-Saharan Africa, then argued widely that only non-Africans could have placed them there. Nineteenth-century scholars attempted to prove the existence of the mythical city of Ophir. They exploited Bibli-

Great Zimbabwe

cal material that described the merchant fleets and the goods used to decorate Solomon's temple—brought from faraway places—to determine if these ancient mariners had been to Ophir. Some scholars chose sites on the Malaccan coast or southern Arabia, but Jean d'Anville in *Géographie Ancienne* suggested that Ophir might be found in southeast Africa, as did the Orientalist Etienne Marc Quatremere in the 1830s in his *Mémoire sur les Pays d'Ophir*.[24] The available Arabic documents reveal virtually no knowledge of the region except that it was a source of gold and that states existed there. The Portuguese had long thought, and said as much, that the ancient kingdom deep in the country of Benamatapa, as they mispronounced Munhumutapa, in southern Africa was Ophir.

As fabulous stories about the abundance of minerals in the Munhumutapa Empire were widely circulated on the East African coast, the Portuguese began to associate it with the Biblical story of the royal visit of the Queen of Sheba, who brought gold and precious stones from the land of Ophir—which was supposed to be in the hinterland of Ethiopia. They were accustomed to calling the Mutapa Empire eastern Ethiopia and romanticized it just as they did Prester John. Based on these legends, George McCall Theal asked:

> Were not these the mines from which the Queen of Sheba got the gold which she presented to the King Solomon? said the Portuguese enthusiasts. Was not Masapa the ancient Ophir? Why even then the Kalanga Kaffirs called the mountain close to the residence of their great chief Fura, and the Arabs called it Aufur, what was that but a corruption of Ophir.[25]

By the mid-nineteenth century, rumors of a massive town of stone ruins circulated widely both in southern

The Munhumutapa emperor as depicted by the French c. 1650

Africa and in Europe through the writings of the geographer Karl Ritter and were noted in H. Kiepert's *Atlas of the Ancient World*. German missionaries were said to have found an ancient town with pyramids, the site of an ancient Egyptian people whose relics lay ignored. H. Rider Haggard made a fortune in his imaginative retracing of King Solomon's visit to his mines in his famous novel, *King Solomon's Mines*.

From these myths it was deduced that the ruins were storage rooms for gold, diamonds, copper, and other ornaments. The Ancient Ruins Company Limited, a joint-stock company, was formed in 1894 under the Honorable Maurice Gifford with the explicit goal of melting down any gold objects found in the *zimbabwes*. With a monopoly to exploit all the ancient ruins south of the Zambezi River, hired hands of the Ancient Ruins Company went about ransacking and pillaging the *zimbabwes* for six years, until the company was dissolved in 1900 because of financial mismanagement and public outrage over its destructiveness.[26] The pillagers went through forty-nine *zimbabwes,* including the Great Zimbabwe, destroying unknown structures and artifacts and looting many precious objects.[27]

But not all travelers, anthropologists, and pseudo-archaeologists adhered to foreign creators in explaining the *zimbabwes* hypothesis. Reverend Samuel S. Dornan, who systematically gathered oral traditions among Shona elders, wrote in 1915, "In face of the internal evidence yielded by the buildings themselves and the confirmatory native traditions, I do not see how one can resist the conclusion that these ruins were built by a race of Negroes, and most likely by the ancestors of those who still live on the country and at no distant date."[28] And he reported to the thirteenth annual meeting of the South African Association for the Advancement of Science in 1915:

> The foreign influence theory must be given up. Zimbabwe was built by natives, inhabited by natives, and recently abandoned, probably not more than 300 years ago. It is just as probable and equally scientific to assume that the old natives could, and did, attain a sufficient degree of intelligence and skill in building, than to postulate some unknown foreign race, who came from where is not clear, nor for what purpose, erected these structures, and then as mysteriously vanished, leaving no other trace of their presence. Such a method of explanation, however, romantic or alluring, is only a modern example of the old fallacy ignotum er ignotus, a reversal of the process of evolution in respect of human culture."[29]

A shift had come among archaeologists at the turn of the century, when, at last, the only two scientifically trained ones, David Randall-MacIver and Gertrude Caton Thompson, offered African answers to formerly unanswerable questions.[30] The British Association for the Advancement of Science sent MacIver to investigate the *zimbabwes* and prepare a special report. He ignored all existing hypotheses and surveyed several *zimbabwes,* not just the great one; and in 1906, his *Medieval Rhodesia* presented proof of autochthonous African development. The *zimbabwes,* he concluded, were "unquestionably African in every detail, and belong to a period which is fixed by foreign imports as in general medieval."[31] He based this judgment on foreign objects, such as Chinese porcelains, Arab glass and beads, and local pottery, which he dated to the European medieval period. As these objects were found within the stone walls, he concluded that the objects predated the walls or were at least contemporaneous to them. He thus became the first trained archaeologist to establish a scientific basis for the theory of the African origins of the Zimbabwe civilization. Succeeding archaeologists were able to establish that there were roughly four successive periods of civilization between the first and sixteenth centuries AD. The civilization that would ultimately build the *zimbabwes* was therefore shown to have begun long before the European medieval period. But MacIver's research was dismissed for a "lack of first-hand knowledge of the Negro."[32] An indignant Richard Nicklin Hall responded, "The Bantu are not a progressive people. Nor is it possible that the primitive Bantu of medieval times had the capacity to suddenly evolve, without the slightest influence from outside, the renaissance which resulted, so Professor MacIver claims, in the Zimbabwe Temple and the oldest rock mine."[33]

Gertrude Caton Thompson also undertook her own archaeological investigation of the *zimbabwes* under the auspices of the British Association for the Advancement of Science in 1929. She dated the *zimbabwes* by the artifacts found within their foundations, to establish the earliest date for the primary human settlement of the area as well as that of the erection of the *zimbabwes* themselves. On the basis of stratigraphical evidence, according to which the bottom layer is assumed to be earliest, Thompson not only established dates for the construction of the *zimbabwes* as being earlier than the general "medieval period" claimed by MacIver, but also confirmed Schofield's suggestion that the founding civilization was the result of successive periods of development. She calculated that the original date for Great Zimbabwe was between the seventh and ninth centuries AD and that its Golden Age was around the fifteenth century.[34] Since then archaeologists have been able to establish an outline of sociopolitical and economic organization contributing to a reconstruction of the rise and decline of Great Zimbabwe. Despite this evidence, the racist government of Rhodesia, and its antecedents, refused to acknowledge the Africans' role in its creation.

Great Zimbabwe is the largest stone structure in Africa south of the pyramids, the grandest achievement of the civilization that founded Mapungubwe three centuries earlier, and, perhaps, the most magnificent architectural feat of any of the Continent's precolonial cultures. At the height of its prosperity in the fifteenth century, this settlement had an estimated population of 18,000, a figure which led the archaeologist Thomas Huffman to refer to it as southern Africa's first town or city.[35] Walking around these grand ruins, I encountered dozens of schoolchildren on field trips, as well as adults on holiday. One woman told me she had been here at least eight times. For people here, Zimbabwe has become a symbol of national unity, an icon of the glory of the past and their hopes for the future. I, too, confess to having a particular

affection for this place, one unlike anything I have felt for few other ruins in sub-Saharan Africa. This is because Great Zimbabwe epitomizes the process of reclaiming African history and culture that is only just beginning in South Africa, and in many other parts of the Continent. But it *will* happen, and with it the final defeat of a tradition of racist intellectual history that views black African peoples as lacking the unique gift of humanity: the capacity to create beauty and to contemplate it. Then the truth I have been able to experience myself throughout these journeys into Africa's hidden past will become apparent even to the great many in the West for whom "Africa" today connotes only poverty, war, famine, and disease: The civilizations created on this continent over the past five millennia were just as splendid, just as beautiful, just as representative of the ennobled human spirit as any on the face of this earth.

The famous conical tower

As I have said, when I was an undergraduate, the cause of freedom for Rhodesia and South Africa seemed more urgent and relevant than any other decolonization struggle, even those in Angola or Mozambique, as important as these were. The struggle with the colonial presence of white minority settlers in these southern African nations seemed to us uncannily like our own daily confrontation with a white majority in the United States. Unlike black nations caught in long-distance relations with their colonial oppressors in Europe, our brethren in South Africa and Rhodesia lived among their oppressors, as we did. It was not uncommon to joke about the parallels between the Union of South Africa (known as the USA) and our very own USA. And years later, friends of mine who attended President Mandela's inauguration would liken it to the great March on Washington—although, in fact, given the status of blacks in South Africa before the end of apartheid compared with our own before the civil rights movement, Mandela's triumph was an even more astonishing stride toward freedom.

Because of this particular affinity that I and other African Americans had felt for the people here, I wanted to end my series of journeys in southern Africa. Had anyone predicted a mere decade ago that at the end of the century—a century that began with the colonial scramble to divide the Continent—South Africa and not Nigeria would be black Africa's largest and most promising democracy, he or she would have been laughed out of the room. The course of Africa's history has proved impossible to anticipate, even in the short term. Today, even after the return of some semblance of democracy in Nigeria following decades of military dictatorship, South Africa is the embodiment of our hopes for the ideal of a democratic, multiracial society in sub-Saharan Africa.

South Africa's and Zimbabwe's new and evolving rela-

A postcard from the days of the Rhodesian government reinforces the false mythology of Great Zimbabwe, with the figure of the Queen of Sheba on the conical tower.

tion to their pasts are the model for reestablishing the agency of Africans in the creation of their own civilizations. And this process is central not only to the establishment of a new political order but to a new metaphysical order as well, to ending the one created by a millennium of European projection, subjugation, and denial of the very humanity of black people. Denial of the African's basic capacity to write, to remember, to philosophize, to create artworks, to build grand architectural monuments, indeed to possess a cultural heritage worth preserving, worth celebrating.

The black newspaper editor T. Thomas Fortune mused nearly a century ago:

> Bloodshed and usurpations, the rum jug and the Bible—these will be the program of the white race in Africa, for, perhaps, a hundred years . . . But in the course of time, the people will become educated not only in the cruel and grasping nature of the white man, but in the knowledge of their power, their priority ownership of the soil, and in the desperation which tyranny and greed never fail to breed for their own destruction.[36]

Fortune could not have imagined that Africa would be so devastatingly ravaged by internal ethnic hatred in a hundred years. As the U.N. Secretary-General Kofi Annan observed recently, today no fewer than seven million Africans are "refugees, displaced persons, and still-vulnerable returnees," including 6.5 million in Angola; 550,800 in Ethiopia and Eritrea; 310,000 within Sierra Leone; and 440,000 more who have fled Sierra Leone for Guinea and Liberia. How important, how urgent, in the face of such statistics—as well as equally disheartening rates of infant mortality, HIV infection, and figures for per capita income—can the restoration of the historical record be? How vital is this process of recovering the truth and richness of the past? For those concerned with the importance of truth for its own sake, and with the less brutally material elements of human dignity, it is important enough per se to answer the legions of philosophers, theologians, scientists, and pseudoscientists engaged in the millennium-old project of vulgar denials and distortions of the record of African cultural and intellectual attainment.

But I would suggest there is a far more practical imperative as well. As Africans struggle to extricate themselves from the Continent's legacy of colonial exploitation, as they strive to promote tolerance and respect for human rights and to embrace democratic principles, what could be more important to their acceptance and fulfillment of a collective purpose than the awareness of a collective past, a sense of a shared place in the continuum of human history? Likewise, what better way to enlist the cooperation of the Western world in this purpose than by defeating condescension to and outright denial of the Africans' capacity to master their own destiny? Whatever Africa's most urgent practical problems, the long-term growth of the Continent will depend on an investment in such education at all levels. The revelation of the African past—heretofore hidden, denied, minimized—must comprise a central place in educational reform, in Africa to be sure, but also throughout the rest of the world. I hope this book and its companion television series can make a modest contribution to this inevitable process. For ignorance about African civilization is the final frontier in the next century's quest to understand the human experience in all its splendor, depth, and vanity. With the restoration of the particularity of Africa's grand past, perhaps a century hence other writers will note that the future, the next millennium, belongs to Africa and to the Africans.

EPILOGUE

In October 1973, I boarded a train in London and "went up" to Clare College at the University of Cambridge, where I hoped to take a degree in English Literature before returning to America to study law or medicine. I knew very little about Cambridge or Oxford, just as I had known very little about Harvard or Yale before I went off to college. But I had long yearned to study at some combination of these schools, and as luck would have it, because of a certain openness created in the late sixties by fledgling programs called "affirmative action," I would enjoy this privilege.

At Yale, where I majored in History, I received one of the prized Mellon Fellowships that enabled students to continue their studies at Oxbridge. Each year two Yalies were sent to Cambridge, and two Cantabridgians to Yale. Because I was the first African American to receive it, my father christened it "the Watermelon Fellowship." Little did we know how prescient that nickname would be. As soon as I arrived at Clare, after a three-month summer internship at *Time* magazine's London bureau as a correspondent, several English students and faculty members, one after another asked if I had met someone called Kwame Anthony Appiah. I had no idea from whence this name "Appiah" hailed, or even how I should spell it. But

one thing I became certain of: Since white people at home rarely asked me if I had met, or knew, a person who turned out to be white, the same probably was true over here. When at the end of that first week I finally did meet this Appiah fellow, I told him that the one thing I was certain about him was that he must be some sort of black man! That meeting marked the beginning of a deep and intimate friendship, an ideal friendship of brothers, that has lasted for the past twenty-six years.

Like just about all of my black friends back at Yale, I had been pre-med or pre-law, depending on the day. And while I found that I had an affinity, and a passionate interest, in the courses being offered by the fledgling program in Afro-American Studies, I never would have declared that as a major. It could be an avocation at best. The last thing my father had said to me when I left home in 1969 for Yale was, "Don't go up there majoring in Black Studies, whatever that is, because your ass has been black for eighteen years." Then he added for good measure, "And don't Jim Crow yourself with black roommates. Get to know the white kids. You just might learn something."

The first thing I did when I arrived in New Haven was to board with three other young black men, and then enroll in a class on the Harlem Renaissance, obedient son that I am. But learning about my blackness was not going to be center stage for me; I wanted to "prove myself" in a standard discipline, and gravitated, by fits and starts, into American political history, working under the great American historian John Morton Blum. But trying to understand the implications of being a black man in the early seventies in America was my silent second discourse, a passion that burned continuously, a low yet steady fire that, try as I might, I could not extinguish.

Oxford and Cambridge were metaphors for me just as were Harvard, Princeton, and Yale. Smart people studied there, and these schools were mentioned whenever the names of the world's great universities were, so I wanted to study at these places, even when I was a little boy. For as long as I can remember, I had wanted to be a Rhodes scholar, even when my friends wanted to be Willie Mays or Bill Russell. What, exactly, a Rhodes scholar was, however, I had not the faintest idea. Crushed when I failed to receive a Rhodes, the Mellon came to my rescue instead, and that made a world of difference.

I decided that I wanted to study—or "read," as they say at Oxbridge—English Literature, but with some sort of comparative focus on African and African American literature. I cannot even begin to explain how anomalous this latter desire seemed to my tutors at Cambridge, nor the hours of debate it caused. Through another African student at Clare, a brilliant philosopher and passionate Pan-Africanist, O. A. "Dapo" Ladimeji, I learned that someone called Wole Soyinka, a Nigerian playwright in political exile, had just come up to Cambridge as a visiting professor at Churchill College. Soyinka had spent twenty-seven months in Nigerian prisons for protesting the Biafran war. Once released, he had again incurred the wrath of Nigerian strongman General Gowon by publishing his prison memoirs, *The Man Died.* Perhaps he would agree to work with me.

I had absolutely no idea who this Soyinka fellow was. I had never studied African literature, but I had studied African Art History through the works of Robert Farris Thompson, one of the few white professors at Yale whose classes the black kids still attended during our "May Day" strike in the spring of 1970. We called Thompson "the blackest man at Yale," even at the height of our blackest cultural nationalism. Thompson, for us, was the real deal: He was fluent in God-only-knew how many African languages; he played the conga drum; he imitated African dances to illustrate his lectures; he knew every form of the "soul handshake," and he called us all "my brother" or "my sister." If there was a key to opening up the secrets of the heart of darkness, Thompson possessed it—or knew where it was hidden. Thompson—a Texan—was our goat path, the Dixie highway, that led to Guinea, as the novelist Jean Toomer once put it. Even the "blackest" among us, the most essentialist, defended Thompson's right to teach in "Afro-Am," as we had nicknamed the new academic field.

But Thompson could not help me now, as I walked from Clare to Churchill College to attempt to persuade Soyinka to supervise my work in African Literature. I had lived and worked in Tanzania for much of the 1970–71 academic year, and I had traveled across the Equator, accompanied by a Harvard student I had happened to meet in Zanzibar. The two of us hitchhiked from Dar es Salaam to Kinshasa without ever leaving the ground. That should help me, I thought, as I passed Cripps Court at St. John's College, named in honor of Anthony Appiah's maternal ancestors.

"Well, I have to say that you don't know very much about African literature," Soyinka told me bluntly after we had chatted awhile, "but at least you aren't polluted by all of that *Muntu* bullshit that so many black Americans are swearing by these days." *Muntu* was the title of a book by German scholar Janheinz Jahn in which he claimed that he had boiled down all of the wide variety of Africa's cultures and belief systems to half a dozen or so eternal recurring principles. What Soyinka did not know was that, in preparation for our own meeting, I had committed these very principles to memory, desperate to impress him with the depth of my knowledge about Mother Africa.

"*Muntu?*" I asked with a straight face. "Never heard of it."

The lure of Soyinka's and Appiah's elegance of mind sounded the death knell for my pre-medical and pre-law fantasies. Slowly, I began to realize that I had wanted to be a scholar all along. Soyinka and Appiah, over the past quarter of a century, have patiently led me through their worlds, the worlds of the Yoruba and the Asante peoples specifically and, by extension, the civilizations that African people have been making for thousands of years. Since our time together at Cambridge, I have traveled with them in Africa, I have attended African ritual ceremonies with them, I have argued, quarreled, and debated with them—endlessly it seems—over the fine points of African history, philosophy, and literature, and their necessarily complex relation both to the worlds that our ancestors created in the New World and the worlds that they left behind on the Continent. The irony of my education is that I went to Cambridge because of a certain Anglophilic urge, only to become captivated by a couple of Africans along with students such as Ladimeji and Ronnie Mutebe, now the *Kabaka,* or king of the Buganda people of Uganda, and the other students who formed the Cambridge African Student Union. My friendships with Appiah and Soyinka have been my gain in the great long run. And this book, and its accompanying film series, are dedicated to them, an exiled native son's attempt to thank them and pay homage to the civilizations that these brothers embody and have opened to me so very generously.

NOTES

CHAPTER I

1. Phillis Wheatley, "On Being Brought from Africa to America," in *The Norton Anthology of African American Literature*, ed. Henry Louis Gates, Jr., and Nellie Y. Mckay (New York: W. W. Norton & Co., 1997).

2. See *The Life and Writings of Frederick Douglass*, Philip S. Foner, ed., vol. 1 (New York: International Publishers, 1950), 351.

3. Berghahn, *Images of Africa in Black American Literature* (Totowa, N.J.: Rowman and Littlefield, 1977), 40. Bradford Chambers, ed., *Chronicles of Black Protest* (New York: New American Library: 1969), 52.

4. Frederick Douglass refering to the African Civilization Society, *Apropos of Africa: sentiments of Negro American leaders on Africa from the 1800s to the 1950s;* compiled and edited by Adelaide Cromwell Hill and Martin Kilson (London: Cass, 1969), 164.

5. Edward Wilmot Blyden, in Marion Berghahn, *Images of Africa in Black American Literature* (Totowa, N.J.: Rowman and Littlefield, 1977), 51.

6. Henry S. Wilson, *Origins of West African Nationalism* (London: Macmillan, 1969), 242, 246.

7. Ibid.

8. Dorothy Sterling, ed., *Speak Out in Thunder Tones: Letters and Other Writings by Black Northerners, 1787–1865* (Garden City, N.Y.: Doubleday 1973), 1.

9. Richard Newman, *African American Quotations* (Phoenix, Ariz.: Oryx Press, 1998), 13.

10. Frederick Douglass, "The Claims of the Negro Ethnologically Considered." An address before the Literary Societies of Western Reserve College at Commencement, July 12, 1854 (Rochester, N.Y.: Lee, Mann and Co., Daily American Office, 1854).

11. Alain Locke, ed.; with an introduction by Arnold Rampersad, *The New Negro* (New York: Maxwell Macmillan International, 1992.).

12. Ulysees Lee, *The ASNLH, The Journal of Negro History, and American Scholarly Interest in Africa,* in *Africa Seen by American Negroes* (Paris: Présence Africaine, 1958), 409.

13. Newman, *African American,* 17.

14. Ibid., 15.

15. Leopold Sedar Senghor, *Selected Poems* (London: Rex Collings, 1976), 33.

16. Berghahn, *Images,* 128–129.

17. Ibid., 130–131.

18. Richard Wright, *Black Power: A Record of Reactions in a Land of Pathos* (New York: Harper Perennial, 1995).

19. Ibid., xxvi.

20. Newman, *African American,* 16.

21. W.E.B. Du Bois, *Dusk of Dawn. An Essay toward an Autobiography of a Race Concept* (New York: Schocken Books, 1969), 117, 123.

22. See Edward H. Mckinley, *The Lure of Africa: American Interests in Tropical Africa, 1919–1939* (Indianapolis, Ind.: Bobbs-Merrill, 1974), 68.

23. Adrian Room, *African Placenames* (Jefferson, N.C.: 1994), 13.

24. Valetin Y. Mudimbe, *The Idea of Africa* (Bloomington, Ind.: Indiana University Press, 1994), 26–27.

25. Ali Mazrui, *The Africans: A Triple Heritage* (Boston: Little, Brown, and Co., 1986), 23.

26. Joseph E. Harris, ed., *Africa and Africans as Seen by Classical Writers. The William Leo Hansberry African History Notebook* (Washington, D.C.: Howard University Press, 1977), 82.

27. Ibid.

28. Homer, *Odyssey,* Book 1; translated by Robert Fagles; Introduction and Notes by Bernard Knox (New York: Viking, 1996), 25–30.

29. *Odyssey,* Book 5, 309 320.

30. Diodorus Siculus 3, 1–5.

31. Mudimbe, *The Idea of Africa,* 78.

32. Ibid., 78.

33. Georg Wilhem Friedrich Hegel, *The Philosophy of History* (New York: Dover Publications, Inc., 1956), 99.

34. C. G. Seligman, *Races of Africa* (London: T. Butterworth, Ltd., 1930), 96.

35. Basil Davidson, *Old Africa Rediscovered* (London: Gollancz, 1964), 29, 37.

36. Hugh Trevor-Roper, *The Rise of Christian Europe* (New York: Harcourt, Brace Jovanovich, 1965), 9, and also see opening remarks of the first lecture of a series by Hugh Trevor-Roper by the same name in *The Listener Magazine* (Nov. 28, 1963), 71.

37. Christopher Stringer and Robin Mckie, *African Exodus: The Origins of Modern Humanity* (New York: Henry Holt, 1997).

Victoria Falls, Zimbabwe

38. Mazrui, *The Africans,* 12.

39. Caroline Neale, *The Idea of Progress in the Revision of African History* in *Writing Independent History: African Historiography* (Westport, Conn.: Greenwood Press, 1985), 112–117.

40. John Reader, *Biography of a Continent* (New York: Alfred A. Knopf, 1997), 4.

41. Ibid., 368.

42. Jared Diamond, *Guns and Germs: The Fates of Human Societies* (New York: W. W. Norton, 1997), 377.

CHAPTER 2

1. Dorothy Sterling, ed., *Speak Out in Thunder Tones: Letters and Other Writings by Black Northerners, 1787–1865* (Garden City, N.Y.: Doubleday, 1973), 4, 28.

2. Scott Macleod, *Time* (international edition), "The Nile Kingdoms" March 24, 1997, 50. "Afrocentric" Egyptology is supported by an international scholarly literature. However, it has been noted by Professor Ann Macy Roth of Howard University in an unpublished paper entitled "A Letter to My Egyptological Colleagues" that in America, Afrocentric Egyptology is seen less as a scholarly field than a political and educational movement, aimed at increasing the self-esteem and confidence of African Americans by stressing the achievements of African civilizations, especially that of ancient Egypt. In this sense, Egyptology is profoundly Eurocentric, and plays to the prevalent cultural background of its intended audience. But she also shows that due to the classical Christian focus of Western culture, the distribution of writing, the unconscious racism of early scholars, and a general ignorance of the rest of Africa, "traditional Egyptology" is a profoundly Eurocentric profession and should strive to find ways to come to terms with "Afrocentric" Egyptologists. For instance, in developing her argument that Egyptologists tend to disregard racial claims too hastily, she makes use of Bruce Williams's observation that few Egyptians, ancient or modern, would have been able to get a meal at a white lunch counter during the 1950s. Also see Frank Snowden, "Images and Attitudes: Ancient Views of Nubia and the Nubians," *Expedition* 35, no. 2 (1993): 40. He shows that the ancients were able to distinguish a continuum of physical features, including color from the Mediterranean into the interior of Africa (along this continuum, Egyptians were clearly distinguished as physically different from the dark and black-skinned peoples designated as Kushites, Ethiopians, and Nubians) and that they were also able to describe a mixed Nubian-Egyptian element in their world.

3. See "Report of the Symposium on 'The Peopling of Ancient Egypt and the Deciphering of the Meroitic Script,' Cairo, 28 Jan.–3 Feb. 1974" in *General History of Africa II: Ancient Civilizations,* ed. G. Mokhtar (Paris: UNESCO, 1990), 38. Abridged edition. And for a historical summary of traditional attitudes prevalent in Sudanese archaeology, see Bruce Trigger, "Paradigms in Sudan Archaeology," *International Journal of African History* (1993): 323–345.

4. E. A. Wallis Budge, "Translation of Diodorus" (iii.2), in *The Egyptian Sudan, Its History and Monuments* (London, 1907), 53.

5. Derek A. Welsby, *The Kingdom of Kush* (Princeton, N.J.: Markus-Weiner Publishers, 1996), 7.

6. Strabo, *Geography,* trans. Horace L. Jones. (first published 1917–1993): 17.1.53ff. Timothy Kendall, "The Kingdom of Kush," *National Geographic,* November 1990, 103.

7. G. A. Gaballa, *History and Culture of Nubia* (Sudan: Ministry of Culture The Higher Council for Antiquities, date unknown), 25.

8. Macleod, *Time,* 51.

9. Gaballa, *Nubia,* 28.

10. Ibid. "The Nile plays a prominent role in Nubian culture, the couple have to go down to the river on their wedding night and wash in its water, to insure prosperity, good health and numerous progeny." Ibid at 46.

11. William Y. Adams, "Medieval Nubia: Another Golden Age," *Expedition* 35, no. 2, (1993): 28–29.

12. For further reading and excellent coverage of this period, see Timothy Kendall, *Kerma and the Kingdom of Kush, 2500–1500 BC: The Archeological Discovery of an Ancient Empire* (Washington, D.C.: National Museum of African Art, Smithsonian Institution, 1997).

13. S. Adam, "The Importance of Nubia: A Link Between Central Africa and the Mediterranean" in *UNESCO General History of Africa II: Ancient African Civilizations,* 141.

14. Chart courtesy of Dr. Timothy Kendall.

15. David Roberts, "Out of Africa: The Superb Artwork of Ancient Nubia," *Smithsonian* 24, no. 3 (June 1993): 90–99.

16. Gaballa, *Nubia,* 19.

17. Margaret Shinnie, *Ancient African Kingdoms* (London: Edward Arnold, 1965), 25.

18. Gaballa, *Nubia,* 28.

19. A. A. Hakem, "The Civilization of Napata and Meroë" in *UNESCO General History of Africa II: Ancient Civilizations of Africa,* ed. G. Mokhtar abridged edition, 180.

20. Stanley Burstein, ed., *Kush and Axum: Ancient African Civilizations* (Princeton: Markus-Weiner Publishers, 1998), 13–14.

21. Ibid., 13.

22. Samia B. Dafa'alla, "Art and Industry: The Achievements of Meroë," *Expedition* 35, no. 2 (1993): 20. A. A. Hakem, *Ancient African Civilizations,* 252–253.

23. Gaballa, *Nubia,* 30.

24. Ibid., 31.

25. Shinnie, *Ancient African Kingdoms,* 28, 29.

26. See Stanley Burstein, ed., "The Rise of Axum and the Decline of Kush" in *Ancient African Civilizations,* 77–97.

27. Jean Leclant, "The Empire of Kush, Napata and Meroë" in *UNESCO General History of Africa II: Ancient Civilizations of Africa,* 293.

28. Letter to author from archaeologist Dr. Timothy Kendall, spring 1999.

CHAPTER 3

1. Robert Benjamin Lewis, *Light and Truth: Collected from the Bible and Ancient and Modern History, containing the Universal History of the Colored and the Indian race, from the Creation of the World to the Present Time* (Boston: published by a Committee of Colored Gentlemen, 1844), 10.

2. Alan Gascon, *Encyclopedia of Africa South of the Sahara,* vol. 2, ed. John Middleton et al. (New York: Simon & Schuster, 1997), 60. Orthodox Monophysite Christianity has been practiced in Ethiopia since the fourth century.

3. For further reading, see Wilson Moses, *The Wings of Ethiopia: Studies in African-American Life and Letters* (Ames: Iowa State University Press, 1991).

4. John Reader, *Biography of an African Continent* (New York: Alfred A. Knopf, 1999), 210.

5. Martin Hall, p. 5. An embassy from the Emperor of Abyssinia had visited Europe in 1706. Letter, Spring 1999.

6. *The Travels of Sir John Mandeville,* translated and edited with an introduction by C.W.R.D. Moseley (New York: Penguin Books, 1983), 170.

7. Tadesse Tamrat, "Church and State in Ethiopia: The Early Centuries," in *African Zion,* eds. Roderick Grierson et al. (New Haven and London: Yale University Press, 1993), 38.

8. Richard Pankhurst, *An Introduction to the Economic History of Ethiopia from Early Times to 1800* (London: Lalibela House, 1961) 138–139.

9. Ibid., 138.

10. Richard Pankhurst, *A Social History of Ethiopia* (Addis Ababa, Ethiopia: Addis Ababa University, Institute of Ethiopian Studies, 1990), 29, 93–94.

11. J. Perruchon, "Histoire des guerres d'Amda Syon, roi d'Ethiopie," *Journal Asiatique* XIV (1889): 271–493.

12. Pankhurst, *A Social History,* 53.

13. Donald E. Crummey, "Church and State in Ethiopia: The Sixteenth to the Eighteenth Century," in *African Zion,* eds. Roderick Grierson et al. (New Haven and London: Yale University Press, 1993), 44.

14. *The Ethiopian Royal Chronicles* (Extracts), ed. Richard Pankhurst (Addis Ababa, Ethiopia: Oxford University Press, 1967), 50.

15. Ibid.

16. Ibid.

17. Pankhurst, *An Introduction to the Economic History of Ethiopia,* 372–374.

18. Unique to the EOC, the *tabot* is a symbolic representation of the Ark of the Covenant. Most often made out of wood, a *tabot* may, however, be carved from stone. It carries the names of the Trinity, Mary, or a saint, depending on the designation of the church. A *tabot* is consecrated over a three day period by a bishop and then may not be destroyed. It nonetheless may be retired to "sleep" for a time in another church until needed once again. See Harold Marcus, ed., introduction to *Haile Selassie, My Life and Ethiopia's Progress,* vol. 2 (East Lansing: Michigan State University Press, 1994), xvi.

19. *Kebra Nagast* (The Glory of Kings), trans. and ed. Miguel F. Brooks (Asmara, Eritrea: Red Sea Press, 1995), xiii.

20. James Bruce, *Travels between the Years 1765 and 1773 through Part of Africa, Syria, Egypt and Arabia into Abyssinia to Discover the Source of the Nile* (London: James Robins & Co. Albion Press, 1812).

21. Ethiopian Christianity has had a long tradition of being under attack for its Sabbath observance and circumcision practices. Sabbath observance was opposed by the Egyptian Coptic Abuns who were at the head of the Ethiopian Church and who condemned it as a Jewish heresy. The monk Ewostatewos attempted to reform it; it came under attack from Roman Catholic Missionaries; in the sixteenth century, Sabbath observance was briefly outlawed under Susneyos and was only reimplemented when King Fasilidas came to the throne.

22. For further reading, see Steven Kaplan, *The Beta Israel (Falasha) in Ethiopia: From Earliest Times to the Twentieth Century* (New York and London: New York University Press, 1992). Harold Marcus also argues that the Beta Israel, or Falasha, might be the descendants of a homegrown Christian Sabbatarian sect who, for the sake of religious purification, somehow or other abandoned Christ as their Messiah. Recent scholarship cites as evidence: Beta Israel holy books are in Ge'ez, not Hebrew; they have monks whose function and activities are uncannily similar to their Christian coun-

terparts; their liturgy and religious music follows Orthodox Church models; and they know nothing about the New Temple holidays and lore and later rabbinic traditions. See also Harold G. Marcus, *A History of Ethiopia* (Berkeley: University of California Press, 1994).

23. Pankhurst, *A Social History,* 244–247.

24. Charles T. Beke, *Abyssinia: A Statement of Facts relative to Transactions between the Writer and the Late British Political Mission to the Court of Sheba* (London: James Madden, 1845), 20–21.

25. M. Abir, "Ethiopia and the Horn of Africa," in *The Cambridge History of Africa,* ed. Richard Gray (Cambridge, England: Cambridge University Press, 1975), 555–556.

26. Bruce, *Travels,* 252.

27. Ibid., 278.

28. Edward Gibbon, *The History of the Decline and Fall of the Roman Empire,* with an introduction by Hugh Trevor-Roper (London: David Campbell, 1993).

29. Edward Ullendorf, *The Ethiopians: An Introduction to the Country and the People* (London: Oxford University Press, 1965), 64.

30. *Ethiopian Royal Chronicles,* 9.

31. Ibid., 10.

32. See Francisco Alvares, *The Prester John of the Indies, 1540* (London: Beckingham and Huntingford, 1961).

33. Harold G. Marcus, "History of Ethiopia and the Horn from 1600 to the Present," *Encyclopedia of Africa South of the Sahara,* vol. 2 (New York: Charles Scribner's Sons, 1997), 68.

34. Reader, *African Continent,* 7.

35. A copy of this letter was sent to the British Museum, and the trustees apparently returned it on December 14, 1872, to King John. *Kebra Nagast,* xxiv.

36. Richard Greenfield, *Ethiopia: A New Political History* (New York: Frederick A. Praeger, 1965), 170.

37. As John Reader describes it in *Africa,* 208.

38. Ibid., 216.

39. Ibid.

40. Ibid.

41. R. Fatovich, "Some Data for the Study of Cultural History in Ancient North Ethiopia," *Nyame Akuma* 10 (1977): 6–18.

42. Conversation with Harold Marcus, June 17, 1999.

43. Stanley Burstein, *Kush and Axum, an Ancient African Civilization* (Princeton, N.J.: Marcus-Weiner Publishers, 1998), 97–98.

44. Stuart Munro-Hay, *Aksum, an Ancient African Civilization,* 70.

45. *Mashafa Senkesar or The Book of the Saints of the Ethiopian Church,* a translation of the Ethiopic synaxarium made from the Manuscripts Oriental 660 and 661 in the British Museum, ed. E. A. Wallis Budge (Cambridge, England: Cambridge University Press, 1928), 15.

46. Stuart Munro-Hay, *Aksum,* 103.

47. Dimetheos Saprichian, *Deux ans de séjour en Abyssinie ou vie morale, politique et religieuse des Abyssiniens* (Jerusalem, 1714).

48. Letter from Roderick Grierson to author, dated spring 1999. Grierson thinks that the odds are not so overwhelmingly stacked against an ark of some kind being in Ethiopia. He argues that if one reads the *Kebra Nagast* carefully one finds its claims are no less credible than those of the Bible. See Roderick Grierson and Stuart Munro-Hay, *The Ark of the Covenant: The True Story of the Greatest Relic of Antiquity* (London: Weidenfeld & Nicolson, 1999).

CHAPTER 4

1. Letter to author from Oscar Straus Schafer dated November 9, 1998.

2. G. S. P. Freeman-Grenville, *Encyclopedia of Africa South of the Sahara,* vol. 2, ed. John Middleton, editor in chief (New York: Charles Scribner's Sons, 1997), 562.

3. *Timbuktu and the Songhay Empire: Al-Sadi's Ta'rikh Al-Sudan Down to 1613 and other Contemporary Documents,* trans. John Hunwick (with an introductory interpretive essay and six appendices) (Leiden, The Netherlands: E. J. Brill, 1999), 280–281.

4. Elias Saad, *Social History of Timbuctou: The Role of Muslim Scholars and Notables, 1400–1900* (Cambridge, England: Cambridge University Press, 1983), 14–21.

5. P. E. H. Hair, research notes, 1997.

6. Felix Dubois, *Timbuctou the Mysterious* (in French), trans. Diana White (1st ed., 1896; 2nd ed., New York: Negro Universities Press, 1969), 218.

7. Research notes 1997.

8. Adu Boahen, J.E. Ade Ajayi, and Michael Tidy, *Topics in West African History* (Burnt Mill, Harlow, Essex, England: Longman Group, 1986) 2–3. See also Nehmiah Levtzion, *Ancient Ghana and Mali* (London: Methuen and Co., Ltd., 1973), 135.

9. Ibid., 55. Islam spread into West Africa with the Arab conquest and occupation of North Africa between AD 639 and AD 708. The first West Africans to be converted were the Berbers, who inhabited the Sahara; by the tenth century, the Sahara was predominantly Islamic. The easiest means of propagating Islam was through the trans-Saharan trade network; through the activities of the Muslim clerics and scholars; and through the individual rulers themselves, who converted and encouraged Muslim institutions and legal systems. Though the Almoravid Empire in the eleventh century did much to strengthen Islam in the Sahara and Senegambia regions, it made little impact on the way of life and beliefs of the farmers, fishermen, and the people in rural areas, according to A. A. Boahen. Boahen et al., *Topics in West African History,* 15–16.

10. D. T. Niane, *Sundiata: The Epic of Old Mali,* trans. G. D. Pickett (Bristol, England: Longmans, Green, and Co. Ltd., 1965), 69.

11. For an in-depth account of Tuareg and Bella relations, see Robin Maugham, *The Slaves of Timbuktu* (New York: Harper, 1961).

12. George A. Corbin, *Native Arts of North America, Africa and the South Pacific, An Introduction,* 1st ed. (New York: Harper & Row, 1988), 120.

13. Roberta Allen, "Mali Adventure, From Timbuktu to Dogon Country," *New York Times,* September 17, 1995.

14. Ashley Montagu, "Mutilated humanity; female circumcision," 55 *The Humanist,* 4 (July 1995): 12.

15. Raymond Maunay defines them as "a despised but feared caste of musician-genealogist-sorcerer parasites," *Research notes, 1997.*

16. *Ibn Battuta in Black Africa,* eds. Said Hamdun and Noël King (Princeton, N.J.: Marcus Weiner Publishers, 1975), 53.

17. Hunwick, *Timbuktu and the Songhay Empire,* 18.

18. Roderick J. MacIntosh and Susan Keech MacIntosh, "The Inland Niger Delta before the Empire of Mali: Evidence from Jenne-Jeno," *Journal of African History* 22 (1981): 1–2.

19. Levtzion, *Ancient Ghana and Mali,* 75.

20. Ibid., 208.

21. Mark de Villiers and Sheila Hirtle, *Into Africa: A Journey through the Ancient Empires* (Ontario: Key Porter Books, 1997), 266.

22. Hunwick, *Timbuktu and the Songhay Empire,* 18.

23. Jean Louis Bourgeois, "The History of the Great Mosques of Djenne," *African Arts* (1987): 54.

24. Niane, *Sundiata,* 83.

25. Mungo Park, *Travels in the Interior District of Africa* (New York: Arno Press and the New York Times, 1971), 194.

26. Brian Gardner, *The Quest for Timbuctoo* (London: Cassell & Co., Ltd., 1968), 14.

27. Boahen, *Topics in West African History,* 31.

28. Hunwick, *Timbuktu and the Songhay Empire,* 29.

29. Ibid., 280–282.

30. Gardner, *The Quest for Timbuctoo,* 120.

CHAPTER 5

1. Richard F. Burton, *Zanzibar: City, Island, and Coast* (London: Tinsley Brothers, 1872).

2. *The Periplus of the Erythraean Sea, by an unknown author; with some extracts from Agatharkhides "On the Erythraean Sea,"* trans. and ed. G.W.B. Huntingford (London: Hakluyt Society, 1980).

3. With notable exceptions, most of the guidebooks used regarded the Swahili as somewhat alien to Africa, whereas scholarship has now successfully demonstrated how East African coastal settlements really are.

4. I do not want to rehash an argument that has in essence been settled, but for hundreds of years, the Swahili were thought of as foreign or as Arabs settled in Africa. Forty years ago, A.J.H. Prins finally recognized the existence of a people called the Swahilis in *The Swahili-speaking peoples of Zanzibar and the East African Coast* (1960); but he, following his time, placed them after "Arabs" and "Persians," and opened the book with the words: "This book is about the Arabs who have settled in Africa, together with the Africanized Persians and coastal Africans." See James de Vere Allen, *Swahili Origins: Swahili Culture and the Shungwaya Phenomenon* (London: James Currey, 1993), 8. And in 1963, Gervase Matthew in the *Oxford History of Africa* suggested that the coastal states were founded by the Swahili themselves.

5. Derek Nurse and Thomas Spear, *The Swahili: Reconstructing the History and Language of an African Society 800–1500* (Philadelphia: University of Pennsylvania Press, 1985), 4.

6. Merrick Posnansky, *Prelude to East African History up to 1700* (London: Oxford University Press, 1966), 106–110. Few historians concerned themselves with tracing the roots of Swahili culture and the nature of its development until the 1980s. Most were content to rely on early accounts by Arab geographers and travelers to trace the spread of an Arab diaspora on the assumption that Swahili culture and society were, in essence, Arab. "The uncritical acceptance of the claims made by the oral legends and chronicles to Arab origin of the cities' founders led some historians to present the East African coast as a historical arena for " 'Arab Vikings.' " Marina Tolmacheva, *The Pate Chronicle* (East Lansing: Michigan State University Press, 1993), 8.

7. Letter from John Middleton to author dated April 21, 1999. Tourism is a

serious problem all the same. In the sixties hippies used to pollute the mosques by sleeping and eating in them until they were forced out. Tourism brings little money to local people, who are often insulted and exploited by the tourists—the hotel keepers are, generally, non-African foreigners.

8. Linda W. Donley-Reid, "A Structuring Structure: The Swahili House," in *Domestic Architecture and the Use of Space: An Interdisciplinary Cross-Cultural Study,* ed. Susan Kent (Cambridge, England: Cambridge University Press, 1990), 119.

9. Letter to author from Ali Mazrui dated April 19, 1999.

10. G.S.P. Freeman-Grenville, *The East African Coast: Select Documents from the First to the Earlier Nineteenth Century* (London: Rex Collings, 1975), 10, 15.

11. Allen, *Swahili Origins.* As a place of Swahili origin, Shungwaya has variously been described in myths as a major empire, a mere town, an impermanent nomadic settlement, and a series of river based states. Traditions represent Shungwaya as an extensive and well-known phenomenon that existed before AD 800 and to which more than twenty-four East African peoples make reference as home. It is thought to have been an alliance of herdsmen, farmers, and hunters who lived within a specific, as yet unknown territory.

12. John Middleton, *The World of the Swahili: An African Mercantile Civilization* (New Haven: Yale University Press, 1992), 9.

13. Freeman-Grenville, *The East African Coast,* 5, 6, 8.

14. Ibid., 8.

15. See the work of archaeologist Mark Horton, particularly, *Shanga 1980: An Interim Report* (Nairobi, Kenya: National Museums of Kenya, 1981); *Shanga: The Archaeology of a Muslim Trading Community on the Coast of East Africa,* with contributions by Helen W. Brown and Nina Mudida (London: The British Institute in Eastern Africa, 1996).

16. Freeman-Grenville, *The East African Coast,* 15–17.

17. Ibid., 20.

18. Ibid., 31.

19. Lamu has a population of around 12,000 people, and about half are immigrants from the Bajun settlements to the north. The Swahili patricians are in the numerical minority, but it is *their* culture that is held as the epitome of Swahili civilization. See Middleton, *The World of the Swahili,* 77.

20. Letter from John Middleton dated April 21, 1999. This Langoni moiety is non-patrician, and largely people of slave ancestry, or of nineteenth-century Hadrahmi descent, hence the attenuated influence of Islam.

21. Nurse and Spear, *The Swahili,* 94–95.

22. Michael N. Pearson, *Port Cities and Intruders: The Swahili Coast, India, and Portugal in the Early Modern Era* (Baltimore, London: Johns Hopkins Press, 1998), 42.

23. Pearson, *Port Cities,* 45.

24. See Donley-Reid "A Structuring Structure: The Swahili House."

25. See *The Pate Chronicle from the MSS 177, 321, 344, & 358 of the Library of the University of Dar es Salaam,* ed. and trans. Marina Tolmacheva (East Lansing: Michigan State University Press, 1993).

26. James Kirkman, *Men and Monuments of the East African Coast* (London, 1964), 22.

27. Freeman-Grenville, *The East African Coast,* 30.

28. Ibid., 33.

29. Ibid., 108–109.

30. Lilyan Kesteloot, *Intellectual Origins of the African Revolution* (Washington, D.C.: Black Orpheus Press, 1972), 86.

31. Basil Davidson, *The African Slave Trade: Precolonial History 1450–1850* (Boston: Little, Brown and Co., 1961), 182.

32. See Edward A. Alpers, "Slave Trade: Eastern Africa" in *Encyclopedia of Africa: South of the Sahara,* ed. John Middleton, vol. 4. For different estimates of the slave trade see: William Gewase Clarence Smith, *The Economics of the Indian Ocean and Red Sea Slave Trades in the 19th Century* (London: Frank Cass, 1987); Thomas M. Ricks, "Slaves and Slave Traders in the Persian Gulf, 18th and 19th Centuries" in *An Assesment of Slave Trades, 1500–1800: Globalization of Forced Labor,* edited by Patrick Manning (U.K.:Variorum, Ashgate Publishing Limited, 1996); Gordon Murray, *Slavery in the Arab World* (New Amsterdam, New York, 1989); Paul E. Lovejoy *Transformations in Slavery: A History of Slavery in Africa* (Cambridge, England: Cambridge University Press).

33. Coastal Muslims have generally been neglected by the Christian government in Nairobi and have aimed for more political recognition and say in their affairs; while in Zanzibar, since the days of the sultanate, overall governmental power has shifted to other ethnic groups from the interior.

34. Letter from Ali Mazrui to author dated spring 1999. The influence from Persia was undoubtedly considerable, being the most powerful empire in the Indian Ocean from about 600 BC until AD 700, but the claims of massive Persian immigration are only partially explained by a historical reality of continuous interaction.

35. John Middleton has argued that claimed origins to Persia was a way of asserting a socially superior position vis-à-vis the ruling Arab houses. It has also been suggested by James de Vere Allen, Nurse and Spear, and Middleton that those who claim Shirazi origins could also have been a more northerly Swahili group whose members moved southward along the coast establishing kingships in the coastal towns. "Shirazi" would have been a metaphor for Shungwaya, or a place or origin in this case.

36. The insights for this paragraph are drawn from a very good study of Swahili identity by Alamin M. Mazrui and Ibrahim Noor Shariff, *The Swahili: Idiom and Identity of an African People* (Trenton, N.J.: Africa World Press, 1994), 48.

37. Mazrui and Shariff, *The Swahili,* 37, 40.

38. Allen, *Swahili Origins,* 1.

CHAPTER 6

1. For further reading, see John Thornton, *Africa and Africans in the Making of the Atlantic World 1480–1680* (Cambridge, England: Cambridge University Press, 1992). Europeans in pre-colonial West Africa were always outnumbered by disease—especially malaria and yellow fever. The absence of natural harbors and the presence of heavy surf, especially along the Slave Coast, meant that slave ships often waited in the roads, while African merchants crossed the surf with their canoes and cargo—including slaves. Along the coast, European forts and castles were built on leased land. With the phase of state formation in the Gold Coast between 1650 and 1750, the "notes" (leases) for these forts changes hands constantly from vanquished to victor. Local people provided the forts with food, labor, and sometimes support in military confrontation with other European powers. Locals could abet the over-

throw of European establishments they disliked, as happened in Elmina in 1637 or the blowing up of the Dutch lodge in Keta in 1737. Europeans also kept "country wives," marrying into local aristocracies, leaving today a distinctive group of people of Afro-European heritage.

2. M. J. Field, *Social Organization of the Ga People* (London: The Crown agents for the colonies, 1940), 72.

3. Imagine this area of West Africa as being divided into two main zones: the coastal states and the interior, hinterland kingdoms.

4. John Reader, *Africa: A Biography of the Continent* (New York: Alfred A. Knopf, 1998), 342.

5. See A. A Boahen, *Topics in West Africa* (Burnt Mill, Harlow, Essex, England: Longman Group, 1986), 106.

6. Letter to author from Professor Emmanuel Akyeampong, spring 1999.

7. Walter Rodney, "The Guinea Coast," in *The Cambridge History of Africa vol. 4: 1600–1790.* General eds. J. D. Fage and Roland Oliver; ed. John Flint (Cambridge, England: Cambridge University Press, 1975–1986), 319.

8. Paul E. Lovejoy, ed, "Africans in Bondage: Studies in slavery and the slave trade": *Essays in honor of Philip D. Curtion, on the occasion of the twenty-fifth anniversary of African studies at the University of Wisconsin* (Madison: University of Wisconsin Press, 1986).

9. Rodney, "The Guinea Coast," 319.

10. Ibid., 320.

11. Ibid., 11.

12. K. Anthony Appiah, "Africa: The Hidden History," *The New York Review of Books* 45, no. 20 (December 17, 1998): 64–72.

13. Ibid.

14. Patrick Manning, *Slavery and African Life: Occidental, Oriental, and African* (Cambridge, England: Cambridge University Press, 1990), 20–24.

15. R. A. Kea "Firearms on the Gold and Slave Coasts," *Journal of African History* 2 (1971): 185–213.

16. Ibid., 194: "Perhaps you wonder how the Negroes came to be furnished with fire-arms, but you will have no reason when you know we sell them incredible quantities, thereby obliging them with a knife to cut your own throats. But we are forced to it; for if we would not, they might be sufficiently stored with that commodity by the English, Danes, and Bradenburghers; and could we all agree together not to sell them any, the English and Zeeland interlopers would abundantly furnish them."

17. Manning, *Slavery and African Life,* 24.

18. Jean Barbot in Freda Wolfson, *Pageant of Ghana* (London: Oxford University Press, 1958), 73.

19. See Dorothy Hammond and Alta Jablow, *Africa That Never Was: The Myth of Africa* (New York: Library of Social Science, 1977).

20. T. Edward Bowdich, *Mission From Cape Castle to Ashantee* (London: John Murray, 1819), 33–38.

21. Ibid., 37–38.

22. F. A. Ranseyer and J. Kuhne, "Four Years in Ashantee" (1875) in Wolfson, *Pageant of Ghana,* 153–154.

23. Richard Burton, *A Mission to Gelele, King of Dahome,* ed. Isabel Burton (London: Tylston and Edwards, 1894), 159–160.

24. I. A. Akinjogbin, *Dahomey and Its Neighbors, 1707–1818* (Cambridge, England: Cambridge University Press, 1967).

25. See Robin Law, "Royal Monopoly and Private Enterprise in the Atlantic Trade: The Case of Dahomey," *Journal of African History* 18, no. 4 (1977): 555–577; Robin Law, "Slave-Raiders and Middlemen, Monopolists and Free-Traders: The Supply of Slaves for the Atlantic Trade in Dahomey c. 1715–1850," *Journal of African History* 30 (1989): 45–68. The kings of Dahomey enjoyed a number of commercial privileges, and controlled the distribution of war captives taken by the Dahomean army, but they were never the sole sellers of slaves. Agaja Trudo, in particular, invaded Ouidah and Allada because he was concerned to secure or reestablish free access to the European trade to safeguard his supplies of European firearms, which the King of Ouidah had just restricted. Law disagrees that Agaja Trudo had either a monopoly of the trade in slaves or of the disposal of war captives, and that there was always an important group of private merchants in Dahomey whose importance grew with the transition from the slave trade to the trade in palm oil during the nineteenth century.

26. Viceroy of Brazil, April 29, 1730, and July 10, 1730, in Pierre Verger, *Flux et reflux de la traite des nègres,* 149–150. But William Snelgrave also wrote that while Agaja Trudo may have been successful in conquering the coastal areas, he had also become "exceedingly cruel towards his people, being always suspicious, that plots and conspiracies are carrying on against him; So that he frequently cuts off some of his great Men on bare Surmises." *New Account of Some Parts of Guinea and the Slave Trade* (London: 1734; reprinted 1971), 154.

27. Frederick E. Forbes, *Dahomey and the Dahomeans. Being the Journals of the Two Missions to the King of Dahomey and Residence at His Capital in the Years 1849 and 1850* (London: Longmans, 1851), 185.

28. Snelgrave, *New Account,* 36–39.

29. See Robin Law, "Slave-Raiders and Middlemen," 54–55. When the Oyo kingdom diverted their slaves from Ouidah to the ports of Badagry and Porto Novo, the shortage became so acute that Tegbesu sold his own subjects, contrary to Dahomean convention, and resorted to judicial enslavement. The organization of the supply of slaves has been controversial. Law establishes that Dahomey operated as a middleman in the supply of slaves, as well as selling its own captives, and that there was a private as a well as a state sector in the Dahomean slave trade.

30. Ulli Beier, *African Mud Sculpture* (London: Cambridge University Press, 1963), 87.

31. Thomas W. Livingston, "Ashanti and Dahomean Architectural Bas-Reliefs," *African Studies Review* 17 (1974): 442.

32. Suzanne Preston Blier, *The Royal Arts of Africa: The Majesty of Form* (New York: Perspectives, Harry N. Abrams, Inc., 1998), 104.

33. Snelgrave, *New Account,* 126.

34. See Stanley B. Alpern, *Amazons of Black Sparta: The Women Warriors of Dahomey* (New York: New York University Press, 1998).

35. See James Lorand Matory, "Man in the City of Women," forthcoming.

36. Robin Blackburn, "Slavery and Anti-Slavery." Lecture delivered at Munster University, March 20, 1999.

CHAPTER 7

1. W.E.B. Du Bois, "Pan-Africa," *People's Voice* (Oct. 4, 1947); Council on African Affairs, "Repression Madness Rules South Africa," *New Africa Newsletter* (May–June 1950).

2. Youssef M. Ibrahim, "Mandela Ends Triumphant Visit to Britain," *New York Times,* July 13, 1996.

3. Martin Hall, "The Legend of the Lost City: Or the Man with the Golden Balls," *Journal of Southern African Studies* 21 (1995): 179–200.

4. Rider Haggard, *King Solomon's Mines* (New York: Longmans, Green, and Co., 1912), 14.

5. Letter to author from Martin Hall dated April 21, 1999.

6. Ibid.

7. Peter Garlake, *Great Zimbabwe* (London: Thames and Hudson, 1973).

8. Sian Hall and Rob Marsh, *Beyond Belief: Murder and Mysteries in South Africa* (Cape Town: Struik, 1996), 8.

9. Ibid., 8.

10. Ibid.

11. See Stanlake Samkange, "The History of Zimbabwe: Source of Inspiration to African Nationalism," in *The Journal of Arts and Civilization of Black and African Peoples,* vol. 5, eds. Joseph Ohiomogben Okpaku et al. (Lagos, Nigeria: Centre for Black & African Arts & Civilization, Third Press International, 1986).

12. Interview in the *Plain Truth, a Magazine of Understanding* 9 (Sept. 1971): 7.

13. For an excellent discussion of Rhodesian historiography, see David Chanaiwa, "The Zimbabwe Controversy: A Case of Colonial Historiography," in *Eastern African Studies,* vol. 8 (New York: Syracuse University, Maxwell School of Citizenship and Public Affairs, 1973).

14. See Stanlake Samakange, *Origins of Rhodesia* (New York: Praeger, 1969).

15. Peter Garlake, "Prehistory and Ideology in Zimbabwe," in *Africa* 52 (1982): 16–17.

16. Nicholas Carroll, *The Sunday Times,* March 3, 1973.

17. John Randal Baker, *Race,* (New York: Oxford University Press, 1974).

18. There were two successors to Great Zimbabwe. One was the lesser-known but wealthier southwest Torwa State, called "Butua" by the Portuguese. Its first capital was at Khami, the second at Danangombe. The second successor to Great Zimbabwe was Munhumutapa in the northeast, founded by a Karanga dynasty related to Great Zimbabwe. At Torwa, the tradition of stone building survived and entered a new phase of development with the construction of the impressive buildings at Dhlo Dhlo, Nalatali, and Khami in the seventeenth and eighteenth centuries. The architectural style of these *zimbabwes* at Butua were characterized by a number of stepped stone platforms around existing hillocks, and the elaborate forms of wall decoration at Great Zimbabwe were repeated. The last Torwa capital, east of Khami, was called Danangombe, which was overthrown by neighboring chief Chanagamire Dombo and his followers, the Rozvi.

19. Graham Connah, *African Civilizations: Precolonial Cities and States in Tropical Africa: An Archaeological Perspective* (Cambridge, England: Cambridge University Press, 1987), 184.

20. David Randall-MacIver wrote in *Medieval Rhodesia* (London: Macmillan and Co.) in 1906, "It is properly speaking, the huts which constitute the really essential part of the ruin in every case; the stone wall which the visitor admires is only the skin, the huts are flesh and bone."

21. David Beach, *The Shona and Zimbabwe: An Outline of Shona History* (New York: Africana Publishing Company, 1980), 46.

22. See Chanaiwa, "The Zimbabwe Controversy."

23. Maylin Newitt, *History of Mozambique* (London: Hurst and Co., 1995), 48.

24. J. O. Vogel, "Merensky and Nachtigal in Southern Africa: A Contemporary Source for King Solomon's Mines" in *The Journal of African Travel-Writing* 4 (1998): 20.

25. George McCall Theal, "Abstracts of Documents Relating to South Eastern Africa from 1569 to 1700," in *Records of South Eastern Africa,* vol. VIII (Cape Town: Government of the Cape Colony, 1898–1903), 364.

26. David Chanaiwa, "The Zimabawe Controversy," 99.

27. John F. Schofield, "The Ancient Ruins Company Limited," in *Man* 35 (1935): 19–20.

28. "Rhodesian Ruins and Native Tradition," in *South African Journal of Science* 12, (1915): 516.

29. Ibid.

30. David Chanaiwa, "The Zimbabwe Controversy," 116–126.

31. David Randall-MacIver, *Medieval Rhodesia* (New York: Macmillan, 1906).

32. Chanaiwa, "The Zimbabwe Controversy," 74.

33. Richard Nicklin Hall, *Prehistoric Rhodesia, and an examination of the Historical, Ethnological and Archaeological Evidences as to the Origin and Age of the Rocks, Mines and Stone Buildings* (Philadelphia. George W. Jacobs, 1909), 13.

34. Gertrude Caton Thompson, *The Zimbabwe Culture: Ruins and Reactions* (Oxford: Clarendon Press, 1931). See also Peter Garlake, "Prehistory and Ideology in Zimbabwe," in *Africa* 53 (1982), for a detailed analysis of Thompson's and Randall-MacIver's work and the inherent limitations of early archaeological work in southern Africa.

35. Thomas N. Huffman, "Zimbabwe: Southern Africa's First Town," *Rhodesian Prehistory* 7 (15), 9–14.

36. Richard Newman, *African American Quotations* (Phoenix, Arizona: Oryx Press, 1998), 14.

INDEX

Italic page numbers indicate illustrations.

Victoria Falls, Zimbabwe

PHOTOGRAPHS BY LYNN DAVIS

i, ii, vi, viii, 2, 14, 15, 26, 30, 31, 33, 51, 52, 53, 56, 57, 58, 61, 64, 73, 81, 85, 90, 100, 101, 105, 106, 108, 120, 121, 123, 124, 125, 130, 134, 135, 141, 147, 148, 153, 154, 156, 157, 159, 163, 167, 168, 173, 174, 179, 180, 181, 184, 185, 188, 191, 192, 202, 203, 205, 220, 221, 222, 227, 228, 230, 245, 248, 250, 251, 254, 260, 268.

ABBREVIATIONS

Author's Photographic Collection = APC
Ernst Mayr Zoological Library, Harvard University = EMZL
Library of Congress = LC
Book used more than twice = Author's name

CHAPTER 1

8 Reprinted from *Great Explorers of Africa* (London: Sampson Low, Marston, 1894) EMZL; 9 Reprinted from Thomas E. Beselow, *From the Darkness of Africa to the Light of America: The Story of an African Prince* (Boston: Frank Wood Printer, 1891); 10 Carl Van Vechten Collection, LC-USZ62-42528; 11 Marcus Garvey Papers; 12 Carl Van Vechten Collection, LC-USZ62-42502; 17 (top left) Reprinted from *How I found Livingstone: Travels, Adventures, and Discoveries in Central Africa* by Henry M. Stanley (New York: Charles Scribner's Sons, 1902), (below left) EMZL, (bottom right) John Boyne "A Meeting of Connoisseurs," Victoria and Albert Museum, London/Art Resource, NY; 18 Unknown; 19 "Death of Paris. Eighth piece in a series of tapestries on the Trojan War (detail). Tournai before 1486." Zamora Museo Catedralico, Spain; 20 The British Museum, England; 23 APC.

CHAPTER 2

35 "Battle against the Nubians," Panel from the Stuccoed and painted wooden chest of Tutankhamen. Egypt, 18th dynasty. Scala/Art Resource NY; 36 Reprinted from *The Egyptian Sudan,* Vol. II by E. A. Wallis Budge (London: Kegan Paul, Trench, Trübner & Co. Limited, 1907); 38 Courtesy of Dr. Timothy Kendall; 39 APC; 40 Museum of Warsaw; 42 Courtesy of Dr. Timothy Kendall; 43 (top left and right) APC; 44 APC; 46 APC; 47 (top left) Courtesy of Dr. Timothy Kendall, (bottom right) The British Museum, England; 48 Museum Expedition, Courtesy of the Museum of Fine Arts, Boston; 49 Museum Expedition, Courtesy of the Museum of Fine Arts, Boston; 50 Courtesy of Tozzer Library, Harvard University, Reprinted from *Egypt & Nubia* by David Roberts, (London: Moon, 1846–1849); 54 Courtesy of Dr. Timothy Kendall; 55 Museum Expedition, Courtesy of the Museum of Fine Arts, Boston; 60 David Roberts; 62 Charles Gleyre, "Jeune Nubienne," Musée Cantonal des Beaux-Arts, Lausanne, Switzerland.

CHAPTER 3

70 Catalan World Map, Scala/Art Resource, NY; 69 Heironymous Bosch (c. 1450–1516). "Balthazar, the African Magus," detail from the *Adoration of the Magi,* center panel. Scala/Art Resource, NY; 71 Conrad Keyser, Queen of Sheba, *Bellifortis,* Bohemia before 1405. Göttingen Niedersachsische; 72 Reprinted from *The Autobiography of Theophilus Waldmeier, Ten Years in: Abyssinia: and Sixteen Years in Syria* by Theophilus Waldmeier, London: S. W. Partridge & Co., 1886); 75 APC; 76 (top right and below right) Langmuir Collection, Peabody Essex Museum, Salem, MA; 77 Theophilus Waldmeier; 79 Institute of Ethiopian Studies, Addis Ababa, Ethiopia; 80 APC; 82 APC; 84 (top left) Reprinted from *Voyage en Abyssinie by* M. M. Ferret and Galinier (Paris: Paulin, 1847), (below left) Theophilus Waldmeier; 87 "A Dinner Party at Adoua," reprinted from *Life in Abyssinia: Being Notes Collected During Three Years Residence and Travels in that Country* by Mansfield Parkyns, photograph by Stephen Sylvester (London: 1868); 88 (top right and below right) APC; 89 APC; 92 APC; 93 "Nineteenth-century representation of a battle between Ethiopian armies" Musée de l'homme, photo. D. Ponsard; 95 (top left) Theophilus Waldmeier, (top right) APC; 97 APC; 102 Theophilus Waldmeier; 107 Unknown.

CHAPTER 4

112 Reprinted from *Tombouctou, la Mystérieuse* by Felix Dubois (Paris: Flammarion, 1897); 113 William James Muller, "The Eastern Letter Writer" Glasgow Museums: Art Gallery & Museum, Kelvingrove; 116 Felix Dubois; 117 APC; 119 (top left) APC, (bottom right) Felix Dubois; 126 APC; 127 APC; 129 Felix Dubois; 131 Felix Dubois; 132 King Mansa Musa, Map of Europe and North Africa from the Atlas of Charles V, Mecia de Villadeste, Spain, ca. 1413. Giraudon/Art Resource/NY; 133 (top left) Felix Dubois, (bottom right) Felix Dubois; 138 (top left) Felix Dubois, (top right) APC; 139 (bottom left) Felix Dubois, (top right) APC; 142–143 Timbuktu chart Courtesy of John Hunwick; 144 Felix Dubois; 145 Felix Dubois; 146 Felix Dubois.

CHAPTER 5

155 Reprinted from *Reisen in Ost Afrika,* Vol. 1 & 2 by Carl Von Decken (Leipzig, 1869); 160 Reprinted from *A Travers le Zanguebar* by R. P. Le Roy (Paris: Bureaux des Missions Catholiques, 1884); 170 (top left) Reprinted from *Zanzibar* by Richard F. Burton (London: Tinsley Brothers, 1872), (bottom right) Carl Von Decken; 175 APC; 177 EMZL; 178 Peabody Essex Museum, Salem, MA; 183 (top left) EMZL, (bottom left) Carl Von Decken; 186 Reprinted from *Zanzibar: The Island Metropolis of Eastern Africa* by Major F. B. Pearce C. M. G. (London: T. F. Unwin, Limited, 1920); 189 Hulton Getty, Liaison Agency, NY 02344839.

CHAPTER 6

196 (top left) François-Auguste Biard "Slaves on the West Coast of Africa" Bridgeman Art Library International WHM 112033, (bottom right) Reprinted from *The Autobiography of Theophilus Waldmeier, Ten Years in: Abyssinia: and Sixteen Years in Syria* by Theophilus Waldmeier, (London: S. W. Partridge & Co., 1886); 198 "Captive" Reprinted from *Trois Mois de Captivité au Dahomey* by E. Chaudoin (Paris: Paris Librarie Hachette, 1891); 206 EMZL; 207 E. Chaudoin; 210 Reprinted from *Mission to Ashantee* by Thomas E. Bowdich (London: John Murray, 1819); 211 APC; 212 Thomas E. Bowdich; 213 Reprinted from *A Journal of a Residence in Ashantee* by Joseph Dupuis (London: H. Colburn, 1824); 214 Thomas E. Bowdich; 216 E. Chaudoin; 218 E. Chaudoin; 219 Reprinted from *Dahomey and the Dahomans* by Frederick E. Forbes (London: Longman, Brown, Green and Longmans, 1851); 222 (top left) E. Chaudoin; 223 (top left) E. Chaudoin, (bottom right) APC; 224 (top left) APC, (bottom left) APC; 225 E. Chaudoin.

CHAPTER 7

233 Guy Tillim, I-Afrika, Cape Town; 236 Reprinted from *The Portuguese in South Africa: From Arab Domination to British Rule,* Edited by R. W. Murray, F.R.G.S. (1891); 239 Reprinted from *The Portuguese in South Africa: From Arab Domination to British Rule,* Edited by R. W. Murray, F.R.G.S. (London: E. Stanford, 1891); 240 APC; 240 Courtesy of Dr. Andre Meyer; 243 (left and right) Courtesy of Dr. Andre Meyer; 244 National Archives of Zimbabwe; 246 *Sunday Mail,* Harare, 1 September 1996; 247 APC; 249 APC; 252 Reprinted from a print by P. Betrand. c. 1650; 255 The Zimbabwe National Tourist Board.

A NOTE ABOUT THE TYPE

This book was set in Adobe Garamond. Designed for the Adobe Corpora-
tion by Robert Slimbach and released in 1989, the fonts are based on types
first cut by Claude Garamond (c. 1480–1561).

Composition and separations by
North Market Street Graphics, Lancaster, Pennsylvania
Printing and binding by R. R. Donnelley & Sons, Roanoke, Virginia
Cartography by Vikki Leib
Design by Peter A. Andersen